Violence
From Theory to Research

Margaret A. Zahn
North Carolina State University and Research Triangle Institute

Henry H. Brownstein
Abt Associates, Inc.

Shelly L. Jackson
Institute of Law, Psychiatry and Public Policy, University of Virginia

 LexisNexis®

 **anderson publishing**
A member of the LexisNexis Group

Violence: From Theory to Research

Copyright © 2004
        Matthew Bender & Company, Inc., a member of the LexisNexis Group

Phone 877-374-2919
Web Site www.lexisnexis.com/anderson/criminaljustice

Violence: from theory to research / [edited by] Margaret A. Zahn, Henry H. Brownstein, Shelly L. Jackson
    p. cm.
    Includes bibliographical references and index.
    ISBN 1-58360-561-4 (softbound)
    1. Violence--Research. I. Zahn, Margaret A. II. Brownstein, Henry H. III. Jackson, Shelly L.
HM886.V563 2004
909'.04--dc22   2004023922

Cover design by Tin Box Studio, Inc.   EDITOR Ellen S. Boyne
                                  ACQUISITIONS EDITOR Michael C. Braswell

Dedications

To the memory of my husband, A. Stephen Lee, and to the hopes
he and I shared for a less violent world
— Margaret A. Zahn

To my wife Cindy, who makes everything possible
—Henry H. Brownstein

To my husband, Thomas Hafemeister, for his unwaivering
support, and to our children, Jackson and Katriana,
who give me hope for the future.
—Shelly L. Jackson

Acknowledgments

We would like to thank Sarah V. Hart, Director of the National Institute of Justice, and Glenn R. Schmitt, Deputy Director of the National Institute of Justice, for sponsoring the violence workshop in December, 2002, without which this book would not have happened. We also wish to thank Richard Rosenfeld for his important contribution at the violence workshop and for his review of an earlier draft of the concluding chapter. Margaret Zahn would like to thank RTI for providing her time to work on the book, and she would also like to thank M. Dwayne Smith for his support of this project. Henry Brownstein wishes to thank the leadership of the National Institute of Justice for its interest in expanding its agenda for the study of violence. He also thanks his colleagues at Abt Associates, Inc., for encouraging his work on this book.

Shelly Jackson would like to thank the Institute of Law, Psychiatry, and Public Policy for providing support while working on this book. Finally, we thank the theorists and researchers who contributed to this book, and we thank each other. We started as colleagues, we became co-authors and co-editors, and now we are friends.

Table of Contents

PART I

Introduction:
Toward a Theory of Violence

Henry H. Brownstein
Margaret A. Zahn
Shelly L. Jackson

A theory is an explanation of the world around us. It provides a context through which we can incorporate what we consider to be facts and tells us how those facts fit together in a meaningful way. It helps us to make sense of what otherwise does not make sense. Consider the case of violence.

After years of beatings at the hands of a man who claims to love her, a woman stabs or shoots him. We might not condone her action, but in the context of self-preservation we can understand why she would do it. In times of war, not only soldiers but also noncombatants, including children, are killed and wounded. Each time it happens it is horrific and we may not agree with it, but in the context of war we can understand why people are killing and wounding each other. Drug dealers often use physical force and brutality to protect their market share or the integrity of their product. We might be offended and frightened by their actions, but in the context of doing business we are able to explain why in the absence of access to legal authority they might act that way.

A young mother watches as her car rolls down a boat ramp into a lake while her two sons, ages three years and 14 months, are strapped inside. We sympathize when we believe her story that a carjacker took her car and killed her children. When we learn that her story is a lie and that she did it herself to be free of her children, our interpretation of the situation and therefore our response to it are likely to be different. A 15-year-old boy in Springfield, Oregon, walks into his school cafeteria one day and opens fire on his classmates, killing two and wounding more than 20. A 14-year-old in

Paducah, Kentucky, fires at a prayer circle of his fellow students, killing three and wounding five. School officials and psychologists theorize that their actions can be explained in terms of motives and circumstances.

The role of theory in social and behavioral science is to help us explain and thereby understand diverse social situations such as those described above. In the case of violence, theory guides the way we think and what we know about why people violate or harm other people. Chapters in this book present a variety of theories about violence and show how these theories are applied to particular social phenomena. Ultimately, the purpose of this book is to help better explain and understand violence.

Toward a Theoretical Explanation of Violence

In its simplest sense, then, a theory is an explanation. A theory can be an explanation for why two or more things are related to each other, or why something happens or does not happen. A theory helps us to make sense of the empirical evidence or facts of our experience and observation. A theory is not itself a set of facts, but it helps us to explain known facts in a way that is believable and compelling.

According to Herbert Blumer, "The aim of theory in empirical science is to develop analytic schemes of the empirical world with which the given science is concerned" (1969:140). The point is that while theory is a means by which to conceive the world in an abstract way, it is of value for scientific inquiry only to the extent that it "connects fruitfully with the empirical world" (Blumer, 1969:143). For Blumer, social science is thus challenged to develop methodological perspectives "congruent with the nature of the empirical world under study" (1969:vii). This is true whether quantitative research methods are employed to provide empirical evidence that is used to verify a theory (Zetterberg, 1963), or qualitative methods are used to search through empirical evidence for a theory that is grounded in the evidence (Glaser & Strauss, 1967).

A particular social theory, then, is an analytic framework. Through the scientific method, the theory connects an abstract way of looking at a social phenomenon with empirical evidence of that phenomenon as derived from the social world in which we live. The theory expands our knowledge and understanding of that world. Effective theories provide guidance for further inquiry, "setting problems, staking out objects, and leading inquiry into asserted relations" (Blumer, 1969:141). For quantitative researchers, theories offer inferences and implications that need to be verified with empirical evidence from research. For qualitative researchers, they are the ground in which to plant newly discovered empirical evidence to see what new ideas emerge.

Theory does these things by "conceiving the world abstractly, that is, in terms of classes of objects and of relations between such classes" (Blumer, 1969:140). Such abstract classes of objects, or *concepts*, are the basic elements from which theoretical propositions about the nature of social phenomenon and their relationships are derived. Abraham Kaplan suggested that concepts "mark out the path by which we may move most freely in logical space. They identify the nodes or junctions in the network of relationships, termini at which we can halt while preserving the maximum range of choice as to where to go next" (1964:52).

As members of society, we experience the abstract world of social experience as an empirical reality. Individually, we each conceptualize that world in a meaningful way that allows us to live our everyday lives (see Kaplan, 1964; Lazarsfeld & Rosenberg, 1955). We form mental images, called *conceptions*, each of which represents "a collection of related phenomena that we have either observed or heard about somewhere" (Maxfield & Babbie, 1998:94). A *concept*, according to Kaplan, is a "family of conceptions" (1964:49), an abstraction that is understood by all participants in a social world to commonly refer to their personal conceptions of the same social phenomenon (Maxfield & Babbie, 1998).

Today, social and behavioral scientists trying to explain theory to students use different words to define theory, but overall their definitions are consistent with traditional views. Trying to define it in a primer for undergraduates, Bohm simply writes that theory helps you to explain "why or how things are related to each other" (1997:1). Maxfield and Babbie expand on that theme a bit when they write that theory is "a systematic explanation for the observed facts and laws that relate to a particular aspect of life" (1998:37).

Focusing more directly on what theory should do, Akers writes that it should help you "to make sense of facts that [you] already know and can be tested against new facts" (2000:1). Wallace, emphasizing what makes a theory a good theory, writes that it can be "taken to mean any set of symbols that is claimed verifiably to represent and make intelligible specified classes of phenomena and one or more of their relationships" (1969:3). Noting that *explanation* is "the key word in the definition," Liska and Messner define theory as "an interrelated set of statements or propositions used to explain the events or things that constitute the subject matter of a perspective" (1999:16).

In writing about what theory does, Akers makes it clear to his readers that theory explains to us what is or what may be, not what ought to be (2000:2). As noted earlier, for explaining what is or what may be, concepts are the building blocks of theory (Chafetz, 1978; Kaplan, 1964; Lazarsfeld & Rosenberg, 1955). To deal with violence in everyday life, we conceptualize it as individuals. To understand it as a social phenomenon, we construct a concept, a word or symbol that represents our conception of empirical reality. To be able to study theory, we have to be able to define it in such a way that it has meaning and can be measured empirically. At that point it is called an *operational definition* (Maxfield & Babbie, 1998:99), and we use that definition to conduct studies that will allow us to test hypothesized relationships between the concept of violence and concepts of other social or behavioral phenomena. *Propositions* are hypothetical statements we make about the relationships we expect to observe between and among such concepts (see Blumer, 1969; Kaplan, 1964).

Theory is not about what ought to be, yet underlying all social theories are philosophical assumptions about the social world (Kaplan, 1964:88). For example, to be able to explain social phenomena, we need to assume that social reality exists (i.e., it is not an illusion) and that there is some order to it (Chafetz, 1978:34-35). For his students, Bohm calls these assumptions the "hidden agenda" of theories, because they cannot be proven scientifically or empirically but have to be accepted for the theory to make sense (1997:4). Besides making metaphysical assumptions about the nature of reality in general, social theorists make epistemological assumptions about how knowledge is acquired, ontological assumptions about human nature, and cosmological assumptions about the nature of society (Gouldner, 1971). These assumptions guide the thinking of the theorist as he or she approaches the study of a particular phenomenon. When a set of assumptions is integrated in a meaningful way, it forms a general orientation toward a subject matter, a way of thinking about the subject. This general orientation is called a *paradigm* (Kuhn, 1970). A particular paradigm represents a coherent set of assumptions that "serves to define what should be studied, what questions should be asked, how they should be asked, what rules should be followed in interpreting the answers obtained" (Ritzer, 1975:7).

During any historical period, science is likely to be dominated by a single paradigm. That paradigm integrates in a meaningful way a set of assumptions about knowledge and reality that is reasonable in the context of the time. The paradigm contributes to scientific advancement by providing an orientation for theory and research, helping contemporary scientists to accumulate knowledge in an orderly and meaningful way. This is what Kuhn called "normal science" (1970). However, over time, the dominant paradigm inevitably becomes inadequate at explaining changing conditions and circumstances, and a new paradigm emerges. According to Kuhn, "Led by a new paradigm, scientists adopt new instruments and look in new places. Even more important, during revolutions scientists see new and different things when looking at familiar instruments in places they have looked before" (1970:111). In this way, science advances when one paradigm replaces another, or when there are competing paradigms.

Theories of violence will vary depending on the paradigm through which a phenomenon is being explained and the underlying assumptions of that paradigm. For example, a paradigm may be rooted in classical or neoclassical philosophy, a product of the Enlightenment. In that case, a theory of violence would be based on assumptions that human beings have free will and are therefore responsible for their actions and will act to maximize pleasure and minimize pain (see Beccaria, 1963; Bentham, 1843). A theory of violence rooted in a positivist paradigm would not agree that violence is reasoned behavior based on free will. Rather, it would view violence from the philosophical assumption that human behaviors are a consequence of biological or cultural factors over which the individual has no control (Fishbein, 1990; Goddard, 1914; Lombroso, 1876). A theory of violence grounded in a critical paradigm would be based on the assumption that human beings both create and are created by the social structures and institutions of their social world (see Bohm, 1982; Lynch & Groves, 1989; Schwartz & Hatty, 2003).

The paradigm that underlies a particular theory of violence inevitably separates that theory from other theories that use different paradigms. In this case, a simple unification of theories of violence, each grounded in a different paradigm, would be challenging at best. Similarly, it is possible for a number of theories to be rooted in the same paradigm but have different explanatory variables, in which case it would be challenging but possible to establish an integrated theory of violence. Finally, a number of theories could be rooted in the same paradigm and use similar or complementary variables, in which case the possibility of theory integration is maximized. In this book we look at a variety of theories of violence and consider how each contributes to a broader understanding of violence.[1] In addition, we provide an analysis of the feasibility of integrating the theories of violence contained in this book.

The Concept of Violence

As noted earlier, Blumer argued that for a theory to be fruitful it needs to be possible for its concepts to be connected to the empirical world (1969). Therefore, it is not surprising that in considering the problem of social theory, he wrote, "Ambiguity in concepts blocks or frustrates contact with the empirical world" (1969:152). His point was made clearer by comparison to the natural sciences "wherein empirical instances are accepted in their concrete and distinctive form" (1969:152). For example, H_2O might have the quality of an abstract concept to it, but we all recognize water when it is presented to us. We cannot so easily say the same for social concepts. Therefore, theories about abstract social concepts, such as violence, inevitably require greater attention to issues of conceptualization. To study violence, then, we need to clearly define what we mean by violence.

Definitions of violence vary. For example, the term *violence* may refer to a number of different behaviors. Yet by speaking of violence as *violence*, we imply that it is one thing. Through that one word all the forms and manifestations of violence are said to represent the same social phenomenon. Is the killing of a rival by a drug dealer the same thing as the killing of a husband by an abused wife? Is the terrorist act of a suicide bomber the same thing as the patriotic act of a soldier? Do measures of violent crime measure the same thing as measures of corporate violence?

In the everyday lives of individuals, violence is experienced in different ways. Given his or her personal experiences and observations of violence, each individual has a particular mental image or conception of what violence is. For theory and research, the question is whether a concept of violence can be formed that lends itself to observation and measurement. If we are to understand and explain violence, this is an important question. We need to be able to define violence as an abstract class of objects that can be commonly understood to refer to the variety of personal conceptions of violence.

On a broad theoretical level, Sorel (1950) reflected on violence in terms of class conflict, and Arendt (1969) thought about violence in terms of the justification of means to accomplish ends. Contemporary definitions of violence more often identify characteristics or conditions that are necessary for any social activity or behavior to be regarded as violence. Weiner, Zahn, and Sagi define violence as "the threat, attempt, or use of physical force by one or more persons that results in physical or nonphysical harm to one or more other persons" (1990:xiii). For Reiss and Roth, violence refers to "behavior by persons against persons that intentionally threatens, attempts, or actually inflicts physical harm" (1993:2). Similarly, for Riedel and Welsh, violence refers to "actions directed toward another in a face-to-face encounter or near-physical contact" (2002:1-2).

Sometimes the definition of violence is connected not only to the activity or behavior of individuals or groups, but also to the intention for the activity or behavior. For example, Newman defines violence as "the use of force to gain dominance over another or others" (1979:1). In defining violence in subjective terms, sometimes the emphasis is on the way members of society interpret or perceive the activity or behavior. For example, Brownstein wrote, "forms of social activity that we consider violent are those that in our judgment symbolize and represent physical force and domination" (2000:7).

Definitions of violence do have certain characteristics or elements in common. In all of these definitions, violence is associated with a form or forms of social activity or behavior. The activity or behavior actually or symbolically involves force, or at least the threat of force. But there are differences as well. The force may be physical or not and result in injury or not. The behavior may be personal, interpersonal, or collective. Violence also differs by degree, type of injury, the object of the force, the intent of the perpetrator, and whether it is an act of commission or omission.

Black addresses some of these differences by distinguishing two categories of violence: predatory and moralistic (1983). The question is whether violence includes behavior or activity that uses force in an acquisitive way (predatory) and behavior or activity that uses force as a form of social control (moralistic). Is the use of force to seize property from a stranger conceptually different from the use of force to avenge intentional harm to a loved one? Is the use of force by dispossessed people seeking control of their nationhood conceptually the same as the use of force by young men seeking to prove their manhood? Is the use of force by an athlete playing a sanctioned sport by the rules of the sport conceptually different from the use of force by a gang member in battle with members of a rival gang?

Given the complexity of the phenomenon that we call violence and the different paradigms that have been applied to its explanation, it might seem futile to try to establish a general theory of violence. As long as violence is accepted as a singular phenomenon, a coherent theory of violence is possible.

The Approach Taken by the Authors of this Book

The authors of the chapters in this book address theories of violence in a variety of ways. Ron Akers and Adam Silverman write about the application of learning theory to violence, and Robert Agnew does the same for general strain theory. Charles Tittle writes that violence is about control, applying the concepts and propositions of social control theory, and Richard Felson writes on rational choice. Robert Bursik writes about the application of social disorganization theory to violence, and Michael Lynch describes an application of critical theory to corporate acts of violence. Marcus Felson focuses on situations and argues that violence is best understood through the ideas of routine activities theory, while Claire Renzetti writes about an application of feminist theory to violence in gender relations. Finally, Donald Black argues for a pure sociological theory of violence, a theory in which structures rather than individuals or even collectivities are violent.

In the next section of this book, authors explore specific areas of social life and try to explain the relevance of different theories of violence to those areas. Mary Ann Dutton writes about violence involving intimate partners, whereas Finn-Aage Esbensen discusses violence by young people. Helene Raskin White writes about drugs and violence, and Roberta Senechal de la Roche examines the phenomenon of modern lynching. Mark Hamm writes about the violence of hate crimes, and Christopher Hewitt concludes this section by writing about terrorism.

Any given theory is grounded in a paradigm built upon assumptions, which leads the theorist to a particular subject area, questions that should be asked to study that subject, and the best way to interpret what is learned from such studies. The paradigm then is not merely a set of assumptions but is rather a "device for specifying meaning with respect to internal vagueness, being presented as the clearest instance of the general category"

(Kaplan, 1984:118). A paradigm encompasses the broadest level of "consensus within a science," differentiating a community of scientists from others, subsuming for them definitions, interrelatedness of "exemplars, theories, and methods and instruments that exist within it" (Ritzer, 1975:7). That is, a paradigm builds from a set of assumptions a worldview and an approach to understanding and explaining the world. For example, the assumptions of the classical or neoclassical tradition resulted in a paradigm built upon the assumption that human beings have free will. How might a theorist build a worldview around such an assumption, and what research questions would be raised? What methods would be used to do that research?

In this book, theories about violence differ in their assumptions. There are differences in ontological assumptions. For example, some of the theorists view human beings as having free will and as being able to choose to act in particular ways. Rational choice, for instance, is clearly allied with this assumption. Others instead assume that structures or institutions, if not totally determining human behavior, set sharp limits on its expression. Social disorganization theory more closely fits this model. Further, the object of observation varies—with one key difference being observation of individual actors, as in social learning theory, versus social structures as in Black's theory.

Yet, while these theories vary in terms of underlying assumptions, overall they tend to be grounded in one variation or another of the objectivist paradigm. According to the objectivist paradigm, society is made up of social facts. The classical sociologist Emile Durkheim wrote that social facts are "ways of acting, thinking, and feeling, external to the individual and endowed with a power of coercion, by reason of which they control him" (1964:3). They are an objective reality independent of individuals. Most of the theories in this book view violence as an objective reality.

Although most theories in this book are grounded in an objectivist paradigm, they use different variables—such as gender, race, class, and social space—to explain violence. Even within a single paradigm, assumptions may vary considerably.

As discussed earlier, some theories of violence are grounded in classical or neoclassical assumptions. They share the assumption that human beings are responsible for their actions, that they have free will and choose to act in ways that maximize pleasure and minimize pain. In this vein, Akers and Silverman write about learning theory and suggests that violence is primarily a product of social exchange. They acknowledge that there may be physiological differences among people that can account for variations in tendencies toward finding violence intrinsically rewarding, but argue that it is more important to understand how others provide reinforcement through which social rewards and punishments are delivered. Similarly, in terms of strain theory, Agnew argues that if you treat people badly they become upset and respond with crime, including violence.

Other theorists argue that classical or neoclassical assumptions support a view that violence serves as a basis for making rational choices in routine situations. Richard Felson reasons that the actions of individuals are the consequence of rational choices. However, routine activities theory focuses on events and situations rather than on the propensities of individual actors. In terms of crime and violence, Marcus Felson suggests that these propensities are best thought of as perhaps peripheral. Whereas routine activities theory emphasizes events and situations, sociological theory focuses on social structures or institutions. In both theories, individuals are a product of their environment. However, when Black writes about moralistic violence, he is suggesting that violence is a mode of conflict management. Individuals are not choosing to act in violent ways but are the product of the structures and institutions that make up their social world. Thus, both theories can be viewed in the context of a positivist paradigm, though not in the traditional sense that outside forces control human behavior.

Traditional positivist theories are based on the philosophical assumption that outside forces control human behavior. Such theories emphasized biological, psychological, or cultural forces. Arguably, those forces could be a social event or situation or products of a social structure or institution. They could be the forces of social interaction. Social control theorists who study violence would not, for example, ask why people commit violence but rather why they do not. Those who do not are responding to the force of society. Tittle argues from the perspective of a positivist paradigm that violence is about control. Everyone has a latent desire or need to overcome control deficits and to extend control surpluses. Violence results when there is a deficit of control.

In the context of a critical paradigm, theorists assume that human beings are both the products and producers of their social world. Violence might result from the forces of a social situation or social structure that dominates or compels an individual, encouraging or limiting his or her action. As the producers of their social world, however, individuals could change those situations or structures. Renzetti suggests that at the core of feminist theory is the social concept of gender. She defines gender as those socially constructed expectations, attitudes, and behaviors associated with females and males that are the central organizing component of social life. Gender is behind the domination or compulsion that forces individuals to act or behave in a certain way. Violence might be a response to those forces in which the individual is guided by the internalization of gender characteristics. On the other hand, violence might be a reaction to those forces, and the individual is driven to act out against them. Similarly, Lynch writes about how the social constructs of class, race, and gender differentiate people in society in terms of power. Violence is a product of such constructs, and individuals act or behave in relation to their social placement.

Using Theory to Guide the Study of Violence

Several themes and questions need to be addressed by a theory of violence. For example, is violence a response or a solution to a problem created by a social event or condition? This question draws attention to the need to study processes by which problems are solved in order to understand violence. It also raises the question about whether violence is something that needs to be provoked. If so, what is the role of provocation, and need we explain violence in terms of individual or group responses to provocation? More broadly, it raises the question of whether all violence can be or needs to be explained in the same way. Must one theory accommodate those who believe that violence is predatory *and* those who believe it is moralistic? Are there other ways to think about violence, such as whether it is instrumental, or perhaps expressive? Must the theorist understand violence in terms of what is going on in the mind of the perpetrator, the victim, or even both? Is violence always about behavior or action? Can organizations or structures be violent, and can an organization or structure be the focus of a study of violence?

The way violence is conceptualized and the paradigm on which a theory about violence is based influences the questions that will be asked and, consequently, how violence will be studied. In that sense, the concept and the paradigm similarly determine what variables should be studied and the appropriate unit and level of analysis of the study.

The problem of identifying the proper unit or level of analysis for the study of violence is of particular concern. By definition, in studies of violence as a concept that is observable and measurable, the dependent variable is *violence*. But is violence best measured as a form of behavior or action, or as a characteristic of a social structure or institution? Is it more productive to think about the unit of analysis as an aspect of behavior or as a characteristic of a social institution? Because it is easier to find observable measures of violence in terms of behavior, and particularly criminal behavior, much of the research that has been done has focused on violent crime as the dependent variable (see Brownstein, 2000:7-10). That does not necessarily make it the best way to study violence.

There are theorists who argue for the importance of nonbehavioral units or levels of analysis for violence research. For routine activities theory, for example, Marcus Felson suggests that the units of analysis should include variables such as time, day, incident, episode, and setting. He argues that these variables enhance the analysis of violence in that they establish a framework within which to analyze the resolution of disagreements. In terms of pure sociological or social geometry theory, Black suggests that the proper unit of analysis for the study of violence is conflict. He argues that because conflict can occur on both the micro and macro levels of social life, it allows for analyses applicable to groups, regions, nation-states, and multinational groups as well as to individuals.

Sociological variables are also valuable in explaining violence, and many theorists consider gender to be an important variable. If we could understand why men commit violence so much more often than women, it might help us to better understand why and how violence occurs. Gender locates individuals in the social structure in terms of power, hierarchy, advantage, and disadvantage. Other variables that have a similar value for analyses of violence include race, class, and age. Theorists who try to understand and explain violence have suggested that gender, along with race, class, and age, affects beliefs, attitudes, behavior, the people with whom one associates, social models for behavior, consequences of behavior, and opportunities. In that sense, these variables have value for studies of violence as defined and explained from different theoretical perspectives.

Another variable that some theorists consider important for the study of violence is *relational space*, which refers to a dimension of social space. It includes the nature and number of ties between people, the frequency of contacts between individuals and groups, and the duration and intensity of a social relationship. Variables such as gender, race, class, and age place an individual in social space in terms of the organizational context of other people and groups. Relational space places the individual in social space in terms of their relationship to these people and groups.

Toward a Coherent Theory of Violence

A coherent theory of violence needs to provide a framework for studying violence as a complex and multifaceted phenomenon. It should enable researchers to explain and study violence defined in a variety of ways and to incorporate seemingly incompatible philosophical assumptions about human nature, the nature of society, and the basis of knowledge. A social theory is a good theory when it successfully integrates verifiable facts to produce a meaningful and compelling explanation of a social phenomenon. To do that, it must meet certain scientific criteria.

First, a good general theory of violence needs to meet the criterion of *simplicity* or *parsimony*. That is, it must be made of simple statements that offer the greatest explanatory power. If a theory is to explain a phenomenon, it cannot be stated in a way that adds confusion rather than clarity. Second, a good theory of violence should be *generalizable*. It must be able to account for as much conceptual and empirical variation in the phenomenon as possible.

Third, a good general theory of violence must be *testable*. That is, it must be possible to define operationally the abstract concept of violence as characterized by the theory. Propositions of the theory must be worded as formulations and hypotheses that can be tested empirically. Otherwise the value of the theory is diminished. It remains on the level of abstraction, and the extent to which it has validity on the level of social experience cannot be known.

Another criterion that some theorists consider important for a good general theory of violence is *originality*. A theory of violence that has originality offers ideas about the phenomenon that provide a better explanation of violent activity or behavior than any previously available. New is not necessarily better, but a new theory of violence should advance our understanding of violence.

In a way, *validity* is central to all these other criteria. For example, the standard of generalizability is really about the theory having external validity. In terms of external validity, the theory needs to be broad enough that findings from research based on its propositions can be generalized to more than one social setting or circumstance. By itself, though, validity is perhaps the single most important criterion for a good theory of violence. In general, validity refers to the need for a match between the propositions of a theory and the empirical observations of the research that test that theory (Campbell & Stanley, 1963:5-6; Maxfield & Babbie, 1998:55-59). Other kinds of validity are also important. In *construct validity*, for example, the way the theory conceptualizes violence must be relevant to the way or ways violence is observed and measured in the experience of the people who are judged by a researcher to be engaged in violence. In terms of *internal validity*, we can determine that the propositions of the theory have been supported by the research findings only if we can feel certain that those findings actually say what we think they say.

Both the theoretical and empirical papers included in this book have been prepared by the most noted researchers and theoreticians of our times. The first part of the book includes chapters by criminological theorists, many of whom apply their theories of crime to violence. The second part includes chapters by researchers who look at the substantive area of their expertise through the lens of theories of violence. Each chapter is original and was written specifically for this book. In the end, the aim of this book is to bring together the most sophisticated and current theory and empirical work in order to advance our understanding of violence.

Endnote

1   In December 2002, the National Institute of Justice (NIJ) convened a meeting in Washington, DC, of prominent criminological theorists and researchers to talk about theories of violence. The original purpose of the meeting was to identify an integrated theory that would guide NIJ's research agenda in the area of violence. The participants represented a variety of ways of thinking about crime and violence. Each of the theorists who attended the NIJ meeting was asked to write a brief paper that would demonstrate how his or her theory of crime could be applied specifically to violence. Those papers ultimately served as first drafts of many of the chapters that follow. For the two days of the meeting, they also served as a foundation for discussion. The discussion showed how different theories of violence have different conceptions of violence and are grounded in different paradigms. This book benefits from what was learned at that meeting.

References

Akers, R.L. (2000). *Criminological Theories*. Los Angeles: Roxbury.

Arendt, H. (1969). *On Violence*. New York: Harcourt, Brace and World.

Beccaria, C. (1963). *On Crimes and Punishments*. Indianapolis: Bobbs-Merrill.

Bentham, J. (1843). *The Works of Jeremy Bentham. Vol. I. An Introduction to the Principles of Morals and Legislation*. Edinburgh: William Tait.

Black, D. (1983). "Crime as Social Control." *American Sociological Review*, 48:34-45.

Blumer, H. (1969). *Symbolic Interactionism—Perspective and Method*. Englewood Cliffs, NJ: Prentice Hall.

Bohm, R.M. (1997). *A Primer on Crime and Delinquency*. Belmont, CA: Wadsworth.

Bohm, R.M. (1982). "Radical Criminology: An Explication." *Criminology*, 19:565-89.

Brownstein, H.H. (2000). *The Social Reality of Violence and Violent Crime*. Boston: Allyn & Bacon.

Campbell, D.T., and J.C. Stanley (1963). *Experimental and Quasi-Experimental Designs for Research*. Chicago: Rand McNally.

Chafetz, J.S. (1978). *A Primer on the Construction and Testing of Theories of Sociology*. Itasca, IL: Peacock.

Durkheim, E. (1964). *The Roles of Sociological Method*. Tr. by S.A. Solovay and J.H. Mueller and edited by G.E.G. Catlin. New York: Free Press.

Fishbein, D.H. (1990). "Biological Perspectives in Criminology." *Criminology*, 28:27-72.

Glaser, B.G., and A.L. Strauss (1967). *The Discovery of Grounded Theory: Strategies for Qualitative Research*. Chicago: Aldine.

Goddard, H.H. (1914). *Feeblemindedness: Its Causes and Consequences*. New York: Macmillan.

Gouldner, A.W. (1971). *The Coming Crisis of Western Sociology*. New York: Avon.

Kaplan, A. (1964). *The Conduct of Inquiry—Methodology for Behavioral Science*. San Francisco: Chandler.

Kuhn, T. (1970). *The Structure of Scientific Revolutions*. Chicago: Chicago University Press.

Lazarsfeld, P.F., and M. Rosenberg (1955). *The Language of Social Research*. New York: Free Press.

Liska, A.E., and S.F. Messner (1999). *Perspectives on Crime and Deviance*. Upper Saddle River, NJ: Prentice Hall.

Lombroso, C. (1876). *The Criminal Man*. Milan: Hoepli.

Lynch, M.J., and W.B. Groves (1989). *A Primer in Radical Criminology*. New York: Harrow and Heston.

Maxfield, M.G., and E. Babbie (1998). *Research Methods for Criminal Justice and Criminology*. Belmont, CA: West/Wadsworth.

Newman, G. (1979). *Understanding Violence*. New York: J.B. Lippincott.

Reiss, A.J., and J.A. Roth (1993). *Understanding and Preventing Violence*. Washington, DC: National Academy Press.

Riedel, M., and W. Welsh (2001). *Criminal Violence—Patterns, Causes, and Prevention*. Los Angeles: Roxbury.

Ritzer, G. (1975). *Sociology: A Multiple Paradigm Science*. Boston: Allyn & Bacon.

Schwartz, M.D., and S.E. Hatty (2003). *Controversies in Critical Criminology*. Cincinnati: Anderson.

Sorel, G. (1950). *Reflections on Violence*. Tr. by T.E. Hulme and J. Roth. Glencoe, IL: Free Press.

Wallace, W.L. (1969). *Sociological Theory*. Chicago: Aldine.

Weiner, N.A., M.A. Zahn, and R.J. Sagi (1990). *Violence: Patterns, Causes, Public Policy*. San Diego: Harcourt Brace Jovanovich.

Zetterberg, H.L. (1963). *On Theory and Verification in Sociology*. Totowa, NJ: Bedminster.

PART II

Theories of Violence

Theories are the product of human endeavor. Ideally, theorists take the *facts* about some phenomenon and organize them in a meaningful way. They put the facts together so they form a narrative that makes sense and enhances our understanding of the phenomenon. A theory of violence, for example, should enhance our understanding of violence. Unfortunately, in the case of social science, this is not so simple.

Some social theorists view society as an objective reality that is made up of social facts. Emile Durkheim argued that the basic unit of society is the *social fact*, which he defined as "every way of acting, fixed or not, capable of exercising on the individual an external constraint" (1938:13). From this perspective, something like violence presents itself to us in social life as an objective facticity. It is what it is, independent of what we think or say it is.

Other social theorists view society as a subjective reality, only present to us through interactions with others involving our decisions and actions in relation to those others. Max Weber argued that the basic unit of society is *social action*, defined as the totality of "all human behavior when and in so far as the acting individual attaches subjective meaning to it" (1947:88). From this perspective there are no facts. Emphatically Alfred Schutz wrote, "Strictly speaking, there are no such thing as facts, pure and simple" (1962:5). The point is that if society is subjectively constructed through social interaction, then what we call facts really are only what we think or believe we know to be factual based on our prior experience. For theorists, there are no facts to study, only claims about what is factual.

This is important because we are talking about the basic building blocks of all theory. For some theorists, those building blocks are considered *facts*; for others, they are merely *claims*. In either case, you as the reader of a theory need to look carefully at the evidence the theorist provides in support of those building blocks. How strong is the evidence that what the theorist claims to be factual is supported by solid social science? You may not be able to review every study from which the theorist drew conclusions and constructed the facts on which the theory is built, but at least you can read closely to see if the theorist has empirical evidence from research to support his or her claims about what is or is not factual.

In some way, producing a theory is like connecting the dots. To preserve the logic of the theory and to adequately explain the phenomenon being explained, the theorist needs to fill the empty spaces and gaps between the facts with preliminary research findings and unverifiable assumptions. So when you read a theory you should continuously ask questions about what you are reading. Once you are confident in the facts, you need to ask questions about the logic of the theory. Assuming the facts are scientifically verifiable, is the explanation logical? Does it make sense to you? Can you see how the theorist got from Point A to Point B? Then, once you are ready to acknowledge that the theory is logical, you need to ask yourself whether you agree that the assumptions are reasonable. As noted earlier, every theory rests in part on untestable assumptions. If the theory you are reading rests on the assumption that people have free will, are you prepared to accept that people do have free will, or at least that it is arguable and possible that people have free will?

Once you are comfortable that a theory is logical, its assumptions are reasonable, and its facts are verifiable, you must ask yourself about its value. Behind every theory is the question, "So what?" The purpose of theory is to enhance our knowledge and understanding. Does the theory you are reading do that? For example, does a particular theory of violence advance our knowledge and understanding of violence? Or, does it offer guidance to practical applications for dealing with violence? However defined, is there any *value* in the theory of violence you have read?

In the chapters that follow in Part I of this book, you have a rare opportunity. These chapters were each written especially for this book. All of the authors are prominent criminological theorists who were asked to apply their theory specifically to violence. Most had written theories of crime or deviance. Some had already written theories of violence or had applied their theories to violence, but others had not. This is the first time that all these theorists together have focused their attention on an explanation of violence.

Each theorist who was invited to submit a chapter for this book was provided with guidelines including a set of areas that they were asked to address. The theorists were asked to include sections on the following: major principles and assumptions of the theory; definitions of violence used in the chapter; application of the theory to violence specifically; application of the theory to both collective and interpersonal violence; and the level of empirical support for the theory.

References

Durkheim, E. (1938). *The Rules of Sociological Method*, 8th ed. Tr. by S.A. Solovay and J.H. Mueller and edited by G.E.G. Catlin. New York: Free Press.

Schutz, A. (1962). *Collected Papers I. The Problem of Social Reality*. Edited with and Introduction by M. Natanson. The Hague: Martinus Nijhoff.

Weber, M. (1947). *The Theory of Social and Economic Organization*. Tr. by A.M. Henderson and T. Parsons and edited with an Introduction by T. Parsons. New York: Free Press.

CHAPTER 1

Toward a Social Learning Model of Violence and Terrorism

Ronald L. Akers
Adam L. Silverman

Introduction and Definition of Violence Used in the Chapter

The purpose of this chapter is to outline an application of Akers's social learning theory of crime and deviance[1] to violent behavior ranging from personal, individual violence to collective, terrorist violence, defined as illegal or illegitimate acts of physical threat and harm against persons and places by individuals or nonstate collectivities. While the principles of the theory apply to both conforming and deviant behavior, for our purpose here, we do not include an effort to account for legitimate acts by political authorities in carrying out law enforcement or control domestically or in carrying out war and peacekeeping operations internationally. We do include all acts of illegitimate violence, use of force, physical aggression, assault, homicide, rape, and property destruction in which injury or death is expected or ignored.

The focus is on the social psychological process of coming to commit and to continue in violence. We are persuaded that most of what we propose here based on social learning theory is compatible with, or at least not contradictory to, what other structural theories of anomie, conflict, collective behavior, or others would propose, and that full models that go beyond the social psychological level should incorporate these other dimensions. However, no effort will be made here to examine that issue specifically.

Major Principles and Application of Social Learning Theory to Violence

Social learning theory is not confined to accounting for the acquisition of novel behavior. Rather it utilizes general principles of social behavior to offer a social psychological explanation of criminal and deviant behavior that embraces variables operating in the acquisition, maintenance, and change in criminal or conforming behavior. The principal explanatory concepts in the theory, under each of which a number of specific variables or measures may be clustered, are *differential association, definitions, differential reinforcement,* and *imitation/modeling* (Akers, 1985; 1998; Akers, Krohn, Lanza-Kaduce & Radosevich, 1979; Akers & Sellers, 2004).

Differential association refers to both the normative dimension (values, attitudes, morality, ethics, justifications, rationalizations, and ideology shared with others) and the interactional dimension of the primary-group (family, peers, friends, and neighbors) and secondary-group (organizations, social, religious, and political reference groups) relationships and affiliations. Through differential association these groups influence (and are influenced by) individuals' values and behavior. These are both immediate and more distant reference groups with which one identifies. If the groups with which one is and has been in differential association (directly or indirectly as identity or reference groups) are more accepting of violence, hold attitudes and beliefs supportive of violence, and disproportionately engage in violence, then the person is, himself or herself, more likely to be ready to do the same in given circumstances.

Definitions favorable or unfavorable to deviance refer to one's own attitudes and beliefs, rationalizations, justifications, and definitions of the situation (learned and reinforced principally through differential association) that hold certain acts as right or wrong, moral or immoral, justified or unjustified, ethical or unethical. General and specific religious, moral, and other conventional values and norms are negative toward deviance, but those values can be distorted, subverted, or misinterpreted to justify deviant behavior, even that which is contrary to those general values. Definitions favorable to deviant acts may be "positive" in that they view the behavior as morally desirable and a good thing to do, or they may be "neutralizing" beliefs that define the act as something that, although undesirable, is justified, excusable, or necessary given the situation. Included in this concept of neutralizing definitions are verbalizations (Cressey, 1953), rationalizations, techniques of neutralization (Sykes & Matza, 1957), accounts (Lyman & Scott, 1970), disclaimers (Hewitt & Stokes, 1975), and moral disengagement (Bandura, 1990). Cognitively, definitions favorable to deviance provide a mind-set that makes one more willing to commit the act when the opportunity occurs or is created. Behaviorally, they affect the commission of deviant behavior by acting as internal *discriminative stimuli*. There are other external discriminative stimuli (setting, physical layout, presence or lack of others, vulnerability of targets, and so on) that provide cues or signals to the person that this is the right or appropriate time and situation in which to engage in the behavior.

For the most part, endorsement or internalization of these positive or neutralizing definitions (or other discriminative stimuli) do not "require" deviant action. Rather, they are conventional beliefs so weakly held that they provide no restraint, or they are simply convenient attitudes that facilitate law violation in the right set of circumstances. Some of the beliefs, however, are so intensely held and so strongly promoted by groups or subcultures that once acquired they seemingly compel one to act on them. The radical, reactionary, or militant ideologies of some terrorist groups are of the type that not only justify but provide strong positive definitions and motivation for extreme violence and acts of terrorism (Barak, 2004; Silverman, 2002a; 2002b) Often these are in the nature of misapplying excuses and norms of evasion found in the general culture or applying them in ways that re-define the context of the behavior. But in the case of extremist and terrorist groups they are in the form of pushing negative in-group norms and attitudes toward out-groups to virulent extremes while discarding, neutralizing, or counteracting whatever norms of constraint on means may be present. Indeed, violence committed by participants in terrorism is an example of "committing a crime solely on the basis of adherence to a set of values or beliefs [that] would occur only in extreme cases of highly ideologically motivated offenses or of intense group loyalty." (Akers, 1998:97; see also Akers, 1996).

Differential reinforcement refers to the balance of rewarding and punishing consequences of behavior (instrumental learning), of anticipated or actual (direct positive reward or avoidance of aversive consequences) and negative (direct or indirect) consequences of behavior (instrumental learning). The greater the extent to which the mix or balance of actual and anticipated positive reward or desired consequences outweigh the undesired consequences, the higher the probability of violence. Differential reinforcement is a separate source of motivation for violence that operates with and without accompanying definitions (as discriminative stimuli), although the congruence or discrepancy between one's beliefs and deeds may also function as positive or negative stimuli (differential reinforcement) that increase or decrease the probability of the deed (see Akers, 1998:98). While recognizing that there may be physiological variations in violent tendencies or susceptibility to finding violence intrinsically rewarding, the theory proposes that violence results primarily from the social exchange in which the words, responses, presence, and behavior of others directly reinforce it, provide the setting for reinforcement (discriminative stimuli), or serve as the conduit through which other social rewards and punishers are delivered or made available. This refers not only to direct reactions of others but to the whole range of actual and anticipated tangible, intangible, and symbolic rewards (and punishments) valued in society or sub-groups. Reinforcing effects can come from the violence fulfilling or believed to be fulfilling ideological, religious, political, or other goals. In some instances, the effects may come from anticipated transcendental rewards in heaven or punishment in hell. The greater the value or amount of rewards for one's violent behavior, the more frequently it is rewarded, and the higher the probability that it will be rewarded (balanced against the amount, frequency, and probability of punishing consequences), the greater the likelihood that it will occur and be repeated. "A child reared in a community espousing nonviolent values and living in a family that professes non-violent attitudes may nonetheless come to engage in and justify violence because he has witnessed abusive behavior in the home, has been the object of abuse himself, or has otherwise learned violent behavior in spite of the nonviolent cultural norms to which he has been exposed" (Akers, 1998:103).

Imitation refers to learning by observing others' behavior (observational learning). The observation of salient models of violence and of the consequences of that violence (directly or indirectly through the factual or fictional depictions of violence in the media) is more important in the initial acquisition and performance of violence, but imitation effects continue to some extent in the maintenance and modifications of violence.

The content and variations in this process operating at the social psychological level have always been seen in social learning theory as functions of, or influenced by, sociocultural factors at the meso and macro levels and by the immediate situational context (Akers, 1973; Burgess & Akers, 1966). We will not review the issue here, but Akers (1998) has recently elaborated a Social Structure Social Learning (SSSL) model that explicates the relationship between social structure, social learning variables, and deviant/criminal behavior including violent behavior. That model posits that the social learning process (and the main variables in that process) mediates most, or at least a substantial portion, of the effects of the social structure and sociocultural milieu on criminal and deviant behavior.

Akers long ago made reference to the cognitive and behavioral principles of social learning as way of analyzing interpersonal violence, including so-called "compulsive" acts of violence. He recounted some of the well known media-reported cases of spouse abuse, child abuse, serial killers, serial rapists, and homicidal violence of lovers, acquaintances, family members, enemies, and strangers and hypothesized that:

> Persons who commit violent acts have come into contact with other persons and social situations which differentially reinforce such action. Through participation and imitation in certain social and cultural contexts they learn that violence is defined as 'all right,' and if it is not rewarded, at least it is not punished . . . When they are confronted with similar situations they are likely to respond violently. Thus, when a person reacts with seemingly

senseless violence to something or someone, on examination we may find that the same behavior, or something similar to it, is an already established part of his or her behavioral repertoire (Akers, 1985:265).

It is no surprise that the two snipers (John Muhammad and Lee Malvo) who shot people in the Washington, DC, area and elsewhere had a history of gun training and violence. It also came as no surprise to find out later that they had justified the killings as righteous vengeance (Muhammad is a convert who took on an extremist version of Islam), wanted to settle personal scores (he was resentful of his wife and defined what he did as a way of responding to a failed marriage), and expected to get some kind of direct or symbolic rewards from it (at one point they attempted to extort money for stopping the killing). The older 2002 sniper had military training in sharp shooting, and his teenage accomplice certainly received from him direct socialization and training in the definitions and techniques of sniper killing and probably had violent leanings even before becoming associated with the older killer.

One does not have to learn the techniques and definitions of the behavior in direct face-to-face interaction in this way, in a specific subculture of violence, or under the influence of a group promoting violence. Further, the nature of the justifications do not have to be invented by or be unique to a particular group. For instance, many of the learned justifications for violence are the application or misapplication of familiar excuses found in the general culture that neutralize the generalized norm against physical attack, maiming, or killing others. Definitions favorable to committing violence that one would usually condemn include defining it as unavoidable, in self-defense, or necessary to achieve justice, or to promote a higher good that has to be achieved by fast social change. Within obvious physical limitations, it makes little difference in the way in which definitions or beliefs function as discriminative for violence whether these reasons are "true" or " untrue." If a rapist defines the actions and struggles of his victims as really wanting to be raped, it makes little difference in understanding his behavior if that is a totally false interpretation of her actions. If militant Islamic groups believe that America is the great Satan and enemy that is waging organized war against all Islam, it does not really matter for purposes of explanation that this is a completely unfounded and erroneous belief.

A Concise Statement of the Theory as Applied to Violence

A concise statement of the social learning explanation of violence summarizing the theoretical analysis thus far is as follows:

> The probability that persons will commit acts of violence is increased when they *differentially associate* directly or indirectly with others who commit violent behavior and espouse

definitions favorable to it (differential association), are relatively more exposed in-person or symbolically through media to *salient models of violence* (imitation), *define it as desirable or justified* (definitions) in a situation *discriminative* for the behavior, and have received in the past and/or anticipate in the current or future situation relatively *greater reward* (either through positive achievement of desired outcomes or avoidance of undesired outcomes) and *less punishment* (either directly or indirectly) for the behavior (differential reinforcement).

This rather complex sentence shows that, while the theory embraces all of the mechanisms of the learning process, it relies principally on the four major explanatory concepts (shown in parentheses and discussed above) of (1) *differential association,* (2) *definitions favorable and unfavorable (and other discriminative stimuli),* (3) *differential reinforcement,* and (4) *imitation/modeling.*

Violent behavior and the readiness (or low level of reticence) to commit acts of violence is acquired, enacted, and changed through variations in association, definitions, reinforcement, imitation, discriminative stimuli, and other variables in the social learning process. This is typically through the nondeliberative process of group and societal influence but often is through deliberate tutelage, training (including militarist training, use of weapons and explosives, suicide bombing, and other terrorist techniques in collective violence), indoctrination, and socialization of children as well as current and new adult members of the group.

There are commonalities across varieties of violence, and those who commit one type (e.g., intimate violence) are more likely to commit another type (e.g., income-producing violence). The same social learning variables are implicated, although their substance, characteristics, and sources may differ. This can be illustrated by brief social learning analyses of rape and terrorism.

Application of Social Learning Theory to Interpersonal and Collective Violence: Rape and Terrorism

Rape is both a sexual and violent act in which nonconsensual sexual intercourse is attempted or consummated through the threat or use of physical force or coercion short of physical force that renders the victim unable to consent. One who is differentially associated with others who are sexually conforming and not involved in violent acts and condemn such behavior is unlikely to commit sexual violence. If the groups with which one is and has been in differential association (kin, fraternities, gangs, and others) are more accepting of and disproportionately have engaged in sexually coercive behavior, then the individual is more likely to be ready to do the same in given circumstances of opportunity. The greater the experienced or anticipated physical and psychological sexual stimulation/gratification, social reward or punishment (informal and formal reactions of others), and pleasure derived from directing coercion against women, the more inclined the man is to use force in sex given the set of circumstances discriminative for it. If the outcome of committing such violent acts is to get what he wants sexually, to control the victim, or gain approval (or at least no disapproval) from associates and to suffer no adverse consequences, he is more likely to repeat it in similar circumstances. General and specific beliefs and attitudes held by the rapist may include seeing sexual coercion as a positive thing that a real man should do when confronted with resistance to his sexual advances. It is, however, more likely to include "rape myths" of excuses and justifications that neutralize the deviant nature of rape, deny that it is really rape, or define the actions of the victim as proving that she really desires forceful sex regardless of what she says or does.

The social sources of these attitudes may be immediate or more distant reference groups, picked up in verbal and behavioral interaction within male peer groups currently and over time as well as in childhood socialization and intrafamilial exposure to violent sexual behavior and attitudes. Observation of and rewarded participation in rape may be direct (as in gang rape). However, this kind of first-person observation of sexual violence is much less likely than exposure to depiction of sexual violence available in books, films, videos, magazines, games, and the Internet, and for rapists this once-removed modeling in various forms of pornographic media probably occurs more frequently than in-person observation (Boeringer, Shehan & Akers, 1991).

Rapists are unlikely to define their acts as serving a higher goal or as carrying out the just deeds of a group with which they strongly identify. Terrorism, on the other hand, is "moralistic" violence (Black, 1976; Cooney, 1998; Senechal de la Roche, 1996; Silverman, 2002b) that seeks to redress the grievances and enforce the norms of the groups and causes with which the terrorists identify against those perceived to have violated them. Terrorists' identities are shaped around strongly held ideologies that define their violence as fully justified acts of "freedom fighters," war, and destroying or defeating the enemy in service of political, social, religious, or ethnolinguistic ideals and objectives (Barak, 2004; Silverman, 2002a). The ultimate intention of the terrorists is to utilize the fear and intimidation created by their actions to bring about sociopolitical change (Schmid & Jongman, 1988). Acts of terrorism are committed with the intent to assert the subcultural norms and world view of the actors onto the larger culture and/or other subcultures. Thus, terrorism is both "identity-based" and "strategic/utility-maximizing" behavior and can be understood in terms of Weber's (1968) notion of value rationality. The terrorist's identity is so strong that it functions to limit the choices of behavior to those permitted by the group context and provides a logic of consequences within those bounds. Moreover, it overcomes the problem of collective action (Olson, 1971). Terrorists take actions with high personal costs because of, not despite, their identity. The identity and the context it provides reduce or overcome the real and potential costs of terrorism for the terrorist (Silverman, 2004).

Our explanation of terrorism posits that terrorists adopt an identity (Wald, 1992) and ideology or "framing" promoted in the movement that include attitudes, beliefs, and values that justify killing, destruction, and injury as means to a noble end. The extremist subculture provides identity, ideational and physical resources, and a more or less coherent perspective on the disputes and grievances that are so important to the person in which violent struggle is an integral part of his life. The terrorist learns that violence is permissible and rewarded by political outcomes and the approbation of both leaders and members of the group. For groups such as al Qaeda, there is direct tutelage and training for specifically planned terrorists attacks on identified targets. In other groups, the learning of violence and appropriate targets is less direct, with the harsh and uncompromising political language used by some leaders and members encouraging, without specifically endorsing or planning, violent actions. These may be extreme expressions of religious and political values that the terrorists ostensibly share with others who do not engage in violence. The others refrain because they have not adopted the self and group identity of the terrorists and subscribe to countervailing nonviolent definitions that the terrorists do not endorse. Our argument here is that the key concepts of "identity" and "framing" found (along with opportunity and organizational resources) in political science, sociology, criminology, and religious studies related to terrorism are linked to the social learning concepts of differential association and definitions and may provide linkages between social learning theory and other perspectives on terrorism (Silverman, 2002a). Social learning is not a simple "cultural deviance" theory, but rather articulates culture and subculture (in this case of violence and terrorism) with the social learning process through the concept of definitions (see Akers, 1996).

Abortion clinic violence may be viewed as a type of terrorism that is also explicable in social learning terms. It is both a contextually bound and instrumental action intended as a way to resolve conflict through extension of one type of social control over a particular conflict (Black, 1976). The moralistic element in abortion clinic violence, based on the norms and definitions espoused in the anti-abortion movement, is intended to bring about social and political change. The pro-life ideology is anti-violence but the horror with which it views taking the life of the unborn is pushed by a few to the extreme for whom killing an abortionist is justified as preventing a murderer from committing any more murders. Abortion clinic violence is rewarded through anticipation of several related outcomes: immediately stopping abortions, intimidating and scaring providers and seekers of abortion from engaging in it, and intimidating society and the polity into restricting/outlawing abortion in order to prevent future acts of violence. Those who do not adopt these extreme definitions favorable to vio-lence and who counter them with nonviolent definitions of acceptable means will not engage in abortion clinic violence.

The terrorist attacks of September 11, 2001, as well as a good deal of the other terrorist incidents that have occurred before and since that time domestically and internationally, can be explained by the same reference to identity-based grievances and definitions favorable to violence as an instru-ment of change (Silverman, 2002b). The self-described martyrs of the Hamas, Hezbullah, Islamic Jihad, and al Qaeda all have specific rational-izations and justifications for their violent actions: the existence of Israel, the lack of an Islamically acceptable society and polity, and the inherent evil of Western (particularly American) culture and Judeo-Christian religions. The Basque terrorists of the ETA (Euskadi Ta Askatasuna), and the terrorists affil-iated with the various Irish Republican movements also have higher goals and ideological justifications for terrorist attacks: the Basque homeland and a united Ireland, respectively. Although he had no direct membership in it, the American Patriot Movement seems to have been a powerful reference group for Timothy McVeigh, who wreaked devastation and murder in bombing the federal building in Oklahoma City.

As part of their subcultural identities, terrorists learn an ideology that the ends justify the means; violence for political ends is accepted and rewarded. These function as definitions favorable to violence. Terrorism becomes a way of life and a means for at least some of the members of the subculture to pursue the conflicts that they perceive between themselves and out-groups. In essence, the "framing" of the conflict teaches the terrorists definitions of the situation and when, where, and how often, it is morally right or justified to engage in political violence. It is important to note that counter-balancing forces such as the dire personal, monetary, life-threat-ening, and life-taking consequences, both immediate and long-term, of actively engaging in terrorism means that not every member who partici-pates in or identifies with and adopts the rationalizations of such a collec-tivity will carry out terrorists acts themselves. Only a tiny portion of those who vehemently oppose abortion have or will take part in any violence not only because of the offsetting negative consequences for them but also because of countervailing norms in the same groups against violence as a means of carrying on the struggle. For similar reasons, only some Islamic fundamentalists actually commit violent acts as part of Jihad.

Empirical Support for Social Learning as a General Theory of Crime and Deviance

The preponderance of empirical research conducted over a great many years on the effects of one or more of the social learning variables (differ-ential association, imitation, definitions, and differential reinforcement) on delinquent, criminal, and deviant behavior has found strong to moderate effects in the expected direction. (See the extensive reviews of the research literature in Akers, 1998; Akers & Sellers, 2004; and the empirical papers in Akers & Jensen, 2003.) Examples of such research findings in the literature can be found in Elliott, Huizinga, and Ageton (1985); Sellers and Winfree (1990); Warr (1993); Winfree, Sellers, and Clason (1993); Agnew (1994); Thornberry, Lizotte, Krohn, Farnworth, and Jang (1994); Benda (1994); Burton, Cullen, Evans, and Dunaway (1994); Catalano, Kosterman, Hawkins, Abbott, and Newcomb (1996); Mihalic and Elliott (1997); Skinner and Fream (1997); Esbensen and Deschenes (1998); Huang, Kosterman, Catalano, Hawkins, and Abbott (2001); Rebellon (2002); and Jang (2002). Research in other societies indicates that social learning is not an American culture–bound or society-specific explanation of deviance (see, for example, Junger-Tas, 1992; Kandel & Adler, 1982; Zhang & Messner, 1995).

Social learning of deviant and conforming behavior in the family is found in research on parental modeling, application of positive and negative sanctions in parental supervision and discipline, and support for values and attitudes favorable or unfavorable to deviance. Children reared in families in which the parents and older siblings are involved in deviance or crime are themselves at higher risk of delinquent involvement while those in conforming families in which parents make consistent use of positive reward for proper behavior and punitive reactions to misbehavior are at lower risk of developing delinquent or criminal behavior (Ardelt & Day, 2002; Capaldi, Chamberlain & Patterson, 1997; McCord, 1991a; 1991b; Rowe & Gulley, 1992; Snyder & Patterson, 1995).

Peer groups are the most important primary group context in which adolescents and young adults are socialized into deviant attitudes and learn delinquent and criminal behavior tendencies and has long been a focus of the differential association dimension in social learning theory. There is a large body of research literature reporting the importance of differential peer associations and definitions in explaining the onset, continuation, or cessation of crime, delinquency, use of alcohol and other drugs, and other forms of deviant behavior. More frequent, longer-term, and closer association with peers who are perceived as engaging in and holding values supportive of deviant behavior than with conforming peers is strongly predictive of one's own delinquent behavior.

> No characteristic of individuals known to criminologists is a better predictor of criminal behavior than the number of delinquent friends an individual has. The strong correlation between delinquent behavior and delinquent friends has been documented . . . using alternative kinds of criminological data (self-reports, official records, perceptual data) on subjects and friends, alternative research designs, and data on a wide variety of criminal offenses. Few, if any, empirical regularities in criminology have been documented as often or over as long a period as the association between delinquency and delinquent friends (Warr, 2002:40).

Haynie (2002) reports strong empirical support for the social learning principle of the balance or ratio of association with delinquent and non-delinquent friends (see also Lauritsen, 1993; Loeber & Dishion, 1987; Simons, Wu, Conger & Lorenz, 1994; Warr, 1993).

One special peer association context in which this balance leans in the deviant direction is participation in delinquent gangs and subcultures. Research continues to find strong effects of gang membership on serious delinquency (Curry, Decker & Egley, 2002; Esbensen & Deschenes, 1998; Winfree, Backstrom & Mays, 1994). Gang membership promotes criminal offending because "group processes and norms favorable to violence and other delinquency within gangs subsequently encourage and reinforce participation in violent and delinquent behavior" (Battin, Hill, Abbott, Catalano & Hawkins, 1998:108). "Gang members reward certain behavior in their peers and punish others, employing goals and processes that are indistinguishable from those described by Akers" (Winfree, Backstrom & Mays, 1994:149). These group processes involve differential association, exposure to delinquent models and definitions, and reinforcement for delinquent behavior that have effects even controlling for "personal-biographical characteristics, including ethnicity, gender, and place of residence" (Winfree, Backstrom & Mays, 1994:167).

In addition to the positive findings consistently reported by other researchers, support for social learning theory comes from research conducted by Akers, his students, and associates over many years in which all of the key social learning variables are measured (Akers, 1998). These include research on adolescent substance use (Akers & Cochran, 1985; Akers, Krohn, Lanza-Kaduce & Radosevich, 1979; Akers & Lee, 1999; Hwang & Akers, 2003; Krohn, Lanza-Kaduce & Akers, 1984), teenage smoking (Akers & Lee, 1996; Spear & Akers, 1988), alcohol consumption among elderly populations (Akers, La Greca, Cochran & Sellers, 1989), rape and sexual coercion among samples of college males (Boeringer, Shehan & Akers, 1991), as well as homicide rates among 82 nations (Jensen & Akers, 2003). These studies have consistently found that the social learning variables of differential association, differential reinforcement, imitation, and definitions, singly and in combination, account for high levels of explained variance (from 31 to 68 percent in the full models) in the various forms of deviant, delinquent, and criminal behavior. The effects of the social learning variables remain across age, sex, race, and class.

This review of empirical support for the theory refers only to representative research and does not attempt to cite the whole body of empirical evidence. However, even if all studies were cited, it would remain true that the great majority of the research has been on adolescent deviance and delinquency. There still has not been much research directly testing the efficacy of social learning theory as an explanation of violent behavior as outlined here. Empirical models built on the social learning concepts have been supported in research on rape (Akers, 1998; Boeringer, Shehan & Akers,

1991), homicide/suicide (Batton & Ogle, 2003), courtship violence (Sellers, Cochran & Winfree, 2003), adolescent violence (Bellair, Roscigno & Velez, 2003), and terrorist attacks on abortion clinics (Silverman, 2002a). However, more research is needed on social learning models of interpersonal or collective violence. The question is to what extent does social learning theory help us understand what is already known about violence and to what extent does it set up hypotheses that can be tested against newly collected data? We contend that it does help to account for at least some of the empirical parameters of violence and terrorism that have already been established, especially with regard to the ideologies and attitudes favorable to violence and the patterns of group and subcultural associations. We leave it to future research to assess further how well models and propositions from social learning theory fit empirical findings.

Conclusion

The basic proposition in social learning theory is that the same social psychological process in a context of social structure, interaction, and situation, produces both conforming and deviant behavior. The difference lies in the direction of the balance of influences on behavior. However horrific they may be, violence and terrorism may be understood by reference to the empirical values and balance of the same cognitive/behavioral variables that relate to learning and committing any behavior. This understanding, however, should be taken as an explanation not as an excuse. To explain is not to accept.

Endnote

[1]   "Social learning" may be used to refer to any social behavioristic approach in social science especially in psychology in the work of Albert Bandura (1977) and others (Patterson, Reid, Jones & Conger, 1975). In the field of criminology and deviance, however, social learning is most likely to mean the theory first proposed by Burgess and Akers (1966) and developed through the years by Akers (1973; 1998) as an integration of Sutherland's (1947) theory of differential association and behavioral principles of reinforcement and imitation.

Discussion Questions

1. How would social learning theory explain violence, rape, and terrorism? In your response refer to the four major dimensions of the social learning process. violence, rape, and terrorism?

2. Explain what happens when an individual differentially associates with deviant groups?

3. Explain the role that recontextualization of events plays in the creation of definitions favorable to terrorism?

4. Explain why having multiple and overlapping associations promotes normative behavior and retards deviant behavior?

5. What part does the concept of definitions favorable and unfavorable in social learning theory play in accounting for criminal and deviant behavior? In what way does this concept relate to that of "rape myths" in explaining rape and sexual aggression and "framing" or "identity" with regard to terrorism?

References

Agnew, R. (1994). "The Techniques of Neutralization and Violence." *Criminology*, 32:555-580.

Akers, R. (1973). *Deviant Behavior: A Social Learning Approach*. Belmont, CA: Wadsworth.

Akers, R.L. (1985). *Deviant Behavior: A Social Learning Approach*, 3rd ed. Belmont, CA: Wadsworth.

Akers, R. L. (1996). "Is Differential Association/Social Learning Cultural Deviance Theory?" *Criminology*, 34:229-248.

Akers, R.L. (1998). *Social Learning and Social Structure: A General Theory of Crime and Deviance*. Boston: Northeastern University Press.

Akers, R.L., and J.K. Cochran (1985). "Adolescent Marijuana Use: A Test of Three Theories of Deviant Behavior." *Deviant Behavior*, 6:323-346.

Akers, R.L., and G.F. Jensen (eds.) (2003). *Social Learning Theory and the Explanation of Crime: A Guide for the New Century*. New Brunswick, NJ: Transaction.

Akers, R.L., M.D. Krohn, L. Lanza-Kaduce, and M. Radosevich (1979). "Social Learning and Deviant Behavior: A Specific Test of a General Theory." *American Sociological Review*, 44: 635-655.

Akers, R.L., A.J. La Greca, J.K. Cochran, and C.S. Sellers (1989). "Social Learning Theory and Alcohol Behavior among the Elderly." *Sociological Quarterly*, 30:625-38.

Akers, R.L., and G. Lee (1996). "A Longitudinal Test of Social Learning Theory: Adolescent Smoking." *Journal of Drug Issues*, 26:317-343.

Akers, R.L., and C.S. Sellers (2004). *Criminological Theories: Introduction, Evaluation, and Application*, 4th ed. Los Angeles: Roxbury.

Ardelt, M., and L. Day (2002). "Parents, Siblings, and Peers: Close Social Relationships and Adolescent Deviance." *Journal of Early Adolescence*, 22:310-349.

Bandura, A. (1977). *Social Learning Theory*. Englewood Cliffs, NJ: Prentice Hall.

Bandura, A. (1990). "Selective Activation and Disengagement of Moral Control." *Journal of Social Issues*, 46:27-46.

Barak, G. (2004). "A Reciprocal Appraoch to Terrorism and Terrorist-like Behavior." In M. Deflem (ed.), *Terrorism and Counter-Terrorism: Criminological Perspectives, Sociology of Crime, Law, and Deviance*, pp. 33-49.

Battin, S.R., K.G. Hill, R.D. Abbott, R.F. Catalano, and J.D. Hawkins (1998). "The Contribution of Gang Membership to Delinquency: Beyond Delinquent Friends." *Criminology*, 36:93-115.

Batton, C., and R.S. Ogle (2003). "Who's It Gonna Be—You or Me? The Potential of Social Learning for Integrated Homicide-Suicide Theory." In R.L. Akers and G.F. Jensen (eds.), *Social Learning Theory and the Explanation of Crime: A Guide for the New Century*, pp. 85-108. New Brunswick, NJ: Transaction.

Bellair, P.E., V.J. Roscigno, and M.B. Velez (2003). "Occupational Structure, Social Learning, and Adolescent Violence." In R.L. Akers and G.F. Jensen (eds.), *Social Learning Theory and the Explanation of Crime: A Guide for the New Century*, pp. 197-226. New Brunswick, NJ: Transaction.

Benda, B.B. (1994). "Testing Competing Theoretical Concepts: Adolescent Alcohol Consumption." *Deviant Behavior,* 15:375-396.

Black, D. (1976). *The Behavior of Law*. London: The Academic Press.

Boeringer, S., C.L. Shehan, and R.L. Akers (1991). "Social Contexts and Social Learning in Sexual Coercion and Aggression: Assessing the Contribution of Fraternity Membership." *Family Relations*, 40:558-564.

Burgess, R.L., and R.L. Akers (1966). "A Differential Association–Reinforcement Theory of Criminal Behavior." *Social Problems*, 14:128-147.

Burton, V., F.T. Cullen, D. Evans, and R.G. Dunaway (1994). "Reconsidering Strain Theory: Operationalization, Rival Theories, and Adult Criminality." *Journal of Quantitative Criminology*, 10:213-239.

Capaldi, D.M., P. Chamberlain, and G.R. Patterson (1997). "Ineffective Discipline and Conduct Problems in Males: Association, Late Adolescent Outcomes, and Prevention." *Aggression and Violent Behavior*, 2:343-353.

Catalano, R.F., R. Kosterman, J.D. Hawkins, R.D. Abbott, and M.D. Newcomb (1996). "Modeling the Etiology of Adolescent Substance Use: A Test of the Social Development Model." *Journal of Drug Issues*, 26:429-456.

Cooney, M. (1998). *Warriors and Peacemakers: How Third Parties Shape Violence*. New York: New York University Press.

Cressey, D.R. (1953). *Other People's Money.* Glencoe, IL: Free Press.

Curry, G.D., S.H. Decker, and A. Egley, Jr. (2002). "Gang Involvement and Delinquency in a Middle School Population." *Justice Quarterly*, 19:275-292.

Elliott, D.S., D. Huizinga, and S.S. Ageton (1985). *Explaining Delinquency and Drug Use.* Beverly Hills, CA: Sage.

Esbensen, F., and E.P. Deschenes (1998). "A Multisite Examination of Youth Gang Membership: Does Gender Matter?" *Criminology*, 36:799-827.

Haynie, D. (2002). "Friendship Networks in Delinquency: The Relative Nature of Peer Delinquency." *Journal of Quantitative Criminology*, 18(2):99-134.

Hewitt, J.P., and R. Stokes (1975). "Disclaimers." *American Sociological Review*, 40:1-11.

Huang, B., R. Kosterman, R.F. Catalano, J.D. Hawkins, and R.D. Abbott (2001). "Modeling Mediation in the Etiology of Violent Behavior in Adolescence: A Test of the Social Development Model." *Criminology,* 39:75-108.

Hwang, S., and R.L. Akers (2003). "Adolescent Substance Use in South Korea: A Cross-Cultural Test of Three Theories" In R.L. Akers and G.F. Jensen (eds.), *Social Learning Theory and the Explanation of Crime: A Guide for the New Century*, pp. 39-64. New Brunswick, NJ: Transaction.

Jang, S.J. (2002). "The Effects of Family, School, Peers, and Attitudes on Adolescents Drug Use: Do They Vary with Age." *Justice Quarterly*, 19:97-126.

Jensen, G.F., and R.L. Akers (2003). "Taking Social Learning Global: Micro-Macro Transitions in Criminological Theory." In R.L. Akers and G.F. Jensen (eds.), *Social Learning Theory and the Explanation of Crime: A Guide for the New Century*, pp. 9-38. New Brunswick, NJ: Transaction.

Junger-Tas, J. (1992). "An Empirical Test of Social Control Theory." *Journal of Quantitative Criminology*, 8:9-28.

Kandel, D., and I. Adler (1982). "Socialization into Marijuana Use among French Adolescents: A Cross Cultural Comparison with the United States." *Journal of Health and Social Behavior*, 23:295-309.

Krohn, M.D., L. Lanza-Kaduce, and R.L. Akers (1984). "Community Context and Theories of Deviant Behavior: An Examination of Social Learning and Social Bonding Theories." *Sociological Quarterly*, 25:353-371.

Lauritsen, J.L. (1993). "Sibling Resemblance in Juvenile Delinquency: Findings from the National Youth Survey." *Criminology*, 31:387-410.

Loeber, R., and Dishion, T. J. (1987). "Antisocial and Delinquent Youths: Methods for Their Early Identification." In J.D. Burchard and S. Burchard (eds.), *Prevention of Delinquent Behavior*, pp. 75-89. Newbury Park, CA: Sage.

Lyman, S.M., and M.B. Scott (1970). *A Sociology of the Absurd.* New York: Appleton-Century-Crofts.

Mihalic, S.W., and D. Elliott (1997). "A Social Learning Theory Model of Marital Violence." *Journal of Family Violence*, 12:21-36.

McCord, J. (1991a). "Family Relationships, Juvenile Delinquency, and Adult Criminality." *Criminology*, 29:397-418.

McCord, J. (1991b). "The Cycle of Crime and Socialization Practices." *Journal of Criminal Law and Criminology*, 2:211-228.

Olson, M. (1971). *The Logic of Collective Action: Public Goods and the Theory of Groups*. Cambridge, MA: Harvard University Press.

Patterson, G.R. (1995). "Coercion as a Basis for Early Age of Onset for Arrest." In J. McCord, (ed.), *Coercion and Punishment in Long Term Perspectives*, pp. 81-105. Cambridge, UK: Cambridge University Press.

Patterson, G.R., J.B. Reid, R.Q. Jones, and R.E. Conger (1975). *A Social Learning Approach to Family Intervention*, Volume 1. Eugene, OR: Castalia.

Rebellon, C.J. (2002). "Reconsidering the Broken Homes/Delinquency Relationship and Exploring Its Mediating Mechanism(s)." *Criminology*, 40:103-136.

Rowe, D.C., and B.L. Gulley (1992). "Sibling Effects on Substance Use and Delinquency." *Criminology*, 30:217-234.

Schmid, A.P., and A.J. Jongman (1988). *Political Terrorism: A New Guide to Actors, Authors, Concepts, Databases, Theories, and Literature*. Amsterdam: North-Holland.

Senechal de la Roche, R. (1996). "Collective Violence as Social Control." *Sociological Forum*, 11:97-128.

Sellers, C.S., J.K. Cochran, and L.T. Winfree, Jr. (2003). "Social Learning Theory and Courtship Violence: An Empirical Test." In R.L. Akers and G.F. Jensen (eds.), *Social Learning Theory and the Explanation of Crime: A Guide for the New Century*, pp. 109-128. New Brunswick, NJ: Transaction.

Sellers, C.S., and T.L. Winfree (1990). "Differential Associations and Definitions: a Panel Study of Youthful Drinking Behavior." *International Journal of the Addictions*, 25:755-771.

Silverman, A.L. (2002a). *An Exploratory Analysis of an Interdisciplinary Theory of Terrorism*. Ph.D. Dissertation. University of Florida.

Silverman, A.L. (2002b). "Just War, Jihad, and Terrorism: A Comparison of Western and Islamic Norms for the Use of Political Violence." *The Journal of Church and State*, 4:73-92.

Silverman, A.L. (2004). "Zealous Before the Lord: The Construction of the Christian Identity Ideology." In L. Snowden and B. Whitsel (eds.), *Terrorism: Research, Readings & Realities*. Upper Saddle River, NJ: Prentice Hall.

Simons, R.L., C. Wu, R.D. Conger, and F.O. Lorenz (1994). "Two Routes to Delinquency: Differences between Early and Late Starters in the Impact of Parenting and Deviant Peers." *Criminology*, 32:247-276.

Skinner, W.F., and A.M. Fream (1997). "A Social Learning Theory Analysis of Computer Crime among College Students." *Journal of Research in Crime and Delinquency*, 34:495-518.

Snyder, J.J., and G.R. Patterson (1995). "Individual Differences in Social Aggression: A Test of a Reinforcement Model of Socialization in the Natural Environment." *Behavior Therapy*.

Sykes, G.M., and D. Matza (1957). "Techniques of Neutralization: A Theory of Delinquency." *American Sociological Review*, 22:664-670.

Spear, S., and R.L. Akers (1988). "Social Learning Variables and the Risk of Habitual Smoking among Adolescents: The Muscatine Study." *American Journal of Preventive Medicine*, 4:336-348.

Sutherland, E.H. (1947). *Principles of Criminology*, 4th ed. Philadelphia: J.B. Lippincott.

Thornberry, T.P., A.J. Lizotte, M.D. Krohn, M. Farnworth, and S.J. Jang (1994). "Delinquent Peers, Beliefs, and Delinquent Behavior: A Longitudinal Test of Interactional Theory." *Criminology*, 32:47-84.

Wald, K.D. (1992). *Religion and Politics in the United States*. Washington, DC: CQ Press.

Warr, M. (1993). "Parents, Peers, and Delinquency." *Social Forces*, 72:247-264.

Warr, M. (2002). *Companions in Crime: The Social Aspects of Criminal Conduct*. Cambridge, UK: Cambridge University Press.

Weber, M. (1968). *Economy and Society: An Outline of Interpretive Sociology*. Tr. by Ephraim Fischoff and edited by G. Roth and C. Wittich. New York: Bedminster.

Winfree, L.T., C. Sellers, and D.L. Clason (1993). "Social Learning and Adolescent Deviance Abstention: Toward Understanding Reasons for Initiating, Quitting, and Avoiding Drugs." *Journal of Quantitative Criminology*, 9:101-125.

Winfree, L.T., Jr., T.V. Backstrom, and G.L. Mays (1994). "Social Learning Theory, Self Reported Delinquency, and Youth Gangs: A New Twist on a General Theory of Crime and Delinquency." *Youth and Society*, 26:147-177.

Zhang, L., and S.F. Messner (1995). "Family Deviance and Delinquency in China." *Criminology*, 33:359-388.

CHAPTER 2

A General Strain Theory Approach to Violence

Robert Agnew

. . . 'what's really important today is not the Arab street, but the Arab basement' . . . The 'Arab Street' is the broad mass of public opinion, which is largely passive and nonviolent. The 'Arab basement' is where small groups of hard-core ideologues, such as Osama bin Laden and his gang, have retreated and where they are mixing fertilizer, C-4 plastic explosives and gasoline to make the bombs that have killed Westerners all over the world. Over the years, Arab leaders have become adept at dealing with the Arab street. . . . They know how to buy off, or seal off, the anger and how to deflect its attention onto Israel . . . The Arab basement, though, is a new and much more dangerous phenomenon. These are small groups of super-empowered angry men who have slipped away from the street into underground cells, but with global reach and ambitions. While issues like Israel and U.S. policy clearly motivate them, what most fuels their anger are domestic indignities—the sense that their repressive societies are deeply failing, or being left behind by the world . . . The only sensible solution is to defeat those in the Arab basement . . . while at the same time working to alleviate the grievances, unemployment, and sense of humiliation that is felt on the Arab street . . . 'It takes many years of political, social, economic and human degradation to create a terrorist . . .' (Friedman, 2002:A23).

Major Arguments of and Evidence for General Strain Theory (GST)

The core idea of general strain theory (GST) is quite simple: if you treat people badly, they may become upset and respond with crime, including violence (Agnew, 1992). GST elaborates on this idea by describing (1) those types of negative treatment most likely to result in crime, (2) why negative treatment increases the likelihood of crime, and (3) why some people are more likely than others to respond to negative treatment with crime. This chapter describes the central arguments of GST in these areas and then discusses how GST might explain various types of criminal violence. Special note is made of areas in which further research is needed.

The Types of Negative Treatment (Strain) Most Likely to Result in Crime

GST focuses on three broad categories of negative treatment or strain. Others may: (1) prevent individuals from achieving their positively valued goals (e.g., money, status, autonomy); (2) remove or threaten to remove the positively valued stimuli that individuals possesses (e.g., loss of romantic partner, theft of valued possessions); and (3) present or threaten to present individuals with noxious or negatively valued stimuli (e.g., verbal or physical abuse). GST focuses on the individual's *personal experiences* with these types of strain, although *vicarious* and *anticipated experiences* with these types of strain may sometimes result in crime as well (Agnew, 2002). For example, individuals may turn to crime when close others like family members and friends are victimized or when they anticipate that there is a strong likelihood they will be victimized.

Literally hundreds of specific types of strain fall into the broad categories of strain listed above. Data suggest that many, *but not all*, of these specific strains increase the likelihood of crime. Recent work on GST specifies the characteristics of those types of strain that are most likely to result in crime (Agnew, 2001a). Such strains (1) are seen as unjust, (2) are seen as high in magnitude (with magnitude reflecting the degree, recency, and centrality of strain), (3) are associated with low social control, and (4) create some pressure or incentive to engage in criminal coping. GST provides guidance on how to identify strains with these characteristics (e.g., how to identify strains likely to be seen as unjust, how to determine if strains are associated with low social control). As illustrations of these characteristics, consider the following two instances of strain.

First, a father has to take a day off from work to care for his sick child. This creates some strain or stress for the father, but this strain is unlikely to lead to crime. The strain is probably not seen as unjust, because the child was not trying to deliberately harm or inconvenience the father. The strain produced by taking a day off from work is probably not high in magnitude; rather, it likely represents a minor to moderate inconvenience for the father. The strain is not associated with low social control; if anything, the child's illness restricts the activities of the father—reducing opportunities for crime. Finally, the strain does not create much pressure or incentive to engage in crime; crime will not cure the child's illness.

Second, a student is assaulted by another student at school. This assault creates much strain for the victim and increases the likelihood of further crime. The assault is probably seen as unjust, because it involved a deliberate effort to harm the victim. The strain produced by the assault is probably high in magnitude; among other things, the assault threatened the physical safety of the victim and reduced the victim's status or standing among other students. The assault is associated with low social control, because peer conflicts among juveniles usually occur away from sanctioning agents like parents and teachers. And the assault creates some pressure or incentive for criminal coping. Among other things, other students may encourage a criminal response, and a criminal response may be seen as the best way to restore the victim's status and reduce the likelihood of further assaults (see Anderson, 1999).

GST lists certain of the specific strains that *should and should not* increase the likelihood of crime (Agnew, 2001a). Those strains that should increase the likelihood of crime include:

- the failure to achieve core goals that are not the result of conventional socialization and that are easily achieved through crime (e.g., the desire for much money in a short period of time, thrills/excitement, masculine status, high levels of autonomy);

- parental rejection;

- supervision/discipline that is very strict, erratic, excessive given the infraction, and/or harsh (use of humiliation/insults, threats, screaming, and/or physical punishments);

- child abuse and neglect;

- negative secondary school experiences (low grades, negative relations with teachers, find school boring and a waste of time);

- work in the secondary labor market (jobs with low pay and prestige, few benefits, unpleasant tasks, little autonomy, coercive control, limited opportunities for advancement);

- homelessness, especially youth homelessness;

- abusive peer relations (insults, ridicule, threats, assaults), especially among youth;

- criminal victimization;

- experiences with prejudice and discrimination based on ascribed characteristics, like race/ethnicity.

Most of these strains have been found to increase the likelihood of crime, with studies often finding that they have their largest effects on violent crime (Agnew, 2001b). However, there has not been much research on the impact of certain of these strains on crime, particularly those strains involving abusive peer relations and experiences with prejudice and discrimination (although see Agnew, 2002; Colvin, 2000; McCord & Ensminger, 2003; Simons, Yi-Fu, Stewart & Brody, 2003). Further, this list is in need of expansion. GST focuses on the explanation of individual crime and violence, especially "common" or "street" crimes (e.g., assault, robbery, theft). The theory needs to include additional types of strain if it is to properly explain other types of violence. For example, the theory must consider the strains or problems associated with globalization in order to properly explain terrorism.

Those types of strain that should *not* be related to crime include:

- the failure to achieve goals that result from conventional socialization and that are difficult to achieve through illegitimate channels (e.g., educational and occupational success);

- the excessive demands associated with conventional jobs that are well rewarded (e.g., the long hours associated with many professional jobs);

- unpopularity with or isolation from peers, especially criminal peers;

- the burdens associated with the care of conventional others to whom one is strongly attached, like children and sick/disabled spouses.

Data suggest that most of these types of strain are not associated with crime.

Why Strain Increases the Likelihood of Crime

Negative treatment or strain generally makes people feel bad. That is, it contributes to a range of negative emotions, including anger, frustration, and depression. These negative emotions create pressure for corrective action, with crime being one possible response. Crime may be a way to reduce or escape from strain. For example, individuals may steal the money they need, shoot the peers who harass them, or run away from the parents who abuse them. Crime may be a way to take revenge on those responsible for the strain or related targets. And crime may be a way to alleviate the negative feelings associated with strain (e.g., illicit drug use).

Several studies have examined the extent to which negative emotions mediate the effect of strain on crime. Such studies focus on the negative emotion of anger, given its central role in GST. Anger is said to be especially conducive to crime and violence because it energizes the individual for action, lower inhibitions, and creates a strong desire for revenge. These studies generally find that anger partly mediates the effect of strain on crime, especially violent crime (see Agnew, 2001b). Such studies, however, tend to focus on "trait" or long-term anger. GST does state that strain may cause individuals to develop an angry disposition, which in turn increases the likelihood of crime. But GST states that the primary reason that strain leads to crime is because it increases short-term or situational anger. That is, individuals respond to particular strains with angry outbursts, which in turn increase the likelihood of crime. Future research, then, should examine the effect of strain on situational anger. In this area, one recent study found that certain strains increased the likelihood of situational anger and that such anger had a large effect on intentions to assault others. In fact, situational anger had the largest effect on intentions to assault among the broad range of independent variables that were examined (Mazerolle, Piquero & Capowich, 2003).

Future research should also distinguish between different types of anger. Broidy and Agnew (1997), for example, argue that the anger of males tends to differ from that of females. Male anger is more often characterized by moral outrage, while female anger is more often accompanied by guilt and anxiety. The anger of males is said to be more conducive to other-directed crime, especially violence. The anger of females is said to be more conducive to inner-directed crime and deviance, like eating disorders. Further, future research should devote more attention to other negative emotions. One recent study, for example, found that strain increased depression and that depression, in turn, contributed to crime (Simons, Yi-Fu, Stewart & Brody, 2003). Still other negative emotions, like hopelessness and frustration, should be examined. Finally, future research should examine the effect of strain on other mediating variables, like attitudes favorable to aggression. Anderson (1999), for example, argues that the strains associated with life in poor, inner-city communities often generate a set of beliefs that justify the use of violence in certain situations. In particular, individuals who are frequently threatened and assaulted by others often adopt beliefs that justify violence against these others (also see Cloward & Ohlin, 1960; Cohen, 1955; Simons, Yi-Fu, Stewart & Brody, 2003).

Factors Affecting the Reaction to Strain

Crime is just one of many possible responses to strain. Individuals may respond to their strain with *behavioral* coping strategies of a legitimate nature (e.g., negotiating with the peers who harass them, notifying the police about the family member who abuses them). They may employ *cognitive* coping strategies in an attempt to minimize the strain they experience (e.g., convince themselves that their strain is "not that bad"). And they may employ *emotional* coping strategies of a legitimate nature, such as exercise and listening to music.

A central question confronting GST, then, is what factors influence whether individuals cope with strain in a criminal versus noncriminal manner? Individuals are said to be most likely to cope with strain through crime when:

- they have a low tolerance for strain; that is, they are easily upset and have intense emotional reactions to strain (this low tolerance is partly a function of personality traits like "negative emotionality");

- they have poor coping skills and resources; for example, they have poor social and problem-solving skills and limited financial resources;

- they have few conventional social supports, who might provide advice, emotional support, financial support, or direct assistance in coping with strain;

- their costs of crime are low; in particular, they have little to lose by engaging in crime, do not believe that crime is wrong in their particular case, and are in situations or environments where their criminal behavior is unlikely to be sanctioned in a meaningful way;

- they are disposed to crime, because they have personality traits conducive to crime such as low self-control and negative emotionality, they have been previously reinforced for crime in similar circumstances, they have been exposed to valued models who have successfully engaged in crime in similar circumstances, they otherwise have reason to believe they will be reinforced for crime, and/or they hold beliefs favorable to crime.

It should be noted that this list includes the key variables associated with many of the leading crime theories, such as theories of social control, self-control, social learning, and rational choice. One way in which GST might be integrated with these theories, then, is by arguing that the effect of strain on crime is conditioned by the key variables in these theories. Agnew (1995) also argues that strain affects many of the key variables in these theories; for example, harsh discipline may contribute to low attachment to parents and beliefs favorable to crime. Further, the key variables in these theories may contribute to strain; for example, individuals who are low in self-control may provoke negative reactions from others.)

There has been a moderate amount of research on those factors said to condition the effect of strain on crime. Such research has produced mixed results (see Agnew, 2001b). These mixed results may stem from the fact that it is very difficult to detect interactions using survey data, for reasons indicated in McClelland and Judd (1993). Nevertheless, a number of significant interactions have been found. For example, Agnew and colleagues (2002) recently found that individuals with the personality traits of negative emotionality and low constraint were more likely to respond to strain with crime. Individuals with these traits are impulsive, overly active, and quick to lose their temper, among other things. This finding is important because it paves the way for the integration of strain theory with the recent biopsychological research on crime (the traits of negative emotionality and low constraint are influenced by a range of biological factors). Further research, including research based on observational, experimental, quasi-experimental, and vignette studies, should shed important light on those factors that condition the reaction to strain.

Among other things, such research might help us better understand why only some of the many strained individuals in the "Arab street" are pushed or drawn into the "Arab basement." Such research, however, needs to consider a broader range of conditioning variables than those listed in GST. For example, the response of political regimes to the strain and social protest of citizens likely has a major effect on the development of terrorist organizations.

A Note on the Explanation of Group Differences in Rates of Crime and Violence

While GST focuses on the explanation of individual crime and violence, recent work has applied GST to the explanation of age, gender, race/ethnic, and community differences in rates of crime and violence (see Agnew, 2001b). Such explanations typically contend that group differences in crime are partly a function of group differences in the amount of strain experienced, the types of strain experienced, the emotional reaction to strain, and/or the factors that condition the effect of strain on crime. For example, males are said to have higher rates of violence than females because they are more likely to experience the types of strain conducive to violence (e.g., criminal victimization), are more likely to react to strain with moral outrage, and are more likely to respond to their strain and negative emotions with violence (e.g., because they are lower in self-control and are more likely to belong to groups where violence is reinforced).

Using General Strain Theory to Explain the Different Types of Criminal Violence

GST focuses on the explanation of a broad range of criminal and violent acts. Most tests of GST reflect this fact and employ crime measures that index theft, violence, and other types of crime. The few studies that have distinguished violent crime from other types of crime, however, generally find that strain and the negative emotions associated with strain have their strongest effects on violence (e.g., Agnew, 1990; Mazerolle, Piquero & Capowich, 2003). Related to this, studies of violent incidents typically find that such incidents begin with one person treating another in a way that is perceived as negative. The recipient of the negative treatment becomes upset, a dispute arises between the involved parties, neither party is willing to back down, and violence is the end result. Lockwood's (1997) study of high school and middle school students, for example, found that almost all violent incidents began with one student provoking another—with the provocations including pushing, grabbing, hitting, teasing, and insulting (also see Wilkinson, 2002). GST, then, is especially relevant to the explanation of criminal violence.

With some elaboration, I think that GST can also help explain why some adult offenders specialize in particular types of criminal violence and why some offenders commit particular types of violence on certain occasions. GST, in fact, has already been applied to the explanation of certain types of violence—such as adolescent violence toward parents (Brezina, 1999), school violence (Agnew, 2000), and the violence associated with hate crimes (Blazak, 2004). Further, studies of still other types of violence frequently make arguments compatible with GST (e.g., Riedel & Welsh, 2002). Before proceeding, however, it is necessary to define criminal violence and discuss the major types of such violence.

Definition of and Types of Criminal Violence

Violence is defined as "the threat, attempt, or use of physical force by one or more persons that results in physical or nonphysical harm to one or more other persons" (Weiner, Zahn & Sagi, 1990:xiii). GST focuses on the explanation of *criminal violence*, or violent acts "which are in violation of legislatively enacted criminal statues and which are subject to a punitive legal response by duly authorized governmental agencies " (Weiner, Zahn & Sagi, 1990:xiv). It is usually the case that such acts are *intentionally committed* or the result of reckless or negligent behavior. Further, such acts usually cause *unwanted harm*. GST, then, does *not* focus on the explanation of all types of violence; for example, GST does not explain those violent acts that result from reasonable accident (e.g., injuries from a car accident in which no one is at fault) or those that are legal (e.g., the physical pain caused by a dentist filling a cavity or the lawful but violent acts of a soldier during war).

The major types of criminal violence are distinguished from one another on one or more dimensions, including (1) the form and degree of violence (e.g., sexual assault, homicide), (2) the characteristics of the victim (e.g., child abuse), (3) the characteristics of the offender(s) (e.g., individual versus collective violence), (4) the relationship between the victim and the offender (e.g., intimate/partner violence), (5) the setting for the violence (e.g., school violence), and (6) the motivation for the violence (e.g., the political motives associated with much terrorist violence).

Using General Strain Theory to Explain the Types of Criminal Violence

Let us assume that individuals are experiencing those types of strain conducive to crime/violence and that they have those characteristics conducive to a criminal/violent response (see above). I believe that whether such individuals engage in a *particular type of violence* is a function of (1) the perceived source of their strain; (2) the nature of the problem(s) created by this strain; (3) the characteristics of the individual and the individual's social environment, as these influence the ability to engage in, the costs of, and the disposition for particular types of violence; and (4) whether the individual regularly interacts with others experiencing the same types of strain.

The Perceived Source of the Strain. The perceived source of strain impacts several dimensions of violence, particularly the choice of the victim and—through the choice of victim—the setting for the violence (e.g., home, school). Other things being equal, offenders are most likely to attack the perceived source of their strain or related targets (e.g., vandalize school property instead of attacking teachers). Attacking the source of one's strain best satisfies the desire for revenge, is more likely to be seen as just by the individual and others, and may have utilitarian value as well—perhaps reducing the likelihood that one will experience further harm from this source. For these reasons, family violence is more likely when the perceived source of strain is another family member, school violence is more likely when the perceived source of strain is other students or teachers, terrorism of the type associated with al Qaeda is more likely when the perceived source of strain is the United States or other nations, and so on. It is important to note that offenders may be mistaken about the source of their strain. For example, members of hate groups may attribute their strain to affirmative action programs that favor African Americans or to the "Zionist Occupation Government (ZOG)." Reflecting this fact, GST needs to devote more attention to those factors that influence the attributions individuals make about the source of their strain, with one critical factor being exposure to subcultural groups that encourage particular attributions (see Blazak, 2004).

The Problem(s) Created by the Strain (i.e., The Goals, Values, Needs, Identities/Statuses, and/or Activities Threatened by the Strain). Strain typically creates a problem(s) for the individuals experiencing it; for example, their identities are threatened, their physical safety is imperiled, or they cannot get the money they desperately need. The nature of the problem strongly influences the nature of and motivation for violence. Individuals prefer those types of violence that they believe will best address the problem they are experiencing. One task for GST is to describe the problems associated with particular types of strain and indicate which types of violence are most likely to result from such problems. For example, a desperate need for money may increase the likelihood of robbery; threats to one's masculine identity may increase the likelihood of assault; and threats to one's religious or national identity may increase the likelihood of terrorist acts.

As Cohen (1955) states, certain problems are difficult to deal with through individual action. For example, this is the case with threats to one's social status or standing. Individuals acting on their own usually cannot obtain social status through illegal channels, create new status systems, or overturn existing status systems. As a consequence, threats to social status sometimes result in collective responses to strain, particularly if several individuals experience the status threat and they are in close contact with one another. Such individuals may set up an alternative status system in which they can successfully compete, they may attack those associated with the dominant status system, and/or they may try to overturn this system. These arguments have been used to explain the formation and appeal of gangs, and they may be applied to hate groups and terrorist organizations. The work of Cohen, however, is in need of further development. In particular, we need to better describe those strains most likely to generate collective responses.

Characteristics of the Individual/Social Environment. The source of strain and the problem(s) it creates may predispose individuals toward one or a few types of violence. However, whether individuals engage in a particular type of violence also depends on their ability to commit that violent act, the perceived costs of that act, and their disposition for the act—as determined by their traits, their social environment, and the perceived benefits of the act. Many of the factors that influence whether strained individuals engage in crime (see above) also influence whether they engage in particular types of violence. Such factors include:

- *The individual's coping skills and resources—particularly his or her aggressive skills and resources.* For example, do individuals have personality traits conducive to violence, such as low constraint and negative emotionality? Are they of sufficient size and strength to physically assault those who treat them in a negative manner? Do they have access to a gun? Do they have the financial resources, knowledge, and connections to launch a terrorist attack against another nation?

- *The individual's level of social support, particularly deviant social support.* Are others available to provide the individual with the advice, material assistance, emotional support, and direct assistance that may be necessary to carry out particular types of violence? Osama bin Laden, of course, both equipped individuals with the skills needed to carry out terrorist acts and provided them with much advice, material support, and direct assistance, allowing them to commit acts that may otherwise have been beyond their reach.

- *The perceived costs of particular types of violence.* Costs depend partly on the perceived ability of the target to resist various types of violence and the likelihood that others will come to the aid of the target. As Felson (1996) notes, for example, small people seldom attack big people. When the perceived costs of violence are high, individuals may attack alternative targets—including vulnerable targets that are not responsible for their strain. Individuals who experience strain at work, for example, may attack family members instead of employers. In addition, the extent to which costs are considered varies across individuals, as demonstrated by recent work in deterrence and rational choice theory (e.g., Piquero & Tibbetts, 2002). For example, the threat of certain death may mean little to individuals with no stake in conformity or hope for the future.

- *The individual's disposition for certain types of violence.* This disposition is partly a function of individual traits; for example, depressed individuals may be predisposed to self-directed violence while angry individuals may be predisposed to other-directed violence. Disposition is also a function of the individual's beliefs regarding the desirability/justification of various types of violence, their past and anticipated reinforcements for different types of violence, and their exposure to valued models who have successfully engaged in various types of violence. These beliefs, reinforcements, and models are in turn heavily dependent on the nature of the individual's associates—as discussed by social learning theorists. Members of al Qaeda, for example, were taught beliefs that justified terrorist action against the United States, were exposed to terrorist models, and were told that terrorist acts would result in great reinforcement—particularly bliss in the afterlife.

Regular Interaction with Others Experiencing the Same Strains. As suggested above, strained individuals who regularly interact with others experiencing the same strains may develop collective responses to their strain, including collective violence. This is especially the case when they are experiencing strains that lend themselves to a collective solutions, like threats to one's social status. Cohen (1955) and Cloward and Ohlin (1960) describe the conditions necessary for strained individuals to develop a collective response to strain, with the key condition being regular interaction between the strained individuals. These theorists, however, did not anticipate the active role that certain groups would play in recruiting and organizing strained individuals (Blazak, 2004). Nor did they anticipate the central role that the World Wide Web would sometimes play in this process. Further, their focus was on gang formation and gang crime, such as gang violence. GST needs to draw on the social movements and other literatures in order to better describe the conditions that contribute to the development of other types of groups and other types of collective violence.

Summary

In sum, the particular type of violence selected by strained individuals who are generally predisposed to crime/violence depends on: (1) the perceived source of their strain; (2) the problem(s) created by their strain; (3) their ability to engage in, the perceived costs of, and their disposition for particular types of violence; and (4) whether they are in regular interaction with others experiencing the same strains. As indicated above, these ideas are in need of much development if GST is to accurately explain and predict individual and collective violence of various types. GST, however, has made much progress in identifying the types of strain that contribute to violence in general, the reasons why these strains increase the likelihood of violence, and the factors that influence whether individuals react to strains with violence.

Discussion Questions

1. How does general strain theory (GST) explain violence? Be sure to indicate which types of strain are most likely to result in crime/violence and why some individuals are more likely than others to respond to strain with crime/violence.

2. Select another theory in this book, such as social learning or routine activities theory. How is the explanation of violence provided by GST similar to and different from that provided by this theory? How might these two theories be combined to provide a fuller explanation of violence?

3. Select a particular type of violence described in this book, such as hate violence or drug-related violence. How might GST explain this particular type of violence? Is it necessary to draw on other theories to fully explain this type of violence? If so, which theories, and how do their explanations go beyond GST?

4. Can you think of any other dimensions that distinguish different types of violence from one another, beyond the six dimensions listed in this chapter (e.g., the form and degree of violence, the motivation for violence)? If so, do you think GST can help explain the different types of violence that fall along your dimension(s)?

5. The second part of this chapter states that whether individuals engage in a particular type of violence is a function of four factors (e.g., the perceived source of their strain, the problems created by the strain, the characteristics of the individual and the individual's social environment, regular interaction with others experiencing the same strain). Drawing on the discussion of these four factors, describe those conditions most likely to result in a collective act of terrorist violence against a nation and those most likely to result in an individual act of family violence.

References

Agnew, R. (2002). "Experienced, Vicarious, and Anticipated Strain: An Exploratory Study Focusing on Physical Victimization and Delinquency." *Justice Quarterly*, 19:603-632.

Agnew, R. (2001b). "An Overview of General Strain Theory." In R. Paternoster and R. Bachman (eds.), *Explaining Crime and Criminals*, pp. 161-174. Los Angeles: Roxbury.

Agnew, R. (2001a). "Building on the Foundation of General Strain Theory: Specifying the Types of Strain Most Likely to Lead to Crime and Delinquency." *Journal of Research in Crime and Delinquency*, 38:319-361.

Agnew, R. (2000). "Strain Theory and School Crime." In S.S. Simpson (ed.), *Of Crime and Criminality*, pp. 105-120. Thousand Oaks, CA: Pine Forge.

Agnew, R. (1995). "The Contribution of Social-Psychological Strain Theory to the Explanation of Crime and Delinquency." In F. Adler and W. Laufer (eds.), *The Legacy of Anomie Theory, Advances in Criminological Theory,* Volume 6, pp. 113-37. New Brunswick, NJ: Transaction.

Agnew, R. (1992). "Foundation for a General Strain Theory of Crime and Delinquency." *Criminology*, 30:47-87.

Agnew, R. (1990). "The Origins of Delinquent Events: An Examination of Offender Accounts." *Journal of Research in Crime and Delinquency*, 27:267-294.

Agnew, R., T. Brezina, J.P. Wright, and F.T. Cullen (2002). "Strain, Personality Traits, and Delinquency: Extending General Strain Theory." *Criminology*, 40:43-72.

Anderson, E. (1999). *Code of the Street.* New York: W.W. Norton.

Blazak, R. (2004). "Strain as a Red Flag for Skinhead Recruiters." In P. Mazerolle and R. Agnew (eds.), *General Strain Theory: Essential Readings*. Belmont, CA: Wadsworth (forthcoming).

Brezina, T. (1999). "Teenage Violence as an Adaptive Response to Family Strain: Evidence from a National Sample of Male Adolescents." *Youth & Society*, 30:416-44.

Broidy, L., and R. Agnew (1997). "Gender and Crime: A General Strain Theory Perspective." *Journal of Research in Crime and Delinquency*, 34:275-306.

Cloward, R., and L. Ohlin (1960). *Delinquency and Opportunity*. Glencoe, IL: Free Press.

Cohen, A.K. (1955). *Delinquent Boys*. Glencoe, IL: Free Press.

Colvin, M. (2000). *Crime and Coercion: An Integrated Theory of Chronic Criminality*. New York: St. Martin's Press.

Felson, R.B. (1996). "Big People Hit Little People: Sex Differences in Physical Power and Interpersonal Violence." *Criminology,* 34:433-452.

Friedman, T.L. (2002). "Under the Arab Street." *New York Times*, (October 23):A23.

Lockwood, D. (1997). *Violence Among Middle and High School Students: Analysis and Implications for Prevention*. Washington, DC: National Institute of Justice.

Mazerolle, P., A.R. Piquero, and G.C. Capowich (2003). "Examining the Links Between Strain, Situational and Dispositional Anger, and Crime." *Youth and Society*, 35:131-57.

McClelland G.H., and C.M. Judd (1993). "Statistical Difficulties of Detecting Interactions and Moderator Effects." *Psychological Bulletin*, 114:376-390.

McCord, J., and M.E. Ensminger (2003). "Racial Discrimination and Violence: A Longitudinal Perspective." In D.F. Hawkins (ed.), *Violent Crime: Assessing Race and Ethnic Differences*, pp. 319-353. Cambridge, UK: Cambridge University Press.

Piquero, A.R., and S.G. Tibbetts (2002). *Rational Choice and Criminal Behavior*. New York: Routledge.

Riedel, M., and W. Welsh (2002). *Criminal Violence*. Los Angeles: Roxbury.

Simons, R.L., C. Yi-Fu, E.A. Stewart, and G.H. Brody (2003). "Incidents of Discrimination and Risk for Delinquency: A Longitudinal Test of Strain Theory with an African American Sample." *Justice Quarterly*, 20:827-854.

Weiner, N.A., M.A. Zahn, and R.J. Sagi (1990). *Violence: Patterns, Causes, Public Policy*. San Diego: Harcourt Brace Jovanovich.

Wilkinson, D.L. (2002). "Decision Making in Violent Events among Adolescent Males: An Examination of Sparks and Other Motivational Factors." In A.R. Piquero and S.G. Tibbetts (eds.), *Rational Choice and Criminal Behavior*, pp. 163-96. New York: Routledge.

CHAPTER 3

Control Balance Theory and Violence

Charles R. Tittle

Introduction

Have you ever wondered why people commit senseless acts of violence? Social scientists develop general theories to explain human behavior, but such theories can also be employed to understand specific acts that might be of interest. In addition, their explanatory principles can be used to predict various outcomes for large sets of individuals or groups. Violence is one of those specific types of behavior in need of explanation.

Definition of Violence

Violence is behavior in which a person or social entity (such as a corporation) does something intended to result in physical pain or damage to one or more living creatures.

Scholars want to know why some individuals or groups engage in violent behavior while others do not, why violence occurs at specific places and times, and why it is recurrent for some people or social entities. In addition, people want to know how to prevent it. Violence is particularly salient because it often makes no sense to observers and sometimes upon reflection not even to its perpetrators. Consider the following cases.

Vignette #1

On a cool morning, Ernest and Ray entered their school early. Underneath unusually heavy coats, strapped to their bodies, were pistols taken from a hardware store when the clerk was distracted. After storing the guns

51

and coats in hall lockers, they made their way to class. At the 10 A.M. inter-mission, they met at the lockers as prearranged, took out the weapons, and began shooting fellow students. During the spree they shouted that the vic-tims deserved to die, that this would teach them a lesson, and, as Ray exclaimed, "We don't look so small now, do we?" After what seemed like an eternity to students who lay wounded and bleeding and to others who were diving for cover and running wildly in all directions, the pistols fell silent. While attempting to reload, the avengers were swarmed by a teacher and two students who were hiding across the hall. Later, the shooters showed no remorse, telling the police they were glad to have settled scores with their tormentors. In fact, both boys commented on how exhilarating it was to shoot those students and that they loved holding the power of life and death. Ernest even said that it was the first time in his life that anybody had taken him seriously. After all, as he more fully explained, they were from poor fam-ilies, their clothes were not fashionable, both were small of stature, and everybody picked on them. Neither could get a date and the mere asking usually invited ridicule. Moreover, because they had no friends except each other and their parents more or less let them roam free, they spent most of their time shooting rifles at animals, torturing small creatures, and talk-ing about how nothing could be worse than their current lot in life. They had been cruelly reminded of these facts four days earlier when Johnny Tol-bert had confronted them, saying "you jerks better clear this hallway because my girlfriend will be coming by shortly and I don't want her hav-ing to look at you." As Ernest put it, "We knew right then that we had to do something to show Tolbert and the others that we matter."

Vignette #2

Arland was the foreman of a five-man construction crew. It was not meet-ing the company's production quota, and there was little sympathy for excuses. Part of the problem was Joe, who had been coming in half drunk for the past two weeks. Nothing Arland said or did seemed to help. Late Fri-day, Toby, the job supervisor, delivered the pay checks and in front of the other men got right up into Arland's face and growled that if things did not improve substantially Arland would be getting his pink slip instead of a pay check. Embarrassed and upset, Arland grew angry as he thought about it on the way home. Not only did he feel powerless to produce the work needed, but he was especially incensed because the job supervisor had under-mined what little authority he had with his crew. He considered punching Toby the next day but knew it might get him fired or even jailed. He also thought about sneaking back that night to sabotage some machinery to show his contempt for the company that demanded so much. However, he did not have a key to the equipment pool and did not know how to disable a large machine without a lot of noise or taking a long time. He even considered trying to seduce Toby's wife, which if successful would show Toby who the real man was. Unfortunately, Toby's wife did not seem susceptible to seduction, especially not by Arland, who was not known for charm or good looks. In this state of turmoil, Arland arrived home in a foul mood. When his wife started her normal complaints about the children's misbehavior, bills having arrived, and her day having been filled with unpleasant chores, Arland just "lost it." First, he yelled at his wife, she yelled back, and before long the children were crying and insults were being exchanged. Finally, Arland hit his wife squarely in the face. He later told the police he loved her but that sometimes she put too much pressure on him. He promised not to do it again, although he had done it before, and his wife declined to press charges.

Vignette #3

Rashad entered the café carrying what appeared to be an ordinary briefcase. After eating, he paid the bill and departed, leaving the briefcase concealed by the table cloth. After boarding the subway, at exactly 12:35 P.M., Rashad pushed a switch inside his pocket, detonating a bomb that killed 37 of the 42 occupants of the café. He smiled in satisfaction, knowing that at the same moment three members of his Ethnic Brotherhood were creating similar destruction in a bus terminal, a crowded department store, and a busy intersection. Later, meeting in the back of an old warehouse, Rashad and his comrades recounted their exploits to the other 91 Brothers. All savored the stories, for they had heard news accounts all afternoon and had witnessed the frenzied reactions of people all over the city. The Brothers were elated that their adversaries had finally been put on notice that oppression would no longer be tolerated. They believed the bombings were appropriate recompense for the slaying of Brother Ishmel who was shot to death the previous week by city police who claimed that, when ordered by an officer to lie on the ground for a search, he had brandished what they had thought was a gun but which turned out to be his wallet.

Application of Control Balance Theory to the Vignette Violence

One way to understand these acts is to apply the principles of control balance (Tittle, 1995; 2004). Ernest, Ray, Arland, and Rashad all suffered from what this theory calls a control deficit. That is, they were the objects of control more often and to a greater extent than they controlled other people or things. All had adapted, but when events brought their weaknesses to the fore, they contemplated deviant behavior as a way to change things; that is, they became motivated toward deviance by a provocation. Ernest and Ray were insulted and reminded of their outcast status by Johnny Tolbert; Arland was demeaned publicly by his supervisor; and Rashad was humiliated vicariously by the unjustified shooting of one of the members of his Ethnic Brotherhood. As a result of their renewed awareness of their control deficits, all became attuned to the possibility that deviance might help overcome their disadvantages. They ended up using violence to try to extend their control and overcome the humiliation of the provocative events.

As they anticipated, Ernest and Ray's extreme violence made others fear them and, for a short time at least, people were all too glad to do whatever the shooters wanted. Though Arland could not realistically enhance his control in the specific situation where he became motivated, punching his wife at least made him feel stronger in the family domain. Similarly, by his terrorist act Rashad elevated his control far beyond where it had been. As a result he was able to control people and events, perhaps long into the future, because nobody could predict when or where he might strike again, and impunity was guaranteed as long as he and the other Brothers maintained secrecy. Thus, violence by the vignette characters was quite advantageous, though it might appear senseless to others.

This simple interpretation using control balance ideas may resonate with you because on occasion, you too no doubt have been unable to control things that mattered, tasted humiliation, and felt an urge to hurt somebody. However, the analysis is an incomplete application of the theory. For one thing, it does not tell why numerous people (or other social entities) with more unfavorable control ratios than the scenario characters do not resort to violence. Many people are humiliated without turning to violence, or at least not to the extent portrayed in the scenarios. In addition, it is not obvious why Ernest and the others became violent on the particular occasions described. These were probably not the only times the characters had been humiliated, and previous insults apparently did not always lead to extreme violence. Ernest and Ray were almost daily confronted with rejection by girls they wanted to date, and they were often denigrated by peers. Arland's orders had been ignored by his crew before, and he probably had been reprimanded previously by the boss, perhaps with the knowledge of his crew. Moreover, Rashad and his comrades had suffered a lifetime of discrimination and oppression.

Further, despite probably knowing that such acts could (for Arland) or were almost certain to (for the school shooters and the bombers) to activate serious counter-control measures, why did the characters nevertheless act? Why, for instance, didn't Ernest and Ray simply continue to put up with their accustomed humiliation out of fear of being killed or jailed for a long period of time? Arland may not have thought there would be legal consequences, because he had hit his wife before without a problem, but why he didn't control himself to avoid his wife's retaliation, even if in subtle ways, is not obvious. Moreover, given the heinousness of their acts, why didn't the bombers refrain out of fear that their identities would eventually become known, with severe consequences?

Finally, even if the characters wanted to do something to overcome their control deficiencies, as the interpretation suggests, why didn't they try to do so in other ways? The shooters could have turned to diligent school work with the ultimate goal of achieving professional status and prestige, which would enhance their control ratios considerably, eventually permitting them to show up their former tormentors. Perhaps Arland could have found a more favorable job, or at least he might have taken up a sport where he could show his dominance over others without hurting his wife. And, the Ethnic Brotherhood might have organized itself politically to gain influence over community events or to lobby for prosecution or public exposure of police brutality.

Major Principles and Assumptions of the Theory

Control balance theory explains three general types of behavior: conformity, submission, and deviance. Here we are interested in violence, which is usually deviant. Deviance encompasses acts that the majority of some group disapproves of or that typically brings about pejorative collective reactions (including actions by officials who act on behalf of a group). Thus, deviance is relative to the social group in question. However, in any given group, deviant behaviors include a vast array of behaviors, including most but not all crimes and many acts of violence.

Control balancing involves weighing, by a potential perpetrator of deviance, the perceived gain in *control* to be achieved from deviant behavior, relative to the potential counter control that a particular act of deviance is likely to provoke. The theory contends that all social actors can be characterized, generally and situationally, by control ratios, which reflect the total amount of control they can exercise against other actors, objects, and circumstances, relative to the control to which they are subject. Control ratios can be balanced, they can vary in a negative direction to show deficits (being the objects of more control than they can exercise), or they can vary in a positive direction to reflect control surpluses (where more control can be exercised than is experienced).

Because the theory concerns control in all of its manifestations, actual control ratios are not always obvious. For example, while Ernest and Ray experienced the disadvantages of adolescence, so did the other students, so on that count all the students were about equal in having control deficits. However, some of the students had money, good looks, or charm to help in attracting members of the opposite sex, or perhaps intelligence that permitted some control over academic officials, so their deficits were not as great as less advantaged adolescents. However, Ernest and Ray probably had even more money to spend than most, which they obtained illegally (as implied by their theft of the weapons), and were freer of parental supervision than most students, so could come and go freely, stay up late, and use alcohol or other drugs. Furthermore, because they were outsiders to conventional social circles, they felt less controlled by the bonds of school, church, and community.

If all information were available, it might show that Ernest and Ray had relatively small control deficits. Furthermore, a full accounting of the facts might show that Arland and Rashad could also be characterized that way, especially considering their relationships with females and youths within their social spheres. The vignettes do not reveal enough to establish control ratios, but it appears that all of the characters probably would score between 30 and 45 on a continuum from zero to 100, with scores below 45 reflecting control deficits, those between 45 and 55 showing relatively balanced control, and those greater than 55 representing control surpluses. Arland, for example, was a work leader with a steady income, he may have been large of stature, and he largely dominated his family, despite not having much wealth, being subordinate to his supervisor, not having a job that permitted him to command large numbers of people, and lacking interpersonal skills to manipulate others well. In addition, even though he was part of a social minority, Rashad was nevertheless a male in a subcultural context where being female was especially disadvantageous, he probably exercised a lot of control over children and women, he may have had reasonably good job skills, and he may have been interpersonally persuasive among his peers. Thus, none of the vignette characters were completely overwhelmed by excessive controls. Specific control deficits like theirs—unbalanced but not hugely unbalanced—loom large in a control balance explanation of violence, while other degrees and types of unbalanced control ratios, including surpluses, help explain other deviance.

The theory assumes that all social entities possess a latent desire or need, rooted in the dependency of infancy, to overcome control deficits and to extend control surpluses. However, this desire does not affect actual behavior unless activated by situational circumstances. Further, the theory contends that deviant behavior is the main device that social entities contemplate in trying to alter control imbalances. It is the preferred choice because of its potency, being widely feared as a threat to social arrangements, and for its potential to wreak harm on individuals or the social environment. It is because of this potency that social groups attempt to restrict deviance. When a control imbalance is brought into awareness, especially through debasement, people want to do something about it, and most of the time they think of deviant behavior as the main way to do that.

Though an unbalanced control ratio is the first of a chain of variables, various conditions affect whether control imbalances actually result in misconduct. Provocation is one of them. It generates, usually by humiliation, acute awareness of a control imbalance and brings to consciousness the notion that deviant behavior can help overcome that imbalance or help relieve feelings of debasement. However, such motivation will not produce deviant behavior unless the person also has an opportunity for it; that is, a deviant act must be possible in the situation. For instance, there were many things the vignette characters simply could not do to try to extend their control. They could not alter school, corporate, or governmental policy to extend their control, they could not hire third parties to act for them, and they were all bound to the circumstances, unable to turn to legitimate alternatives.

Further, for motivation to result in deviance, constraints (actual chances of counter-controlling reactions by the object of the deviant act, by circumstances, or by others, including police or other authorities) must not be so great (or perceived as so great) to negate the gain in control stemming from potential deviant behavior. Arland anticipated that he could dominate his wife without counter-control because she would not press charges and he largely controlled the conditions of her life. Rashad believed he and his Brothers could escape capture and certainly their victims could not retaliate. Ernest and Ray, however, knew they would suffer because of their actions but, as their story reveals, in their minds nothing that happened would be worse than what they already were experiencing. Even though most people might think the consequences of a school shooting would outweigh any gain in control, the shooters *perceived* a favorable trade-off.

Because opportunities for some forms of deviance are almost always present and the perceived or actual chances of counter-control are highly variable, and linked particularly to control ratios, the seriousness of particular deviant acts, and risk elements in various situations, an individual or organizational entity will balance the type of deviance with the likely counter-control. As a result, when people become motivated, the chances of *some form* of deviance are high. The stronger the motivation, the greater are those chances. Because the vignette characters were all highly motivated toward deviance, having been reminded of their control weaknesses in particularly poignant ways that made them feel insignificant and debased, they were almost certain to engage in some form of deviance.

The specific form of deviance likely to be exhibited, however, is a product of control balancing, which takes place with respect to particular categories of potential deviance, not with respect to all forms of deviance. Because some deviance (usually the more serious acts) have the most appeal as a way for extending one's control, a motivated person will contemplate committing one or more of them. However, serious forms of deviance, especially acts of violence, also imply the greatest potential counter-control. Therefore, only those people with small control deficits or actual control surpluses can realistically resort to the most serious forms of deviance in response to motivation. Hence, each social entity motivated toward deviance will cognitively slide up or down a continuum of what is called *control balance desirability* in search of an appropriate deviant act. It is important to note that those with balanced control ratios are not likely to deviate because they are less likely to become motivated toward deviance and even when motivated they are more likely to face nullifying counter-control. By contrast, those with overwhelming control deficits lose the ability to imagine alternatives, leading them to simply submit or capitulate. Those with control surpluses, like those with deficits, become motivated for deviance fairly often because they encounter situations in which their control surpluses do not produce the expected outcomes. Thus, a control surplus is as liable to generate deviant behavior as is a control deficit, although the form of deviant behavior that is likely to ensue differs considerably. Simply stated, for those with unbalanced control ratios, the fact of a control imbalance is linked to the chances of deviance of some kind while the degree of control imbalance affects the specific type of deviance likely to be committed. The specific type of deviance likely to be selected is, in turn, a reflection of the control balance desirability of various deviant possibilities.

Control balance desirability is a characteristic possessed in different degrees by various potential deviant acts. Empirically, it is composed of two indicators: (1) the likely long-range effectiveness of the deviant act in question for altering a control imbalance, and (2) the extent to which a given form of misbehavior requires the perpetrator to be directly and personally involved with a victim or an object that is affected by the deviance. Deviance that is greatest in control balance desirability potentially has the greatest long-range impact in altering control imbalances, and it is most impersonal (that is, it can be done without direct, hands-on action by the individual practicing it). Long-range gain in control is important because social entities inherently need or desire to control things. This is theorized to drive much of human conduct (compare Sullivan, 1953), particularly deviant conduct. Control gained through deviance is control of things external to the individual and if the deviance is impersonal, the possibility of counter-control is reduced. However, impersonality also bears on control of internal psychic states such as self-esteem and self-concept. "Hands-on" deviant behavior generally has less long-range potential for modifying a control imbalance, and it is likely to produce disreputable public images. Because self attitudes and concepts appear to be rooted in the reactions of social audiences (Blumer, 1969; Kaplan, 1980; Mead, 1934, Stryker, 1980), risking a bad reputation has important implications for the person's ability to control his or her own psychic states. Hence, the end product of deviance that is highly control-balance desirable is a gain in external and in internal control.

Control-balance desirability is a theoretical construct. It may not correspond at all to the "inherent appeal" or "attractiveness" of a given deviant act to the person contemplating such an act, nor does it necessarily encompass aspects of deviance that various other theorists and researchers have assumed make deviance alluring. This theory interprets deviant behavior as a way of managing control, a way of altering a control imbalance. Hence, control-balance desirability concerns aspects of deviant behavior that bear on maximization of control manipulation, which involves long-range outcomes and effective escape from counter-control. In the heat of provocation, people often want to do things that have low control-balance desirability (McCall, 1994; Scheff & Retzinger, 1991; Short, 1963). Such was true for Ernest and Ray, for whom the school shooting had high "personal desirability" but relatively low control-balance desirability.

Control balance theory contends that motivated individuals or social entities choose forms of deviance located within various ranges of a continuum of control-balance desirability. The theory does not purport to allow accurate predictions of a specific act such as the assault that Arland committed or the setting off of bombs in public places, as Rashad did. However, it does claim to explain selection of some deviant act from among those with similar control-balance desirability scores.

Imagine that all the deviant acts that Ernest, Ray, Arland, or Rashad might have committed were arrayed on a continuum of control-balance desirability from zero to 100. The violence they committed might have scores in the range of perhaps 25 to 40 on a control-balance desirability scale; all enhanced control for their perpetrators, but for the shooters and Arland, only temporarily and in limited ways. In addition, those violent acts required direct, hands-on action by the perpetrators, allowing, at least if caught, public identification of the actor with the unacceptable acts. However, hypothetically they might have committed many other deviant acts, some with very different degrees of control balance desirability and some with similar degrees. Deviance ranges widely, from using mind-altering drugs to applying corporate power to destroy a pristine environment, and includes things such as robbery, hiring an assassin, prostituting oneself, embezzlement, spitting on the sidewalk, overcharging for loans, neglecting children, and many, many more. Every potential deviant act has some degree of control-balance desirability, so all possible deviant acts can be arrayed on a continuum from low to high. Motivated people, like our vignette characters, might do any of them. The theory predicts, however, that given the control ratios of the vignette characters, and other variables, they were likely only to commit acts that fell within a fairly narrow range of the control balance desirability continuum, a range that includes the violent deeds actually committed in addition to many nonviolent acts. For purposes of illustration, that range might be considered to be approximately 30 to 45 on a continnum that begins at zero and ends at 100.

For example, Arland might have tried to force motorists off the road on his way home, he might have muscled ahead of shoppers in a cashier's line, he might have denigrated his work crew and denied them breaks, or he might have punitively and unnecessarily rotated players on the Little League team he coached. The theory suggests that each of the potential acts Arland could have performed in response to the dramatization of his own control weaknesses were fairly similar in control-balance desirability to the assault of his wife. That is, given his control ratio, opportunities available, and other contingencies (to be described later), only some deviant acts were realistic possibilities, and they could all be characterized by similar degrees of control-balance desirability. Like the assault, all would provide some increase in control, at least temporarily, but all would require a high degree of personal involvement with the objects of the action. The theory, thus, contends that Arland's control ratio will predict commission of one or more of the acts within a corresponding zone of the control-balance desirability continuum. Arland's control ratio alone, or even in combination with other variables in the theory, however, will not predict which exact act within the specified range he will commit, although with an increase in the number of variables from the theory one can predict acts within narrower ranges of the control balance desirability continuum.

The main problem the theory addresses is how to identify the range of that continuum from which Arland will choose a deviant act. Four main variables, along with several contingent variables, are said to influence that "desirability" range for those who are provoked and realize that deviance can favorably alter their control imbalances. The main variables are: (1) the entity's control ratio, (2) opportunity, (3) constraint, and (4) self-control (which for social entities such as business organizations is the extent to which internal structural arrangements constrain impulsive action by decisionmakers).

Control Ratio

The *control ratio* is relevant to the range of control-balance desirability from which a deviant act will be selected because only those with surpluses or low deficits can realistically contemplate acts that may generate great counter-control and because some kinds of deviance are possible only for people with given control ratios. The most deviant acts are, for the most part, also the acts that are most effective for altering a control imbalance, and because they have the greatest consequences for others, they are likely to lead to great resistance and therefore imply much potential effort at counter-control. Further, social entities with control deficits usually *cannot* employ deviant behavior that is really effective in a long-range sense. Corporate heads can with impunity defraud the government or consumers of millions, thereby gaining control of financial resources, but people like Ernest and Ray can at best steal small amounts from cash registers or individuals. Powerful people can enlist armies of subordinates to do their bidding, while Arland probably could not even find somebody to beat up his boss for him. Moreover, those with financial resources and political connections can array their forces to oppose even small derogatory remarks, while Rashad and his compatriots ordinarily could not even resist blatant discrimination.

Thus, a control imbalance—either a deficit or a surplus—stands at the beginning of the causal chain that ultimately results in deviant behavior. Initially, the most relevant aspect of a control ratio is simply the fact of imbalance. In the beginning, surpluses and deficits have the same practical consequences—they help to predispose a person or social entity to become motivated for deviance. However, the magnitude of a control imbalance is also important because when provocative situations are encountered, humiliation will be greater for those with the largest imbalances and what they can realistically imagine is linked to the degree of imbalance. Those with deficits are provoked by realizing that they do not have enough control to manage life circumstances or to avoid humiliation, while those with surpluses are provoked by recognition that the control they have become accustomed to exercising or expect to exercise is not sufficiently acknowledged.

Different amounts of exposure to circumstances potentially leading to humiliation or debasement and different actual levels of humiliation or debasement are obviously important influences on motivation, but they work hand in hand with the control ratio. One's gross control ratio sets the parameters within which those other influences operate. Further along the sequential chain, where choices to commit specific deviant acts are made, the exact degree of control imbalance (the control ratio) becomes more critical. There, whether an imbalance is large or small and whether it is in the deficit or the surplus direction, is crucial. Moreover, as will be shown shortly, the control ratio intersects and interacts with other variables, particularly constraint, to influence the range of control balance desirability from which a deviant act is chosen.

Opportunity

Opportunity for specific types of deviant action is crucial for control balancing because deviant acts cannot occur unless they are possible. A perpetrator must have access and means to commit the actions that are being contemplated. Assaulting a challenger not only requires arm movement and strength, there must also be physical convergence of the assaulter and the victim in time and space and in circumstances in which others cannot or will not restrain the attack and where physical barriers do not get in the way (for example, one cannot punch a victim in a passing automobile). Clearly, the means to every form of deviance are not available to all people or social entities at the propitious time, nor is it possible to employ such means, even if available, in all circumstances. Physical confrontation is simply not always possible, personal manipulation sometimes cannot happen, and most people are not in a position to employ third parties or abstract entities (such as social structural arrangements) in accomplishing deviance. Hence, opportunities may affect what people can do and thereby what will likely occur.

Indeed, opportunity for deviance is one of the key factors that helps determine which deviant act within a range of control balance desirability is selected for commission. Consider Arland again. He could not realistically expect to extend his control by going back to college to become a professional engineer so that he could come back to rudely command his old boss. Not only would it be extremely difficult for him to do, given his station in life, but it would take a very long time. Even if it could be accomplished, by the time it was achieved, the temporary insult would probably be long forgotten. Moreover, given his control ratio, he has no opportunity to buy the company and fire the boss. Murdering the boss is not usually realistic because of the potential counter control it is likely to invoke. However, as noted before, there are a number of deviant things Arland had the opportunity for and could realistically expect to do, and they all had reasonably close control-balance desirability. Among them was slowing down his work, sabotaging a machine, gossiping about the boss, stealing something from the project, verbally denigrating a coworker, going home and abusing his own wife, or the acts described earlier involving boorish behavior in the grocery, overbearing behavior to the Little Leaguers, and so on.

Arland's choice about which act (or acts) to commit from among the possibilities was dependent on its (their) availability and possible achievability. Sabotaging a machine may have been difficult because he was not assigned to operate a machine, there may have been no machines in the area of his work, or he may not have known how to render one inoperable without complete destruction. On the day in question he might have taken the bus home and therefore been unable to express road rage; he may have found the grocery line empty, and the Little Leaguers may not have been scheduled for practice that day. He did, however, have the opportunity to assault his wife.

Constraint

The third main variable influencing the specific deviance likely to be chosen by a motivated person is *constraint*. Constraint is a composite variable reflecting the perceived seriousness of an offense (possible magnitude of counter-controlling consequences) and situational risk (actual chances of experiencing those counter-controlling consequences). Constraint is important because an actor theoretically weighs the potential gain from a deviant act against the loss of control it is likely to evoke. The theory assumes that almost everybody is sensitive to the potential consequences of their acts. However, control balance theory sees that sensitivity as revolving around concerns about how deviant actions might stimulate or bring about additional controls, both in the present and the future. It focuses on the *control* implications of deviant acts, not on things like fear of pain or threats to financial resources, although each of these costs can be interpreted in terms of their implications for control.

Self-Control

Self-control is the fourth main variable. So far, the argument has portrayed people as rationale and self-controlled. In reality, however, many are not (Baron, 2003; Baumeister, Heatherton & Tice, 1994; Gottfredson & Hirschi, 1990; Pratt & Cullen, 2000). Provocation impels the person who has a control imbalance toward immediate, "hands on" action. However, such acts usually have less effect in the long run in altering a control imbalance, and "hands on" actions have greater likelihood of invoking counter-controls. Therefore, those with low self-control, who are incapable of deferring the immediate urge for deviance, and who cannot visualize and take into account the long-range consequences of their acts will more likely choose the less control-balance desirable actions. Therefore, those with weak self-control may not behave exactly according to the principles of control balance theory, instead regressing to acts with less control-balance desirability than would otherwise be expected.

Contingencies

The full operation of control balancing is also affected by contingent variables such as moral commitments, intelligence, habits, personality, and others. For instance, a person who, because of the operation of the variables of the theory, is liable to commit a violent act, may have strong moral feelings against violence. Such a person likely will choose one of the other deviant acts within the appropriate control-balance desirability range that does not involve violence. Hence, a man who, given his particular control-balance situation, might otherwise commit violence against somebody may habitually lord it over his children in nonviolent but no less controlling ways. As a result, instead of turning to violence, he will probably do one of the things he usually does, such as dominate his children. Alternatively, some individuals may have aggressive personalities, making it more likely that their choices of deviant acts within a range of control balance desirability will involve violence.

Back to the Vignettes

Why, then, did Ernest and Ray shoot up the school? The answer the theory gives is that they suffered a control deficit but not an overwhelming one. When they became motivated toward deviance by an encounter that rendered them acutely aware of their weakness, they sought a deviant means of extending their control. The likely possibilities, given their control ratios and the nature of the deviant acts they could have accomplished, all fell in a fairly narrow range of control-balance desirability (with limited ability to extend control long-range and involving personal involvement in application). Within that range, they chose the act for which they had opportunity, that seemed to offer the most advantage, and that reflected the particular contingencies relevant to them, such a lack of moral inhibition against violence. Their choice was especially colored by their weak self-control. Because Ernest and Ray could not realistically evaluate the potential consequences of their acts, "rational" control balancing was not possible for them. In addition, in their minds, their control was already so low, no matter what the consequences, things could not be worse. Further, among the possibilities for extending their control, they were drawn to the violent option by habit, having spent a lot of time perpetrating violence against animals and other creatures.

Arland, too, suffered a small control deficit, so was liable for deviant acts within the lower middle of a control-balance desirability range, which included assaulting his wife but other things as well. He turned to assault of his wife because his degree of self control (as evidenced by his responsible job position) enabled him to avoid the more dangerous act of immediately assaulting his boss; his wife was a more opportune target whose assault, based on past experience, implied little counter-control. Moreover, he had a habit of mistreating his wife.

Finally, Rashad, who suffered a modest control deficit, vicariously faced a provocative situation in which an Ethnic Brother had been killed. With increased awareness of his control situation and the visualization that violence could alter things, he balanced the gain from bombing against the potential cost, which, given the organizational arrangements of the Ethnic Brotherhood and the surreptitious nature of the act, were perceived to be small. Such an act fell within a range of control-balance desirability that was possible and likely for someone with Rashad's control ratio, and he had opportunity to do it. Moreover, he seemed to have sufficient self-control to plan and carry it out, he was not restrained by moral considerations, and his other options offered less in control gain.

But, what about the ancillary questions raised at the beginning of this essay? First, why did the vignette characters resort to violence while others with greater control deficits do not? The theory contends that large control imbalances imply too much possibility of counter-control for the action to be feasible, except for those who like Ernest and Ray have lost the ability to "balance controls," usually because of weak self-control, mental illness, or some genetic defect. Thus, those who are totally, or more than modestly, controlled are not likely to engage in acts higher up on the control-balance desirability continuum than is commensurate with their control ratios. Direct violence is one such ill-fitting form of deviance for those with greater control deficits; instead, they are likely to commit acts of defiance or capitulate altogether. Violence is not a tactic for the totally suppressed.

Second, though the characters all felt humiliated by recurrent and recent events, why don't others who may be even more demeaned turn to violence? Those who are debased by social and other circumstances cannot employ any form of deviance in response. (1) They may not have the opportunity to employ it; (2) The potential counter-control may be too great to make it feasible; (3) Various personal contingencies may lead them away from violence toward other forms of deviance; or (4) Random events may lead to one or more other deviant act with a similar control-balance desirability. For example, other students (even those with control ratios similar to

Ernest and Ray's), who become provoked may not have access to firearms like Ernest and Ray did; because they may be more capable of appreciating future possibilities than the shooters, other students may recognize and fear the massive and likely counter-control from a school shooting; and many other provoked students, because of chance, resources, personal characteristics, and opportunities, resort to alternative, nondeviant acts with similar control-balance desirability.

Third, why weren't they deterred? This theory accepts as valid the notion of deterrence (Andenaes, 1974; Gibbs, 1975; Tittle, 1980; Zimring & Hawkins, 1973), contending that people often guide their own behaviors in anticipation of potential counter-control, though they do not suppress deviance totally but instead shift to alternative forms that are more favorable. However, appreciation of potential counter-control requires some intelligence, self-control, and awareness. Ernest and Ray lacked all three, so for them no amount of "consequent" counter-control would suffice; only that which physically restrained them from their actions would have been relevant. In effect, their personal deficiencies created what others would regard as "irrational" acts but which they thought at the time made sense. Arland, apparently accurately, anticipated that there would be minimal counter-control to his act of violence. Rashad imagined that the situational risk was so small that counter-control would be unlikely.

Fourth, why violence instead of something else? The theory contends that violence was selected from among a set of potential deviant actions falling within a restricted and designated range of a continuum reflecting the potential long-range effectiveness of acts for extending control and the necessity for personal involvement in perpetrating the deviant act. Selection of specific ones of the potential deviant acts within the designated zone of control-balance desirability is partly due to chance, to opportunities, or to various personal contingencies, such as moral commitments and personality, and is therefore not easily predicted. The zone of possibility, however, can be narrowed by taking into account larger numbers of relevant variables.

Level of Empirical Support for the Theory

It is one thing to explain a specific instance retroactively and another thing to make predictions about it for a large set of individuals, such as saying that, under conditions x, y, and z, the probability of a given violent act is some specific, high number. The theory implies that good but not totally accurate predictions are to be expected. For example, Arland's choice of deviant act, as well as the choices of all other people with similar control-balance characteristics, can be predicted to fall within a range of likely ones, but it cannot be exactly predicted. However, the range of possibilities can be more or less narrow depending on how many of the theoretical variables are taken into account, and the narrower the range of possibilities, the more accurate the corresponding predictions of outcomes. Similarly, Ernest and Ray's violence, and that of others with similar control-balance characteristics could not be specifically predicted, but the range of possible acts they were likely to have committed could be small, provided we knew their control ratios, the provocative situations they encountered, their level of self-control, and other variables, such as their habitual use of violence against animals and other creatures.

At this point, however, the argument rests on logic, plausibility, and scattered anecdotal evidence. The original statement appeared in 1995. Though it has been recognized as worthy of attention (Akers, 2000:250-251; American Society of Criminology, 2000; American Sociological Association, 1998; Braithwaite, 1997; Crutchfield, Bridges, Weis & Kubrin, 2000:408-421; Jensen, 1999; Savelsberg; 1999), little research testing its adequacy was stimulated (but see Curry & Piquero, 2003; Hickman & Piquero, 2001; Piquero & Hickman, 1999; Wood & Dunaway, 1997-1998). That may be partly because its variables were new or unfamiliar to the criminological community and because it proposed a complex explanatory scheme with nonlinear relationships among variables, both of which required unusual and especially difficult work to test. The limited research that was generated suggests that control imbalances are important predictors of deviance, though it challenges some aspects of the theory. Those empirical challenges and logical critiques, however, led to a major revision (Tittle, 2004). The application described in this essay is based on a refined version of control balance theory, one that has not yet been tested at all. Therefore, whether the theory turns out in practice to fulfill its theoretical promise remains to be seen.

Application of the Theory to Both Collective and Interpersonal Violence

Within control balance theory, violence is a device to help overcome a control deficit or to extend a control surplus. It emerges in response to humiliating or debasing provocations experienced either personally or vicariously. Thus, ordinary "individualistic" violence (when people are acting on their own behalf and not as part of organized activities such as terrorism, gang conflicts, or nationally sponsored warfare) is committed mainly by those with small control deficits or small control surpluses, or by those with larger control imbalances who possess relatively weak self-control. Such acts are usually direct (the action itself produces the violence rather than the action affecting something else that ultimately results in violence) and personally involving (that is, the individual responsible is the one who confronts the victim or the object of the violence). They include raping, beating, assaulting, and many others. However, the decision to employ such violence involves selection from among a set of possible behaviors within a restricted range of acts, most of which involve no violence. That restricted range concerns control-balance desirability, which is defined by the likely long-range potential effectiveness of deviant acts in altering a control imbalance along with the extent to which a given deviant act requires direct, hands-on confrontation. As noted before, concerning Arland, the relevant range in a given instance may include acts as different as assaulting one's wife, running somebody off the road, breaking line at a grocery, or unnecessarily punishing Little Leaguers.

Individuals can also act on behalf of organized entities while not them-selves having control imbalances or weak self-control. Violence perpe-trated by organized groups may be carried out by people who are hired but have no emotional stake in the situation, or it may be perpetrated by mem-bers of a group who act out of loyalty or to fulfill normative expectations. "Collective violence" includes terrorism, intimidation by hate groups, gang-related drive-by shooting, and armed warfare among nations.[1] Unless spe-cific acts within a larger context of "collective violence" are perpetrated by individuals who vicariously experience control imbalances, provocations, and so on, as in the case of Rashad, control-balance variables must be applied on the group or organizational level. Thus, collective violence is likely when: (1) a group as a whole can be characterized as having a small control deficit or surplus, relative to other collectivities, (2) provoking events that *symbolically* humiliate or debase the group occur to remind the mem-bers of the collectivity of its control weakness and to suggest that deviance, including collective violence, could help alter that imbalance, and (3) the group has at least modest levels of organization and discipline. As with indi-viduals, opportunity and potential counter control are relevant so that the same control-balancing process occurs on the collective level to explain a resort to deviance in general and violence in particular.

Collective violence also involves acts with greater control-balance desirability than those we have been considering and perpetrated by per-sons with control surpluses rather control deficits. Influential persons who are members of groups engaging in collective violence can be respon-sible for acts that are carried out by third parties. Sometimes they act as bureaucratic agents without personally experiencing the control balance conditions that lead to individual level violence or that lead the group to undertake collective violence. At other times, however, collective vio-lence is set in motion by individual persons with large control surpluses who become provoked by a failure of their control to evoke the expected response and so use their positions to deploy others on their behalf.

Thus, "individualistic" violence will generally reflect a small control deficit or a small control surplus while violence by an emissary of a group that has a small control deficit or a small control surplus will not necessarily have a personal control ratio to match the group's and may have much stronger self-control than perpetrators of violence typically display. More-over, group leaders may bring about collective violence to meet their own control-balancing needs.

Endnote

[1]   It is interesting to contemplate whether armed warfare among nations is actually deviant behavior according to the definition employed in control balance theory. Collective judgments of "unacceptability" may presuppose a collectivity that supersedes the warring parties, which would imply some type of world collectivity. In cases of war, the warring parties and their respective allies certainly regard the behavior of their adversaries as bad or dangerous. However, we are left to assume that noncombatants who are part of the world collectivity come to regard the actions of one or both warring parties as having pejorative qualities.

Discussion Questions

1.   Why, according to control balance theory, is violence unlikely for those with extreme control imbalances?

2.   What three specific categories of human behavior does control balance try to explain (predict)?

3.   What are the main variables used by control balance theory?

4.   Can a particular, concrete act of violence be predicted using control balance theory? Why or why not?

5.   What is a "contingency"? What part do contingencies play in control balance theory?

References

Akers, R.L. (2000). *Criminological Theories: Introduction, Evaluation, and Application.* Los Angeles: Roxbury.

American Society of Criminology (2000). "Investigating Control Balance Theory." Session 3 of the annual meeting of the American Society of Criminology. San Francisco, CA.

American Sociological Association (1998). "Author Meets Critics." Session 280 of the annual meeting of the American Sociological Association. San Francisco, CA.

Andenaes, J. (1974). *Punishment and Deterrence.* Ann Arbor: University of Michigan Press.

Baron, S.W. (2003). "Self-Control, Social Consequences, and Criminal Behavior: Street Youth and the General Theory of Crime." *Journal of Research in Crime and Delinquency*, 40:403-425.

Baumeister, R.F., T.F. Heatherton, and D.M. Tice (1994). *Losing Control: How and Why People Fail at Self-Regulation.* San Diego: Academic Press.

Blumer, H. (1969). *Symbolic Interactionism: Perspective and Method.* Englewood Cliffs, NJ: Prentice Hall.

Braithwaite, J. (1997). "Charles Tittle's Control Balance and Criminological Theory." *Theoretical Criminology,* 1:77-97.

Crutchfield, R.D., G.S. Bridges, J.G. Weis, and C. Kubrin (eds.) (2000). *Crime Readings,* 2nd ed. Thousand Oaks, CA: Pine Forge.

Curry, T.R., and A.R. Piquero (2003). "Control Ratios and Defiant Acts of Deviance: Assessing Additive and Conditional Effects with Constraints and Impulsivity." *Sociological Perspectives,* 46:397-415.

Gibbs, J.P. (1975). *Crime, Punishment, and Deterrence.* New York: Elsevier Scientific.

Gottfredson, M.R, and T. Hirschi (1990). *A General Theory of Crime.* Stanford, CA: Stanford University Press.

Hickman, M., and A.R. Piquero (2001). "Exploring the Relationships between Gender, Control Ratios, and Deviance." *Deviant Behavior,* 22:323-351.

Jensen, G.G. (1999). "A Critique of Control Balance Theory: Digging into Details." *Theoretical Criminology,* 3:339-343.

Kaplan, H.B. (1980). *Deviant Behavior in Defense of Self.* New York: Academic Press.

McCall, N. (1994). *Makes Me Wanna Holler.* New York: Random House.

Mead, G.H. (1934). *Mind, Self, and Society.* Chicago: University of Chicago Press.

Piquero, A.R., and M. Hickman (1999). "An Empirical Test of Tittle's Control Balance Theory." *Criminology,* 37:319-342.

Pratt, T.C., and F.T. Cullen (2000). "The Empirical Status of Gottfredson and Hirschi's General Theory of Crime: A Meta-Analysis." *Criminology,* 38:931-964.

Savelsberg, J.J. (1999). "Human Nature and Social Control in Complex Society: A Critique of Charles Tittle's Control Balance." *Theoretical Criminology,* 3:331-338.

Scheff, T.J., and S.M. Retzinger (1991). *Emotions and Violence: Shame and Rage in Destructive Conflicts.* Lexington, MA: Lexington Books.

Short, J.F., Jr. (1963). "The Responses of Gang Leaders to Status Threats: An Observation on Group Process and Delinquent Behavior." *American Journal of Sociology,* 68:571-579.

Stryker, S. (1980). *Symbolic Interactionism.* Menlo Park, CA: Benjamin/Cummins.

Sullivan, H.S. (1953). *The Interpersonal Theory of Psychiatry.* H.S. Perry and M.L. Gawel (eds.). New York: Norton.

Tittle, C.R. (2004). "Refining Control Balance Theory." *Theoretical Criminology* (in press).

Tittle, C.R. (1995). *Control Balance: Toward a General Theory of Deviance.* Boulder, CO: Westview.

Tittle, C.R. (1980). *Sanctions and Social Deviance: The Question of Deterrence.* New York: Praeger.

Wood, P.B., and R.G. Dunaway (1997-98). "An Application of Control Balance Theory to Incarcerated Sex Offenders." *Journal of the Oklahoma Criminal Justice Research Consortium,* 4:1-12.

Zimring, F.E., and G. Hawkins (1973). *Deterrence: The Legal Threat in Crime Control.* Chicago: University of Chicago Press.

CHAPTER 4

A Rational-Choice Approach to Violence

Richard B. Felson

There are arguably two basic theoretical approaches to violence and crime: rational choice perspectives and frustration-aggression approaches. The first assumes that behavior has a purpose or goal. Offenders harm others and break laws because they can achieve outcomes they value (the rewards) at not too high a cost. Costs include external consequences (e.g., punishment) as well as internal, psychological consequences (e.g., guilt) resulting from the violation of moral beliefs. Rational choice theorists use the name reluctantly because they know that rationality is "bounded," that is, that behavior reflects subjective judgments about payoffs, and that individuals often make careless decisions that can have disastrous outcomes.

The second major approach treats at least some violence and crime as an irrational response to aversive stimuli. According to frustration-aggression approaches, people lash out after experiencing stress, pain, failure, or suffering of any sort (Berkowitz, 1989; Dollard, Doob, Miller, Mowrer & Sears, 1939). Aversive stimuli leads the person to experience negative affect, which instigates "reactive" or "expressive aggression." Expressive aggression satisfies an innate desire to harm others when one is feeling bad or frustrated. It is different from instrumental aggression where harm is a means to an end rather than an end itself. From a frustration-aggression perspective, a rational choice perspective can explain only instrumental aggression. A biologically based frustration-aggression mechanism is necessary to explain expressive aggression. From a rational choice perspective, all aggression is instrumental.

Frustration-aggression scholars are more eclectic in that they include a bit of rational choice in their approach. They recognize that some aggression is instrumental (although they think that most of it is expressive). In addition, they emphasize the role of costs as an inhibitory factor even for expressive aggression. If the costs of attacking the source of the aversive

71

stimuli are too high, the person displaces the aggression onto an innocent third party. However, the instigation for expressive aggression is a biological urge, and not a reward. Without the biological connection, expressive aggression is difficult to explain, because it is difficult to argue that people are rewarded for aggression following exposure to most aversive stimuli.

In general strain theory, Agnew (1992) uses a frustration-aggression approach to explain all forms of crime, not just those involving aggression. People violate the law in response to any type of aversive stimuli. Why bad experience leads people to misbehave is unclear. General strain theory is a sociological theory, and sociology often ignores the more proximate causes of individual behavior. In addition, sociologists loathe biological explanations, so they are unlikely to buy any biological connection between aversive stimuli and aggression. They rely, at least implicitly, upon some sort of frustration-aggression mechanism to explain the effects of negative experience. For example, a frustration-mechanism is offered to explain the correlation between inequality and crime (e.g., Blau & Blau, 1982).

The other major criminological theories can be classified as rational-choice perspectives. Control theories emphasize the cost side of the equation, treating the rewards of crime as constant. Bonds with conventional others, efficacious neighbors, and the presence of capable guardians all increase the costs of crime (Felson, 1998; Hirschi, 1969; Sampson, Raudenbush & Earls, 1997). In addition, those people who lack self-control are sometimes too careless in their decisionmaking to consider or adequately assess the costs (Gottfredson & Hirschi, 1990). Social learning theory is an alternative version of the rational choice approach. It emphasizes socialization and the role of models as a source of information about what behavior is likely to provide a good payoff (Akers, 1998). Cultural theories and differential association emphasize the learning of attitudes from other group members that affect what people think is rewarding and/or costly (e.g., Sutherland, 1947). Finally, some versions of strain theory imply that offenders rationally turn to crime (for money or status) when they anticipate that the probability of achieving success using conventional means is too low (e.g., Cohen, 1955).

Definitions of Violence, Aggression, and Crime

When people intentionally harm others, social psychologists call it aggression. When aggression involves the use or threat of physical force, they call it violence. Crime, or violation of law, also involves behaviors that are harmful, at least according to the judgment of lawmakers. However, while some crimes involve intentional harmdoing (or aggression), other crimes do not. For example, thieves and violent offenders deliberately harm their victims, while no harm is generally intended by drunken drivers, illegal drug users, and prostitutes.

The relationship between harm-doing, violence, and crime is depicted in Figure 1. Crime in which *no harm is intended* includes victimless crimes and accidents resulting from the offender's negligence. Harming others is not on the mind of these offenders and is irrelevant to their motivation. These offenders are engaged in crime (or, in some cases, a civil wrong), but they are not engaged in aggression or violence.

Figure 1
The Relationship between Crime, Harm-doing, and Violence

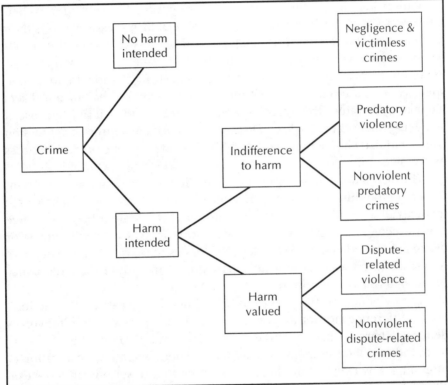

For other crimes—crimes involving aggression—harm *is* intended. Some of these acts of aggression are *predatory*, and some are *dispute-related*, depending on the offender's attitude toward harming the victim. Harm is incidental to predatory offenders, and not their goal. They deliberately harm victims but do not have a particular desire to harm them. Rather, they have some other goal in mind, and they are willing to harm the victim in order to achieve it.[1] For example, robbery and rape typically involve predatory violence. Most robbers and rapists are indifferent to the victim's suffering. They use violence to force the victim to comply because compliance will allow them to get something else they want (e.g., money or sex). Other predatory offenders use nonviolent methods (e.g., theft or fraud).[2] Harm is incidental to most thieves; they desire the stolen object but do not care whether the victim's insurance can replace it. Note that those scholars who take a frustration-aggression approach treat offenses in which harm is deliberate but incidental to the offender as instrumental aggression.

In dispute-related aggression, harm is the proximate goal and the offender's desired outcome. These offenders have grievances with their victims, they are angry, and they want to see their victims suffer. Most homicides and assaults stem from disputes, but so do some robberies, rapes, thefts, and frauds (Black, 1983). Insults and other verbal attacks also stem from disputes, although they are not usually considered violations of law.

Rational choice and frustration-aggression perspectives differ in their interpretation of the motivation for dispute-related aggression; this is their battleground. From a frustration-aggression perspective, these behaviors involve expressive aggression: harm has intrinsic value for a person who has experienced negative affect *for any reason*. From a rational choice perspective, dispute-related aggression is instrumental behavior and harm has extrinsic value: the aggressor values harm to the victim because it achieves some other purpose. Disputes are a critical source of aggression from a rational choice perspective, while they are just one of many sources of aversive stimuli from the point of view of frustration-aggression.

The distinctions between crime, aggression, and violence are important for understanding the causes of violent crime, because violent crime involves all three. Thus, an offender's proclivity to commit illegal violence may reflect: (1) a willingness to violate norms or laws; (2) a willingness or desire to harm others; or (3) a willingness or desire to use physical coercion. As a result, theories of conformity, harm-doing, and physical coercion may be needed to explain criminal violence. [3]

The evidence on the versatility of offenders suggests that some individual-difference factors are common to all offending, whether it involves deliberate harm or not. Gottfredson and Hirschi (1990) attribute versatility to individual differences in self-control. There is some specialization in offending, however. While those who commit more serious offenses usually commit less serious crimes, the reverse is not necessarily true. Thus, serious crimes occur much less frequently than minor crimes. In addition, some offenders commit property or drug offenses but avoid violence unless they are strongly provoked. Some may use illegal drugs but would prefer not to harm others. Most offenders are inhibited, at least to some extent, in the crimes they are willing to commit. They may take a "cafeteria style" approach to crime, but they won't put everything on their plate.

If a variable is correlated with violent crime, but not other crime, then a theory of violence, not of crime, is needed to explain the relationship. For example, theories of crime cannot explain why the United States has a relatively high rate of violence, because American rates of nonviolent crime are not particularly high (Zimring & Hawkins, 1997). In addition, race is primarily associated with violence among adolescents, particularly armed violence (Felson, Armstrong & Deane, 2001). It is not associated with serious or minor nonviolent offending, nor is it associated with verbal aggression. The race difference is apparently a difference in the use of violence, one method of harm-doing. Theories of violence, not crime, or aggression are necessary to explain the pattern.

Similarly, if a variable is correlated with crime in general, not just violent crime, then a theory of crime, not violence, is needed to explain the relationship. For example, testosterone is associated with a variety of crimes, not just violence, so we need to understand why testosterone leads males to break rules (not intentionally harm others) to explain the pattern (e.g., Booth & Osgood, 1993). In addition, evidence suggests that the modeling of parental violence by children cannot explain the intergenerational transmission of violence. Adults who as children were physically abused by their parents are just as likely to engage in nonviolent offending as violent offending. Physical abuse has no greater effect than parental neglect on the likelihood that the child will become a violent adult (e.g., Widom, 1989). These studies suggest that any type of parental mistreatment results in a greater likelihood of misbehavior by offspring.

Clearly, some of the causes of violence and other crime are similar, and some are different. Low self-control, or any characteristic that makes a person more willing to violate laws or conform, should lead to criminal behavior generally, not just violence and not just violations involving harm-doing. Empathy, hostility biases, punitiveness, selfishness, or any characteristic that increases a person's desire or indifference to harming others is likely to lead to crimes involving deliberate harm. Physical strength and skill, and attitudes about the efficacy and morality of violence, should be associated primarily with violence, not other crime.

Major Principles and Assumptions of a Rational Choice Approach

Dispute-related violence might be considered the last frontier for a rational choice approach: "if one can take it there, one can take it anywhere." The existing alternative—the frustration-aggression approach—is weak competition, however, because it seems clear that most aversive stimuli do not instigate aggressive responses. For example, death is infinitely more aversive than a verbal insult, yet a person is likely to respond with aggression when insulted, not when they are told that they have a terminal illness or a loved one has died. If aversive stimuli were important, homicides would be more common at funerals and hospitals than during recreational activities (Luckenbill, 1977). In addition, we feel worse when we blame *ourselves* for a problem, not the other person, but blaming others, not self-blame, leads to aggression. Finally, why would aversive stimuli have a biological link to aggression from an evolutionary standpoint? If such a link exists, it must have contributed to the survival of the species at some point in human history; it must have been instrumental aggression in the past. It is difficult to imagine how hitting people when one is in a bad mood would have contributed to human survival.

A rational choice approach says we should look at the incentives for aggression and the decision-making process that precedes it. The rationality of decisionmakers is particularly limited, because violent encounters often involve quick decisions, strong emotions, and alcohol. People who are angry, hurried, lacking in self-control, and drunk often fail to consider costs, morals, or alternative approaches. Those who are upset after experiencing aversive stimuli may also make careless or impulsive decisions. Thus, stressors are facilitators, not instigators, of aggression—a much more limited role. In addition, people may strike out habitually in certain circumstances, based on past rewards rather than the anticipation of future ones. In general, ill-considered decisions rather than inner compulsions result in behaviors that seem irrational (i.e., costly and immoral) to the objective observer.

People's inhibitions may be overwhelmed when they are angry and have a strong desire to hurt someone, but the source of that desire is not a biological urge caused by aversive stimuli. Anger can be a strong emotion, but it is a response to being mistreated and humiliated, not a response to all types of aversive stimuli (Averill, 1983). Of course, people respond emotionally when they have other bad experiences, but they tend to respond with sadness and other emotions, not anger.

While offenders may behave impulsively in the sense that they fail to consider long-range consequences, they are still making decisions. Even when people use violence in a rage, they must still decide how and when to attack and how to respond to their adversary's counter-attack. The hockey player, no matter how angry, remembers to drop his gloves *and* stick. He is more effective without his gloves and with stick in hand, but the use of the stick would get him into serious trouble.

A rational choice perspective has also been described as a social interactionist approach, because it emphasizes the social interaction between antagonists and third parties in disputes that culminate in violence (Tedeschi & Felson, 1994). When people express their grievances or exchange insults, they often do not anticipate that the conflict will escalate to physical violence. Verbal conflicts sometimes spiral out of control when adversaries fail to anticipate how each other will respond. For example, someone makes an off-hand threat, and then feels compelled to carry it out when the target does not back down. To understand the violent outcome it is important to understand the *interim decisions* that lead up to it.

Incentives for Violence

The question then is what are the incentives for violence? The use of violence is related to basic human desires. People want to influence others because many of our rewards are provided by other people. They want to be treated fairly, and they think those who fail to do so should be punished. They want the esteem of others and to think favorably of themselves. Finally, some people enjoy activities that are exciting and entail some risk. These basic goals of human behavior are also the goals of aggression and violence.

Getting one's way. People often attempt to influence the behavior of others. They use persuasion, they promise rewards, or they threaten or administer punishment. Aggression is a social influence tactic—sometimes used as a last resort, sometimes as a first resort. It can *compel* targets to do something they would otherwise not do, or *deter* targets from what they are doing. For example, predatory offenders, such as robbers and rapists, often use threats to compel their victims to comply. Parents use threats and punishment as a deterrent when their children misbehave or disobey them.

Sometimes targets comply and the violent actor is successful; at other times targets retaliate and the conflict escalates. Those who resist with violence sometimes deter further violence and sometimes encourage it. Violence involves an interaction between at least two parties, and the cooperation of both is required for a peaceful solution. This basic dilemma is the subject of game theory and the basis for strategic thinking.

Interpersonal conflict is a ubiquitous aspect of social life and an important source of aggression and violence. The dependence of family members on each other and the necessity for joint decisions create opportunities for conflict. Thus, siblings fight over the division of labor, and about ownership and the use of tangible goods in the home (Felson, 1983). In addition, routine activities that lead to conflict are likely to result in violence (Felson, 1998). For example, acquaintance rapes typically occur during consensual sexual activity when partners disagree about how far to go (Kanin, 1985).

Getting justice. We punish those who offend us in order to deter them, but also to achieve retributive justice. When someone does wrong—particularly when they wrong us—we believe they deserve an appropriate punishment. Thus violent behavior is often motivated by a desire for retribution or justice when a person has a grievance. Note that this motivation can be described using the language of rational choice, but it also can be described as normative behavior. Either way, people are choosing to behave in a way that achieves something they value.

It is ironic that people who engage in dispute-related violence often feel self-righteous and view their behavior as an act of justice (see Black, 1983). To fail to punish the misdeeds of others would be morally wrong. While pacifists view violence as a clear moral evil, for most people, moral values regarding the use of violence are ambiguous and context-dependent. They describe harm-doing as just punishment when they approve of it and as aggression or violence when they do not.

If justice restoration is important in dispute-related aggression and violence, then the attribution of blame is critical. We punish people when we blame them for negative outcomes. We assign blame when we think that they have misbehaved, intentionally or recklessly. We wish to harm people when we believe that they have wronged us, not when we believe that they have harmed us through no fault of their own.

People are often careless in their attributions of blame—sometimes they can be described as "blame-mongerers." That is, they tend to assign blame even when it is undeserved. They may fail to understand their adversary's perspective, or they may ignore exonerating circumstance, committing the fundamental attribution error (Ross, 1977). Sometimes they blame others to avoid self-blame. Sometimes blaming others can help explain traumatic events that are otherwise difficult to understand. Finally, some people have a "hostility bias" and are quick to assign blame and respond with aggression (Dodge & Coie, 1987).

Grievances are common in social life because people frequently break rules and offend each other. However, people often do not express their grievances to the offending party (Averill, 1983; Goffman, 1959). They do not confront the person, either because they want to avoid an embarrassing scene or because they want to avoid damaging their relationship. Rules of politeness help regulate interpersonal relations by preventing aggression, although sometimes they prevent conflicts from being resolved. Grievances accumulate, and the offended person may be particularly angry when they finally respond. From a rational choice perspective, the accumulation involves a cognitive summing of grievances, not a build-up of aggressive energy, drive, or arousal.

An aggrieved party may rely on the criminal justice system to punish the person who provoked them *if* that person engaged in a criminal offense. However, most grievances are not a response to illegal behavior, or the illegality cannot be proven, so the use of the criminal justice is not an option. Even when it is, the criminal justice system may not be available if the aggrieved party also has engaged in some illegal activity. For example, violence may occur in conflicts over illicit drug sales because the police are not available to handle related grievances (Goldstein, 1981). Black (1983) focuses on the antagonists' relative social status and the closeness of their relationship as factors in the availability of the criminal justice system, but the evidence is mixed at best (see, e.g., Felson, 2002).

Displaying power. People also use aggression to enhance or protect their identities, that is, their self or social image. For example, by using violence, a young man demonstrates that he is powerful, tough, and courageous. By showing skill with his fists, he can increase his status among his friends. If winning is impossible, standing up to the antagonist maintains some level of honor and provides a measure of satisfaction.

An insult or "put-down" dishonors the target and makes him appear weak and ineffectual, while a counter-attack nullifies that image. Retaliation is a form of defensive self-presentation, a way of "saving face" or maintaining one's honor when one has been attacked. However, the counter-attack "puts-down" the adversary who may retaliate in turn, creating a "conflict spiral." When these face-saving contests occur, adversaries try to win rather than limit their punishments to fit the offense. Sometimes small disputes escalate into physical violence.

Escalation is particularly likely to occur when an audience is watching, because the threat to face is greater. Sometimes third parties egg on the adversaries, making it difficult for them to back down without losing face. Sometimes third parties act as mediators, allowing both sides to back down without losing face (Felson, 1978). The response of third parties is a key factor in the escalation of aggressive interactions.

School-aged bullies are typically attempting to promote or assert an identity rather than defend one. Their behavior is typically predatory rather than dispute-related. Bullies prey on vulnerable targets, usually in the presence of third parties, in order to show how tough they are (see Olweus, 1978). For the bully, dominating the victim is an accomplishment, a way of demonstrating power to himself and others. The bully targets other boys, presumably because dominating girls will not make him look strong, and may have the opposite effect.

Thrill-seeking. Many people enjoy activities that involve or appear to involve risk. They like to gamble, play competitive sports, and ride roller coasters. Many prefer to avoid taking real risks themselves but enjoy watching others do so. Thus, viewing violence on television and film is a popular activity in most parts of the world.

The desire for thrills and the enjoyment of risk provide an incentive for predatory violence, particularly among young men (see Katz, 1988). They may enjoy a certain degree of physical danger or the risk of getting caught by the police. From this perspective, individuals view risk itself as a value rather than as an reflection of potential costs. They seek it rather than avoid it. Note that individual differences in thrill-seeking provides an alternative explanation for the versatility of offenders. Versatility is not necessarily due to low self-control or careless thinking.

Research suggests that individual differences in sensation-seeking reflect, at least in part, biological differences (see Raine, Brennan, Farrington & Mednick, 1997). People who engage in antisocial behavior tend to be physiologically underaroused, as indicated by lower resting heart rate levels. These persons may seek out exciting activities to compensate for their physiological underarousal and bring some physiological balance to their system. Resting heart rates have also been shown to be lower for violent offenders than nonviolent offenders (e.g., Farrington, 1987), suggesting that thrill-seeking may be a more important motive for violence than for other criminal behavior.

Level of Empirical Support for the Theory

From a frustration-aggression perspective, any type of aversive stimuli leads to aggression. From a rational choice perspective, only personal attacks and other behavior the person finds offensive instigate aggression. There must be an attribution of blame, a loss of face, or a concern for deterrence. Aversive stimuli produced by nonhuman sources or accidental behavior should not instigate aggression, unless the person attributes negligence or intent to harm. Other forms of aversive stimuli may facilitate an aggressive response, but they are not instigators. They are neither necessary nor sufficient to produce aggression, and if they have any effect it is likely to be weak.

In testing the rational choice approach, it is unnecessary to show that incentive and costs can affect aggressive behavior, because everyone agrees that some violence is instrumental and that perceived costs inhibit all forms of aggression. The challenge for a rational choice perspective is to show that only aversive stimuli stemming from disputes, not aversive stimuli generally, instigate aggression. It is also important to show that instances that appear to be expressive aggression are really instrumental aggression. If the empirical basis of frustration-aggression approaches is undermined, rational choice is all that is left standing.

Laboratory studies show that the key determinant of aggressive behavior is an intentional attack by a confederate, not generally aversive stimuli. Subjects will not deliver shock or cause harm to a confederate unless they have been shocked or insulted themselves (Tedeschi & Felson, 1994). Some studies do show small effects of physical pain, or losing contests, if the subject is also attacked, but an aversive stimulus has no effect by itself. Berkowitz (1993) argues that aversive stimuli do instigate aggression in laboratory studies but that the attack is necessary to overcome inhibitions. However, a more likely explanation is that that aversive stimuli are a weak facilitator and not an instigator of aggression.

Laboratory research also shows that the attribution of blame is critical in determining whether a negative experience leads to aggression. It is primarily negative experiences that are perceived as *unjustifiable* that lead to aggression. Berkowitz (1989) explains this well-known finding by claiming that unjustifiable frustrations are more aversive than justifiable frustrations. However, research also shows that subjects retaliate for intended shocks even when they do not actually receive the shock (Epstein & Taylor, 1967). The results suggest that "bad intentions," not bad experiences, lead to aggression, because they imply blame. Other laboratory studies show that subjects are more likely to retaliate when a person shocks them than when a machine shocks them (Sermat, 1967). The pain is the same, but the meaning differs. When someone zaps them, and subjects think that they have been wronged, they retaliate.

Research on the sequence of events leading to homicide and assault suggests that events begin when someone believes they have been wronged or personally attacked (Felson, 1984; Luckenbill, 1977). When someone provides an excuse or justification for their behavior—reducing the level of blame assigned—the conflict is less likely to escalate to violence (Felson, 1982). Aversive stimuli of a general sort are never mentioned in descriptions of actual violent events. Nor is displaced aggression; the motive almost always has something to do with the victim. That is why the police are able to catch offenders and prosecutors "establish motive" and get convictions. They show that the defendant had a grievance with the victim.

Research showing a relationship between the experience of stressful life events and violence appears to provide support for the frustration aggression approach. However, stress also interferes with competent performance, and the tendency to be polite and friendly. That may anger others. Thus, evidence shows that individuals who experience stressful life events are more likely to be the victims of violence (Felson, 1992; see also Silver, 2002). The relationship between stress and their own aggression disappears when the victimization measure is controlled. This finding suggests that the relationship between stress and violence generally reported in the literature may be due to the fact that people under stress are more likely to generate grievances, get into conflicts, and then engage in aggression themselves.

The frustration-aggression approach appears to be supported by evidence of displaced aggression in laboratory studies. However, there are alternative social psychological explanations. Attacks on "innocent" third parties may be an attempt to salvage some face, an attempt to restore equity when people think someone else has been unfairly rewarded (i.e., jealousy), or an attack on someone who is a member of a group with whom one feels aggrieved (see Tedeschi & Felson, 1994, for a review). Outside the laboratory, many acts of what appear to be displaced aggression are not: the person is irritable but has no intent to harm, or the person does in fact have some grievance with the victim.

Application: Violence Against Women

The social activists who study violence against women as a separate discipline rely, to some extent, upon a rational choice approach. They claim that men who rape or who assault their wives are attempting to dominate them or display their power, while women who assault their husbands are motivated by self-defense. Men's violence toward women stems ultimately from sexism in the larger society that motivates men to commit violence against women, and tolerates it when they do. The activists do not mention frustration-aggression, probably for ideological reasons: it implies less blame to offenders and more for victims.

To understand how violence against women is different one must compare it to violence against men. A comparative approach reveals that violence against women is more likely to involve family members and more likely to involve sexual coercion. However, it also reveals that men who assault women are no more likely to have traditional attitudes about women than men who commit violence against men (see Felson, 2002, for a review). In addition, most rapists and men who hit their wives commit other crimes as well. They are more likely to be versatile criminals, not sexists who specialize in violence toward women.

Men engage in violence much more often than women, yet wives hit their husbands as often as husbands hit their wives (though with less effect). In addition, during a verbal conflict, a man is less likely to become violent if the adversary is his wife than if it is another man. Something is inhibiting men from assaulting their wives. If we examine violence generally, we find that women's victimization rates are lower than men's, in spite of the fact that women tend to be much smaller and weaker, and therefore more vulnerable. Low victimization rates for women, not high rates, require explanation. We should ask not why men hit women, ask why they don't do it more often.

One reason that women are victimized less often than men is that they are less likely to provoke violence. However, the main reason women have lower victimization rates is the belief that harming women is worse than harming men—the chivalry norm. The tendency is to protect women, not harm them. Thus, the criminal justice system treats violence against women more severely and violence by women more leniently (see Felson, 2002, for a review). While women who violate gender roles or engage in deviant behavior are not treated as well, they tend to be treated better than men who violate gender roles or are deviant. These patterns suggest that sexism—defined as traditional attitudes toward women—actually inhibits violence against women. However, the privacy of family life can increase women's vulnerability to their husbands (and children's vulnerability to their parents).

To a large extent, men and women have similar motives when they engage in assault, and men and women are victimized for similar reasons. There are some differences in motivation in violence involving women, however. At least two studies suggest that men who assault their wives are particularly likely to have a control motive (Felson & Messner, 2000; Felson & Outlaw, n.d.). However, these controlling husbands are not necessarily attempting to achieve long-term dominance. Men who assault their wives are more likely than other violent offenders to be drunk, suggesting that they are not strategic thinkers with a long-range perspective (Burchfield & Felson, 2003). In addition, husbands tend to be slightly less controlling than their wives (e.g., Stets & Hammons, 2002). Thus, gender appears to be related to the methods used to control a spouse, not the motive. Because men are stronger and have a greater proclivity to use violence, they are more likely to use violent means. When a woman wants to control her husband, she is more likely to use other methods.

Johnson (1995) argues that only a minority of violent husbands are motivated by a desire for dominance stemming from sexist beliefs. These "patriarchal terrorists" commit violence that is more serious—that is, more injurious, frequent, and unilateral—than the "common couple violence" that is typically committed by both husbands and wives. However, evidence suggests that the violence of controlling husbands is not particularly likely to be injurious, frequent, and unilateral (Felson & Outlaw, n.d.).

Violence by wives against their husbands is typically attributed to self-defense and victim-precipitation. However, the evidence suggests that husbands are no more likely than wives to be the first to use violence in domestic conflicts (Cares & Felson, 2003). In addition, women who kill their husbands are no more likely to kill in self-defense than women who kill in other circumstances, and they are just as likely to have criminal records (Felson & Messner, 1998). The evidence is not consistent with the image of an otherwise peaceful wife who only kills because of "battered wife syndrome."

Face-saving is probably more likely to motivate men's aggression than women's. Men care more about not looking weak or cowardly, so they are more likely to retaliate when attacked, particularly if an audience is watching (Felson, 1982). Violence between men is more likely to involve displays of power and contests over image. Attacking females implies weakness, which is why some people call a man who is violent toward a woman a coward. In addition, males often publicly display their violence against other males (recall the schoolyard bully), while they usually hide violence toward females. This argues against the idea that rapists are attempting to demonstrate power.

On the other hand, there are good reasons, as well as evidence, to suggest that sexual coercion is usually sexually motivated. Dramatic sex differences in sexuality provide the context. Males are much more likely than females to be indiscriminate and casual in their attitudes toward sexual relations, and their interest is greater (see Baumeister, 2000, for a review). These sex differences in sexuality lead to conflict between the sexes. Men attempt to influence women to have sex, using a variety of techniques including coercion. Rape allows a man without moral qualms or fear of consequences to have sex with anyone he wants.

Most date rapes occur during consensual sexual activity when the man is sexually aroused (Kanin, 1985). He wants intercourse, but she doesn't want to go that far. Men who engage in date rape tend to use it as a last resort after persuasion and other techniques have failed. In addition, sexually coercive men tend to be young men with high sexual aspirations. They masturbate frequently and spend a lot of time searching for sexual partners. Rapists express a preference for attractive victims, and they overwhelmingly choose young women (Felson & Krohn, 1990). Their violence is usually tactical, not gratuitous: they use the force necessary to complete the crime but no more. On the other hand, men who rape their ex-wives and ex-girlfriends are more likely to beat up the victim during the rape. These rapists have a preference, not an indifference, to harming the victim. Their motive is more likely to involve retribution and revenge, not sexual compliance. It is also possible that some men find forced sex arousing. However, evidence suggests that most rapists do not find coercive sex more arousing than consensual sex. They differ from other men in that their arousal is not inhibited by the fact the sex is forced; they are indifferent to the victim's suffering.

Application: Collective Violence

The importance of third parties as mediators, instigators, and audience, was discussed earlier. However, third parties also act as allies or co-offenders in violent encounters, particularly those involving youths (see Warr, 2002, for a review). When the offenders are part of a larger gathering of people, the event is sometimes referred to as a riot. However, theorists have had difficulty distinguishing riots from other forms of collective violence or co-offending (see McPhail, 1991). Perhaps that is because they are not very different.

In a riot, the presence of a large crowd makes it more difficult for the police to identify individual offenders and make arrests. In addition, if the crowd tolerates the violence of individuals, they are unlikely to serve as capable guardians. As a result, violent offenders anticipate low costs. Unlike the typical criminal offender, participants in riots often commit their offenses in the presence of the police, although out of their reach. The situation creates opportunities for violent conflict, when the police attempt to make arrests.

Originally, frustration–aggression approaches dominated the study of riots and other forms of collective violence. Scholars emphasized the irrationality of "mobs" who operated out of control and as a group (e.g., Le Bon, 1895). The current position emphasizes the purposive behavior of individuals or small groups within the larger gathering (McPhail, 1991). In most riots only a minority of the participants engage in property destruction and looting, and an even smaller percentage engage in violence (McPhail, 1991). The police are much more likely to injure participants than participants are to injure police. Most crowd members engage in other actions or watch the event for entertainment. Thus, it is a mistake to view the crowd as acting in uniformity or as following a single norm that emerges during the event.[4] In addition, those participants who do engage in property destruction, looting, and violence are selective in their targets (Berk & Aldrich, 1972). Their behavior does not appear to involve an irrational outburst, nor does it involve individuals overcome by mob psychology.

The motives for participants in collective violence are similar to the motives for individual violence. Participants in protest riots often have grievances with the government or the police: a common precipitating event is some violent action by the police (Tilly, 2003). Participants in communal riots have grievances against some other group. Lynchings involve grievances with the accused and vigilante justice, just like homicides committed by individuals. On the other hand, some participants in riots have no grievance, but view the decline in guardianship as an opportunity to loot for profit or to destroy property for entertainment. Thrill-seeking is probably the motivation for participants in celebration riots, as well as for the large number of people who come to watch any civil disorder. It is more exciting to see it in person than to watch it on television.

The social interaction leading up to collective violence is important, as it is for dispute-related violence involving individuals (e.g., Tilly, 2003). The outcome of the event is often unpredictable regardless of whether individuals or groups are involved. Participants may have no plans or at least no shared plans beforehand, and their goals may change in response to the behavior of the police and other participants. Grievances may develop during the event in response to police action. Conflicts may escalate as participants engage in illegal actions and the police respond with force. Face-saving may become involved if participants view violent actions by the police as a threat to face or if the police view taunts and resistance as a lack of respect for their authority. These same motivations have been described in discussions of violent encounters between individual citizens and the police (Westley, 1970).

In protest demonstrations, participants express a shared grievance publicly in an attempt to influence authorities. Participants may be attempting to dramatize their complaint, disrupt operations, show they have support, or provoke a police response that increases that support. However, they do not necessarily have practical goals. People sometimes express complaints either individually or groups, out of a sense of justice, even when they believe their actions have no hope of success. Like individual violence, collective violence may be a form of justice restoration. However, there is evidence that collective actions, including violence, are more likely when actors think they can effect change (Muller & Weede, 1994).

Collective violence is different from individual violence in that group processes play a more central role. Issues related to conformity, group cohesion, and leadership become important. For example, numerous studies of conformity suggest that people are reluctant to question what they think is the popular position (e.g., Janis, 1982). In addition, leaders may use violence against out-groups to increase group cohesion and maintain their power. Finally, the literature on group polarization suggests that groups often make more risky decisions than individuals (although the opposite is sometimes true), in part because there is a diffusion of responsibility (e.g., Diener, 1977; Friedkin, 1999).

Conclusion

A rational-choice perspective suggests that it is important to consider incentives and costs when studying any type of violence. Violence has a purpose whether the offender acts alone or in a group, and whether the victim is a man or a woman. While group processes are more important for collective violence, and family conflict and sexual motives are more important for violence against women, the general principles are the same.

Those of us who study violent crime must figure out what we are attempting to explain. In studying individual and group differences, it is important to understand that violent crime involves crime, aggression, *and* violence. We need to understand why people violate laws, why they deliberately harm others, and why they sometimes use physical violence as their method. We cannot rely upon criminological theories to explain correlates of violent crime when those variables are not associated with other crime, and we cannot rely upon theories of aggression and violence to explain correlates of criminal behavior generally.

While some of the causes of violence and other crime are similar, some are different. The versatility of many offenders implies that common causes, such as low self-control and thrill-seeking, are important. However, the reluctance of some offenders to commit violent crimes implies that inhibitions about harming others or using physical violence are also important.

My focus has been on motives and other situational factors involved in aggression (or deliberate harm-doing). I have challenged the distinction between instrumental and expressive aggression, arguing that all aggression is instrumental. Motives include effecting compliance, retribution, producing favorable identities, and thrill-seeking. These motives can explain why people engage in what is sometimes called expressive aggression. They can explain why only certain types of aversive stimuli—perceived wrongdoing and intentional attack—lead to anger and dispute-related aggression. Pain, illness, and death, the most aversive stimuli in the human experience, do not have this effect. They do make people unhappy, which may facilitate aggression if mood affects decisionmaking. However, a strong biological link between aversive stimuli and aggression has not been demonstrated. Even if a rational choice perspective proves to be an inadequate explanation of all forms of aggression, it seems unlikely that frustration-aggression approaches can fill the gap.

From a rational-choice perspective, the distinction between predatory and dispute-related aggression is useful. In predatory aggression, offenders intentionally harm their victim, but that is not their goal. They want to force compliance, promote an identity, or have some fun at the victim's expense. In dispute-related aggression, the proximate goal of offenders is to harm, but their motives are deterrence, retribution, and saving face. A special frustration-aggression mechanism is not necessary to explain why participants in social conflicts want to see their adversaries suffer.

Endnotes

[1]   Behavior has multiple consequences; some of these consequences are goals, while others are incidental outcomes. In addition, a consequence that is incidental to the offender, may be quite costly for the victim. The victim's experience of harm should be the focus in treating the victim, but it is irrelevant to an understanding of the offender's behavior.

[2]   Behaviors involving deception or stealth are not generally treated as examples of aggression, although they fit the definition.

[3]   To some extent, individual differences in the proclivity to break laws, do harm, or use violence may reflect differences in the willingness to commit *serious* crime. However, violence and aggression are only considered serious violations when they are perceived as unprovoked or disproportionate to the provocation (e.g., Kane, Joseph & Tedeschi, 1976).

[4]   Sometimes the offenders coordinate their actions, sometimes they act independently.

Discussion Questions

1.   Think back to the last time you were involved in an incident in which someone was violent or verbally aggressive. Describe the sequence of events. What theoretical approach is most useful in understanding what happened?

2.   What variables should be associated with violence if violence is considered as deliberate harm-doing? What variables should be associated with violence if violence is considered a type of deviance? Can criminological theories or theories of aggression and violence better explain the actual patterns that we observe?

3.   Suppose one believed that, because of sexism, violence against women was different from violence involving men. How would one test such a perspective?

4.   When college women indicate on surveys that someone they know forced them to have sex, they often say that what happened was not rape. Why don't they label it rape? Are they mistaken? What is probably happening in these incidents?

References

Akers, R. (1998). *Social Learning and Social Structure: A General Theory of Crime and Deviance*. Boston: Northeastern University Press.

Agnew, R. (1992). "Foundations for a General Strain Theory of Crime and Delinquency." *Criminology*, 37:47-87.

Averill, J.R. (1983). "Studies on Anger and Aggression: Implications for Theories of Emotion." *American Psychologist*, 38:1145-1160.

Baumeister, R.F. (2000). "Gender Differences in Erotic Plasticity: The Female Sex Drive as Socially Flexible and Responsive." *Psychological Bulletin*, 126:347-374.

Berk, R., and H. Aldrich (1972). "Patterns of Vandalism during Civil Disorders as an Indicator of Selection of Targets." *American Sociological Review*, 37:533-547

Berkowitz, L. (1993). *Aggression: It's Causes, Consequences, and Control*. Philadelphia: Temple University Press.

Berkowitz, L. (1989). "The Frustration-Aggression Hypothesis: An Examination and Reformulation." *Psychological Bulletin*, 106:59-73.

Black, D.J. (1983). "Crime as Social Control." *American Sociological Review*, 48:34-45.

Blau, J., and P. Blau (1982). "The Cost of Inequality: Metropolitan Structure and Violent Crime." *American Sociological Review*, 47:114-129.

Booth, A., and D.W. Osgood (1993). "The Influence of Testosterone on Deviance in Adulthood: Assessing and Explaining the Relationship." *Criminology*, 31:93-117.

Burchfield , K.B., and R.B. Felson (2003). "Who Gets High and Who Gets Assaulted? Alcohol and Drug Use in Domestic and Other Violence." Paper presented at the annual meeting of the American Society of Criminology, Denver, CO.

Cares, A.C., and R.B. Felson (2003). "Gender, Victim-Offender Relationship and the Frequency of Violence." Paper presented at the annual meeting of the American Society of Criminology, Denver, CO.

Cohen, A.K. (1955). *Delinquent Boys: The Culture of the Gang*. New York: Free Press.

Diener, E. (1977). "Deindividuation: Causes and Consequences." *Social Behavior and Personality* 5:143-155.

Dodge, K.A., and J.D. Coie (1987). "Social-Information-Processing Factors in Reactive and Proactive Aggression in Children's Peer Groups." *Journal of Personality and Social Psychology*, 53:1146-1158.

Dollard, J., L.W. Doob, N. Miller, O.H. Mowrer, and R.R. Sears (1939). *Frustration and Aggression*. New Haven, CT: Yale University Press.

Epstein, S., and S.P. Taylor (1967). "Instigation to Aggression as a Function of Degree of Defeat and Perceived Aggressive Intent of the Opponent." *Journal of Personality*, 35:265-289.

Farrington, D.P. (1987). "Implications of Biological Findings for Criminological Research." In S.A. Mednick, T.E. Moffitt, and S.A. Stack (eds.), *The Causes of Crime: New Biological Approaches*, pp. 42-64. New York: Cambridge University Press.

Felson, M. (1998). *Crime and Everyday Life*, 2nd ed. Thousand Oaks, CA: Pine Forge.

Title: Violence: From Theory to
            Research
Cond: Good
User: mcsales
Station: Esmeralda-PC
Date: 2021-05-26 16:56:13 (UTC)
Account: Benjamins Bookshelf
Orig Loc: 2-B
mSKU: BBM.VIZ
Seq#:   1039
QuickPick   0IG
unit_id: 2060003
width: 0.68 in
rank: 3,786,835

delist unit# 2060003

XXXXX

Felson, R.B. (2002). *Violence and Gender Reexamined*. Washington, DC: American Psychological Association.

Felson, R.B. (1992). "Kick 'em When They're Down: Explanations of the Relationship between Stress and Interpersonal Aggression and Violence." *Sociological Quarterly*, 33:1-16.

Felson, R. B. (1984). "Patterns of Aggressive Social Interaction." In A. Mummendey (ed.), *Social Psychology of Aggression: From Individual Behavior to Social Interaction*, pp. 107-126. New York: Springer-Verlag.

Felson, R.B. (1983). "Aggression and Violence between Siblings." *Social Psychology Quarterly*, 46:271-285.

Felson, R.B. (1982). "Impression Management and the Escalation of Aggression and Violence." *Social Psychology Quarterly*, 45:245-254.

Felson, R.B. (1978). "Aggression as Impression Management." *Social Psychology*, 41:205-213.

Felson, R.B., D.A. Armstrong, and G. Deane (2001). "Race and Adolescent Crime and Violence: An Incident-based Analysis." Paper presented at the annual meeting of the Eastern Society of Criminology. Philadelphia, PA.

Felson, R.B., and M.D. Krohn (1990). "Motives for Rape." *Journal of Research in Crime and Delinquency*, 27:222-242.

Felson, R.B., and S.F. Messner (1998). "Disentangling the Effects of Gender and Intimacy on Victim Precipitation in Homicide." *Criminology*, 36:405-423.

Felson, R.B., and S.F. Messner (2000). "The Control Motive in Intimate Partner Violence." *Social Psychology Quarterly*, 63:86-94.

Felson, R.B., and M. Outlaw (n.d.). "The Control Motive and Marital Violence." Unpublished manuscript.

Friedkin, N.E. (1999). "Choice Shift and Group Polarization." *American Sociological Review*, 64:856-875.

Goffman, E. (1959). *The Presentation of Self in Everyday Life*. New York: Doubleday Anchor.

Goldstein, P.J. (1981). "Drugs and Violent Crime." In N.A. Weiner and M.A. Zahn (eds.), *Violence: Patterns, Causes, Public Policy*, pp. 295-302. San Diego: Harcourt Brace Jovanovich.

Gottfredson, M.R., and T. Hirschi (1990). *A General Theory of Crime*. Stanford, CA: Stanford University Press.

Hirschi, T. (1969). *Causes of Delinquency*. Berkeley, CA: University of California Press.

Janis, I.L. (1982). *Groupthink*, 2nd ed. Boston: Houghton Mifflin

Johnson, M. P. (1995). "Patriarchal Terrorism and Common Couple Violence: Two Forms of Violence Against Women." *Journal of Marriage and the Family*, 57:283-294.

Kane, T.R., J.M. Joseph, and J.T. Tedeschi (1976). "Person Perception and an Evaluation of the Berkowitz Paradigm for the Study of Aggression." *Journal of Personality and Social Psychology*, 33:663-673.

Kanin, E.J. (1985). "Date Rapists: Differential Sexual Socialization and Relative Deprivation." *Archives of Sexual Behavior*, 14:219-231.

Katz, J. (1988). *Seductions of Crime: Moral and Sensual Attractions of Doing Evil*. New York: Basic Books.

Le Bon, G. (1895). *The Psychology of the Crowd. Translation 1960*. New York: Viking.

Luckenbill, D.F. (1977). "Criminal Homicide as a Situated Transaction." *Social Problems*, 25:176-186.

McPhail, C. (1991). *The Myth of the Madding Crowd*. New York: Aldine de Gruyter.

Muller, E.N., and E. Weede (1994). "Theories of Rebellion: Relative Deprivation and Power Contention." *Rationality and Society*, 6(1):40-571

Olweus, D. (1978). *Aggression in the Schools: Bullies and Whipping Boys*. Washington, DC: Hemisphere.

Raine, A., P.A. Brennan, D.P. Farrington, and S.A. Mednick (1997). *Biosocial Bases of Violence*. New York: Plenum.

Ross, L. (1977). "The Intuitive Psychologist and his Shortcomings: Distortions in the Attribution Process." In L. Berkowitz (ed.), *Advances in Experimental Social Psychology*, Volume 10, pp. 174-221. New York: Academic.

Sampson, R.J., S.W. Raudenbush, and F. Earls (1997). "Neighborhoods and Violent Crime: A Multi-Level Study of Collective Efficacy." *Science*, 277:918-924.

Sermat, V. (1967). "The Possibility of Influencing the Other's Behavior and Cooperation: Chicken vs. Prisoner's Dilemma." *Canadian Journal of Psychology*, 21:204-219.

Silver, E. (2002). "Mental Disorder and Violent Victimization: The Mediating Role of Involvement in Conflicted Social Relationships." *Criminology*, 40:191-212.

Stets, J., and S.A. Hammons (2002). "Gender, Control, and Marital Commitment." *Journal of Family Issues*, 23:3-25.

Sutherland, E. (1947). *Principles of Criminology*, 4th ed. Philadelphia: J.B. Lippincott.

Tedeschi, J.T., and R.B. Felson (1994). *Violence, Aggression, and Coercive Actions*. Washington, DC: American Psychological Association.

Tilly, C. (2003). *The Politics of Collective Violence*. New York: Cambridge University Press.

Warr, M. (2002). *Companions in Crime: The Social Aspects of Criminal Conduct*. New York: Cambridge University Press.

Westley, W.A. (1970). *Violence and the Police: A Sociological Study of Law, Custom, and Morality*. Cambridge, MA: MIT Press.

Widom, C.S. (1989). "Does Violence Beget Violence? A Critical Examination of the Literature." *Psychological Bulletin*, 106:3-28.

Zimring, F., and G. Hawkins (1997). *Crime is Not the Problem: Lethal Violence in America*. New York: Oxford University Press.

CHAPTER 5

Social Disorganization and Violence

Robert J. Bursik, Jr.

Introduction: Historical Context

Michael and Adler (1933) characterized the state of criminology after the first third of the twentieth century in blunt and unflinching terms: "There is no theory or analysis to be found in the literature of criminology" (p. 61); "The findings constitute a body of descriptive knowledge with extremely limited significance and completely incapable of yielding scientific conclusions" (p. 61). Luckily, their conclusion was premature and overstated, for two intellectual movements already had been unfolding in the Department of Sociology at the University of Chicago that culminated jointly in the social disorganization model of crime and delinquency, arguably the first criminological theory to have been developed almost exclusively in the United States. This perspective continues to have an enduring effect on our conceptualization and understanding of the social factors associated with neighborhood rates of violence.

The early twentieth century was a period of rapid population change in Chicago as people moved into the city to take advantage of the jobs provided by the stockyards, steel mills, railroads, and other local industries (see Bursik, 2000; Bursik & Grasmick, 1993). In addition to the waves of white ethnic immigrants that were arriving from Europe, many African Americans from the South were relocating to Chicago in pursuit of not only work but also the greater degree of racial tolerance that they had been led to believe existed in this thriving Northern city. The extreme diversity of lifestyles, languages, and cultural traditions that were found in Chicago at this time fascinated the sociologists Robert Park and Ernest Burgess (1924; Burgess, 1925) and led to their research into urban life in general, and neighborhood development in particular. On the basis of a wide-ranging series of neighborhood case studies conducted mostly by their students, they produced a model of human ecology that assumed that competition over the control of scarce but desirable space was the fundamental form of social interaction, and that this competition determined the parts of the city in which different populations could reside as well as the degrees of economic deprivation, residential mobility, and racial/ethnic heterogeneity in those areas.

In addition to the work of Park and Burgess, the social disorganization theory of crime and delinquency also had its roots in the more general social disorganization research of W.I. Thomas and Florian Znaniecki (1920) that focused on the adaptation of Polish immigrants to Chicago (see Bursik, 2005). Thomas and Znaniecki clearly demonstrated that there was a far different basis of organization than that found in the "old country," which "centered around the family and the primary community and the fundamental principles of direct personal solidarity and conformity with public opinion" (p. 241). For many of the immigrants they studied, pre-existing primary group ties either were severed or greatly weakened by the relocation to the United States, and most were not able to enter into new relationships that were "as strong and coherent" as those left behind (p. 258). That is, immigrants were in a doubly weak position, unable to establish deep and meaningful associations with members of the host population as well as with the members of their own ethnicity that in the past had given them a sense of responsibility, security, and belonging. According to Thomas and Znaniecki, the resulting "passive demoralization" among many immigrants resulted in the condition to which they famously and controversially referred as "social disorganization," formally defined as a decrease in the influence of existing social rules of behavior upon individual members of the group.

Park and Burgess and Thomas and Znaniecki explicitly noted that immigrant communities characterized by disorganization would have relatively high rates of crime during the period of accommodation. Thomas and Znaniecki provided detailed descriptions of several homicides that occurred among the Polish residents. However, since these sociologists were primarily interested in the urban structures and dynamics that facilitated assimilation, crime *per se* was a secondary consideration. The first well-known effort of the Chicago school to focus specifically on disorganization and crime was Frederick Thrasher's (1927) landmark dissertation on gangs. However, the classic social disorganization theory of crime was most closely identified by far with the studies of Clifford Shaw, Henry McKay, and their colleagues.

Major Principles and Assumptions of the Theory

In 1921, Clifford Shaw and his associates began compiling a record of the home addresses of all male juveniles referred to the Cook County (Illinois) Juvenile Court that eventually spanned the years 1900 to 1965 (see Bursik, 1988; 2001; Bursik & Grasmick, 1993). On the basis of spatial maps of the residential locations of each of these referrals, Shaw and McKay reached two very important conclusions (1929; 1931; 1942; 1969). First, the relative distribution of delinquency rates remained fairly stable over time among Chicago's neighborhoods despite dramatic changes in the ethnic and racial composition of these neighborhoods. That is, they argued that the observed community variation in delinquency rates primarily was a function of certain features of the neighborhoods in which adolescents resided and not due to differences in the racial and ethnic composition of the juvenile population.

The second pattern suggested by these data was equally important: delinquency rates were negatively correlated with the distance of the neighborhood from the central business district. Because Burgess's earlier (1925) Chicago research had documented a strong positive association between the economic status of residential areas and distance from the center of the city, this finding suggested that delinquency rates were negatively correlated with the economic composition of local communities. However, Shaw and McKay did not propose a simple direct relationship between such economic processes and the likelihood of delinquency. Rather, drawing from the model of Park and Burgess, they argued that areas characterized by economic deprivation tended to have high rates of population turnover because they were undesirable residential communities and people abandoned them as soon as it became economically feasible. In addition, because poor neighborhoods were more likely to serve as the locations of initial settlement for new immigrant groups, economically depressed areas also tended to be characterized by racial and ethnic heterogeneity. Shaw and McKay argued that, in turn, rapid population change and heterogeneity were likely to result in *social disorganization*. Shaw and McKay considered this weakened influence of rules of behavior, and not economic deprivation in itself, to be the primary cause of high neighborhood delinquency rates.

Although the social disorganization framework was a central component of American criminology for many years, several important conceptual and analytic shortcomings led to its temporary demise (see Bursik, 1988; 2001; Bursik & Grasmick, 1993) and it came to be seen by many as a framework of only historical interest with little contemporary relevance. However, the model experienced a dramatic revival during the 1980s when a number of criminologists recognized that some of these shortcomings could be resolved by reframing the concept of social disorganization within the context of recent developments in the social sciences. Most current studies in the Shaw and McKay tradition have focused upon one or both of two closely related reformulations: the systemic model of social disorganization (Bursik & Grasmick, 1993; 1996), and the social capital/collective efficacy framework of Robert Sampson and his colleagues (Sampson, Morenoff & Earls, 1999; Sampson, Raudenbush & Earls, 1997). Although there are subtle but critical differences in these two approaches, both conceptualize disorganization in terms of the existence of interactional networks that tie community residents to one another and to institutions outside of the area, the ability of these ties to effectively regulate the nature of the activities that occur within a neighborhood's boundaries, and the residents' willingness to use the networks for those purposes.

The systemic variant of disorganization focuses on the effects on crime of structural variation in three basic types of networks: the private (intimate friendship and kinship relationships), the parochial (less intimate and secondary group relationships), and the public (linkages to groups and institutions located outside of the neighborhood; see Bursik, 1999). As such, the systemic approach formalizes the conceptual differences and causal linkages among social disorganization, the ecological processes that make these three sources of internal self-regulation problematic, and the rates of crime and delinquency that may be a result; all of these were somewhat vague in the original Shaw and McKay presentations.

While the existence of structural linkages is a necessary condition for the exercise of regulatory control, the social capital/collective efficacy framework of Sampson and his colleagues argues that it is not sufficient (see Bursik, 1999). Rather, this variant assumes that the structural relationships that link actors into networks can be an effective source of social control only if they facilitate the exchange of expressive and instrumental social capital that fosters and maintains trust and solidarity among the residents as well as the belief that the residents can effectively control the likelihood of undesirable behavior within the neighborhood (Sampson, Morenoff & Earls, 1999; Sampson, Raudenbush & Earls, 1997). This trust, solidarity, and belief are the defining elements of collective efficacy. Especially critical in this process are the development of intergenerational networks, the mutual transferral of advice, material goods, and information about child rearing, and expectations for the joint informal control, support, and supervision of local children (Sampson, Morenoff & Earls, 1999:635).

Definition of Violence

Given Shaw and McKay's reliance on court referrals generated almost exclusively by law enforcement agencies, their research focused primarily on violations of the criminal law. Therefore, they distinguished between law violations and "the still broader category of 'problem behavior,' including mischief, aggression, and personality problems of the type which often bring about a child's referral to a behavior clinic or other agency" (1969:45), and cautioned that the delinquency rates should not be used as indices of these other types of problematic activities. Most contemporary work on social disorganization and violence has maintained this legalistic orientation, focusing upon those activities that officially have been designated as "crimes against persons," that is, illegal activities that place a victim in danger of physical injury or the loss of life.

Application of the Theory to Specific Forms of Violence

The violent offenses most likely to be examined from a disorganization perspective are those classified by the Uniform Crime Reports as Part I, that is, murder and non-negligent homicide, forcible rape, robbery, and aggravated assault. However, there has been a growing tendency to move beyond this restriction. Sampson and colleagues (1997), for example, examine fights in which a weapon was used, violent arguments among neighbors, gang fights, sexual assaults, and muggings, while the delinquency scale analyzed by Elliott and colleagues (1996) included arson, carrying a concealed weapon, attacking someone with a weapon, and involvement in gang fights. Van Wyk and colleagues (2003) focused on throwing things at, hitting, or shoving intimate partners. In addition, some researchers have explored the degree to which one or more components of social disorganization heighten the likelihood of broader forms of violence, such as civil disturbances (Spilerman, 1976), genocide (Smith, 2002), legalization of the death penalty (Jacobs & Carmichael, 2002), political insurrections (Pizzaro Leongomez, 2002), prison riots (Useem, 1985), suicide (Bachman, 1992), terrorism (Savitch & Ardashev, 2001), and violent intergroup school disorders (Lieske, 1978). However, despite similarities in the components of their models, some of these studies do not formally characterize their models as being in the social disorganization tradition *per se*.

Application of the Theory to Both Collective and Interpersonal Violence

Shaw and McKay did not discuss the phenomenon of collective violence. Nevertheless, they stressed the group nature of most delinquent and criminal activity throughout their writings, and emphasized the degree to which their framework complemented Thrasher's findings that intergroup conflict resulted in the development of gang traditions, solidarity, and attachment to a local neighborhood (1927:46; see Shaw, Zorbaugh, McKay & Cottrell, 1929, Chapter I, footnote 10). For example, they stated that "(T)he play group is a spontaneous form of primary relationship which reflects community life and is very significant in determining attitudes, habits, and standards of conduct in the juvenile. In certain areas of the city these groups become delinquent gangs . . ." (1929:7). In fact, the Conclusion of *Juvenile Delinquency and Urban Areas* (1942:315) emphasizes that group delinquency constitutes a preponderance of all officially recorded offenses committed by boys and young men" (p. 315). With the few exceptions noted above, gang behavior continues to be the primary form of collective violence studied by disorganization researchers (see, for example, Bankston, 1998; Curry & Spergel, 1988; Hagedorn, 1991; Spergel, 1990; Wang, 2002).

Given Shaw and McKay's macrosociological orientation, the bulk of interpersonal violence research has been conducted on the basis of aggregations such as neighborhoods (Patterson, 1991), cities (Baumer, 1994), counties (Kposowa & Breault, 1993), or (rarely) countries (Neapolitan, 1999). However, especially since the publication of the landmark 1997 study by Sampson and his colleagues there has been an increasing tendency to study the social disorganization–interpersonal violence association at the individual and neighborhood levels simultaneously (Elliott, Wilson, Huizinga, Sampson, Elliott & Rankin, 1996; Sampson, Morenoff & Earls, 1999).

Level of Empirical Support for the Theory

The fullest test to date of the systemic social disorganization theory is the study of Chicago by Sampson and colleagues (1997). As predicted, the degree of collective efficacy in a neighborhood was determined by levels of economic disadvantage, residential instability, and population heterogeneity ; in turn, it had a very strong effect on the violent crime rate found in these neighborhoods. Yet, while the findings of Sampson and colleagues generally are consistent with their variant of the social disorganization model, it has become apparent that some problematic conceptual issues have not yet been satisfactorily addressed.

Most notably, the dynamics underlying both forms of the systemic model clearly are far more complicated than originally assumed (Bursik, 2002). Due to the influence of control theory on the development of the initial systemic models, it originally was expected that the effectiveness of informal social control would be a linear (or at least monotonic) function of the size, strength, and density of local social networks. Unfortunately, this proposition failed to recognize that extensive ties to family members, fictive kin, and other neighbors could tie individuals simultaneously to law-abiding *and* law-violating citizens (Pattillo, 1998). For example, a sizeable number of the gang members interviewed by Decker and Van Winkle (1996) reported that their neighbors had nothing but contempt for the gang to which they belonged, but did tend to like them as individuals. Pattillo (1998) observed a similar pattern, and documented how the presence of gang members and drug dealers in otherwise conventional networks complicates the processes of social control. In particular, due to personal ties to gang members, some residents are reluctant to solicit police intervention into what are perceived as essentially local matters. Therefore, the matter is not nearly as straightforward as the systemic social disorganization model's emphasis on the *inability* of impoverished areas to set the processes of public control into motion would suggest. Rather, disadvantaged neighborhoods with a dense set of relational networks also may be *unwilling* to do so. In addition, Rose and Clear (1998) argue that the incarceration of local offenders can have a debilitating impact on informal networks of social control. That is, the effective exercise of systemic control at one level may decrease the effectiveness of control at another.

There are further difficulties. Hirschi's version of control theory (1969) argues that constraints on illegal behavior are strongest when there are strong bonds to significant others. Given the intensely personal interactions that characterize private networks, one would assume that the social control that is exercised within such relationships would have much stronger effects on behavior than that which occurs during more impersonal interactions (see Bursik, 2000). However, Bellair (1997) presents evidence that the social control that emanates from nonintimate relationships may be at least as effective in the control of gang activities as that which is derived from primary groups.

An equally intriguing theoretical complication involves the relationships among economic deprivation, residential mobility, population heterogeneity, and crime. Warner and Pierce (1993) show that in Seattle, racial heterogeneity is associated with high crime rates in neighborhoods with little poverty, but with lower crime rates in impoverished areas (see also Rountree & Warner, 1997). In addition, they present evidence that the effects of stability and homogeneity on the level of informal social control depends on the socioeconomic status of the neighborhood, that is, control is relatively weak in homogenous, stable neighborhoods if those neighborhoods also are economically deprived. An equally complicated situation can be found in the 1997 Sampson et al. study analysis of Chicago: once the effects of the characteristics of the residents are controlled, residential stability is positively associated with the homicide rate, although the relationship is fairly weak.

While such findings are surprising from a systemic viewpoint, they are consistent with Wilson's (1987) observations about the concentration of problems found in extremely poor, socially isolated underclass neighborhoods. In particular, residential stability may be achieved in two very different ways. The image that has dominated the systemic and efficacy social disorganization theories is that stable communities arise when residents of desirable areas develop long-term stakes in those neighborhoods, including the formation of strong networks. However, many members of the economic underclass have been stranded in undesirable, high-crime areas, abandoned by former neighbors who were financially able to relocate into better communities. As opposed to the first type of stable community, the low level of population turnover in such neighborhoods does not reflect freely made residential choices. Thus, there are few incentives to invest time and energy into the development of social ties. The fact that such contemporary urban dynamics have not yet been more fully integrated into the systemic model is an important shortcoming of modern disorganization approaches.

Conclusion

Although it is one of the oldest theoretical traditions of American criminology, Shaw and McKay's social disorganization theory of crime still continues to have a major influence on contemporary community studies of violence, although it has been significantly expanded to include the roles of networks, social capital, and collective efficacy. While tests of the theory have been generally supportive of its predictions, the evidence also indicates that additional conceptual work is needed. Nevertheless, it continues to be one of the more powerful explanatory models in the field.

Discussion Questions

1. The social disorganization framework was once characterized as a group-level version of control theory. Why might one draw that conclusion?

2. How would the model described in this chapter have to be modified to be relevant to noncriminal collective violence?

3. Would the disorganization model be relevant for criminal activities for which consensus about their seriousness cannot be demonstrated?

4. The theory of social disorganization initially was developed as an explanation of crime and delinquency in urban neighborhoods, and that continues to be its primary orientation. Would it be a relevant perspective for the study of rural communities?

References

Anderson, E. (1999). *Code of the Street: Decency, Violence, and the Moral Life of the Inner City*. New York: Norton.

Bachman, R. (1992). *Death and Violence on the Reservation: Homicide, Family Violence, and Suicide in American Indian Populations*. Westport, CT: Auburn House.

Bankston, C.L., III (1998). "Youth Gangs and the New Second Generation: A Review Essay." *Aggression and Violent Behavior*, 3(Spring):35-45.

Baumer, E. (1994). "Poverty, Crack, and Crime: A Cross-City Analysis." *Journal of Research in Crime and Delinquency*, 31(August):311-327.

Bellair, P.E. (1997). "Social Interaction and Community Crime: Examining the Impact of Neighborhood Networks." *Criminology*, 35(November):677-704.

Burgess, E.W. (1925). "The Growth of the City." In R.E. Park, E.W. Burgess, and R.D. McKenzie (eds.), *The City*, pp. 47-62. Chicago: University of Chicago Press.

Bursik, R.J., Jr. (forthcoming, 2005). "Rethinking the Chicago School of Criminology in a New Era of Immigration." In R. Martinez and A. Valenzuela (eds.), *Beyond Racial Dichotomies of Violence: Immigrants, Ethnicity, and Race.* New York: New York University Press.

Bursik, R.J., Jr. (2002). "The Systemic Model of Gang Behavior: A Reconsideration." In C.R. Huff (ed.), *Gangs in America*, 3rd ed., pp. 71-81. Thousand Oaks, CA: Sage.

Bursik, R.J., Jr. (2001). "Community." In S.O. White (ed.), *Handbook of Youth and Justice*, pp. 265-275. New York: Kluwer Academic/Plenum.

Bursik, R.J., Jr. (2000). "The Systemic Theory of Neighborhood Crime Rates." In S.S. Simpson (ed.), *New Advances in Criminological Theory*, pp. 87-103. Los Angeles: Pine Forge.

Bursik, R.J., Jr. (1999). "The Informal Control of Crime Through Neighborhood Networks." *Sociological Focus,* 32 (February):85-97.

Bursik, R.J., Jr. (1988). "Social Disorganization and Theories of Crime and Delinquency: Problems and Prospects." *Criminology,* 26 (November):519-551.

Bursik, R.J., Jr., and H.G. Grasmick (1996). "Neighborhood-Based Networks and the Control of Crime and Delinquency." In H. Barlow (ed.), *Criminological Theory and Public Policy*, pp. 107-130. Boulder: Westview Press.

Bursik, R.J., Jr., and H.G. Grasmick (1993). *Neighborhoods and Crime.* New York: Lexington.

Curry, G.D., and I.A. Spergel (1988). "Gang Homicide, Delinquency, and Community." *Criminology*, 26 (August):381-405.

Decker, S.H., and B. Van Winkle (1996). *Life in the Gang: Family, Friends, and Violence.* Cambridge, UK: Cambridge University Press.

Elliott, D.S., W.J. Wilson, D. Huizinga, R.J. Sampson, A. Elliott, and B. Rankin (1996). "The Effects of Neighborhood Disadvantage on Adolescent Development." *Journal of Research in Crime and Delinquency*, 33 (November):389-426.

Hagedorn, J.M. (1991). "Gangs, Neighborhoods, and Public Policy." *Social Problems,* 38 (November):529-542.

Hirschi, T. (1969). *Causes of Delinquency.* Berkeley, CA: University of California Press.

Jacobs, D., and J.T. Carmichael (2002). "The Political Sociology of the Death Penalty: A Pooled Time-Series Analysis." *American Sociological Review*, 67 (February):109-131.

Kposowa, A.J., and K.D. Breault (1993). "Reassessing the Structural Covariates of U.S. Homicide Rates: A County Level Study." *Sociological Focus*, 26 (February):27-46.

Lieske, J.A. (1978). "Group Disorders in Urban Schools" *Urban Affairs Quarterly*, 14 (September):79-101.

Michael, J., and M.J. Adler (1933). *Crime, Law and Social Science.* New York: Harcourt, Brace.

Neapolitan, J.L. (1999). "A Comparative Analysis of Nations with Low and High Levels of Violent Crime." *Journal of Criminal Justice*, 27 (May):259-274.

Park, R.E., and E.W. Burgess (1924). *Introduction to the Science of Sociology.* Chicago: University of Chicago Press.

Patterson, E.B. (1991). "Poverty, Income Inequality, and Community Crime Rates." *Criminology*, 29 (November):755-776.

Pattillo, M.E. (1998). "Sweet Mothers and Gangbangers: Managing Crime in a Black Middle-Class Neighborhood." *Social Forces*, 76 (March):747-774.

Pizarro Leongomez, E. (2002). "Colombia: Toward an Institutional Collapse?" In S. Rotker (ed.), *Citizens Of Fear: Urban Violence in Latin America,* pp. 55-71. New Brunswick, NJ: Rutgers University Press.

Rose, D.P., and T.R. Clear (1998). "Incarceration, Social Capital, and Crime: Implications for Social Disorganization Theory." *Criminology,* 36 (August):441-480.

Rountree, P.W., and B.D. Warner (1997). "Local Social Ties in a Community and Crime Model: Questioning the Systemic Nature of Informal Social Control." *Social Problems,* 44 (November):520-536.

Sampson, R.J., and W.B. Groves (1989). "Community Structure and Crime: Testing Social Disorganization Theory." *American Journal of Sociology,* 94 (January):774-802.

Sampson, R.J., J.D. Morenoff, and F. Earls (1999). "Beyond Social Capital: Spatial Dynamics of Collective Efficacy of Children." *American Sociological Review,* 64 (October):633-660.

Sampson, R. J., S.W. Raudenbush, and F. Earls (1997). "Neighborhoods and Violent Crime: A Multilevel Study of Collective Efficacy." *Science,* 277 (August 15):918-924.

Savitch, H.V., and G. Ardashev (2001). "Does Terror Have an Urban Future?" *Urban Studies,* 38 (December):2515-2533.

Shaw, C.R., F.M. Zorbaugh, H.D. McKay, and L.S. Cottrell (1929). *Delinquency Areas.* Chicago: University of Chicago Press.

Shaw, C.R., and H.D. McKay (1931). *Social Factors in Juvenile Delinquency. National Commission on Law Observation and Enforcement,* No. 13, *Report on the Causes of Crime,* Volume II. Washington, DC: U.S. Government Printing Office.

Shaw, C.R., and H.D. McKay (1942). *Juvenile Delinquency and Urban Areas.* Chicago: University of Chicago Press.

Shaw, C.R., and H.D. McKay (1969). *Juvenile Delinquency and Urban Areas,* 2nd ed. Chicago: University of Chicago Press.

Smith, R.W. (2002). "Scarcity and Genocide." In M.N. Dobkowski and I. Wallimann (eds.), *On the Edge of Scarcity: Environment, Resources, Population Sustainability, and Conflict,* pp. 138-148. Syracuse, NY: Syracuse University Press.

Spergel, I.A. (1990). "Youth Gangs: Continuity and Change." In M. Tonry and N. Morris (eds.), *Crime and Justice: A Review of Research,* Volume 12, pp. 171-275. Chicago: University of Chicago Press.

Spilerman, S. 1976. "Structural Characteristics of Cities and the Severity of Racial Disorders." *American Sociological Review,* 41 (October):771-793.

Thomas, W.I., and F. Znaniecki (1920). *The Polish Peasant in Europe and America,* Volume IV. Boston: Gorham.

Thrasher, F.M. (1927). *The Gang.* Chicago: University of Chicago Press.

Useem, B. (1985). "Disorganization and the New Mexico Prison Riot of 1980." *American Sociological Review,* 50 (October):677-688.

Van Wyk, J.A., M.L. Benson, G.L. Fox, and A. DeMaris (2003). "Detangling Individual-, Partner-, and Community-Level Correlates of Partner Violence." *Crime & Delinquency,* 49 (July):412-438.

Wang, J.Z. (2002). "A Preliminary Profile of Laotian/Hmong Gangs: A California Perspective." *Journal of Gang Research*, 9 (Summer):1-14.

Warner, B.D., and G.L. Pierce (1993). "Re-examining Social Disorganization Theory Using Calls to the Police as a Measure of Crime." *Criminology*, 31 (November):493-517.

Wilson, W.J. (1987). *The Truly Disadvantaged: The Inner City, the Underclass, and Public Policy.* Chicago: University of Chicago Press.

Zatz, M.S., and E.L. Portillos (2000). "Voices From the Barrio: Chicano/a Gangs, Families, and Communities." *Criminology*, 38 (May):369-401.

CHAPTER 6

Toward a Radical Ecology of Urban Violence

Michael J. Lynch

This article examines explanations of violent crime from a critical criminological perspective. Some readers may get no further than the title of this chapter because criminologists generally believe that critical criminology is theoretically abstract, anti-empirical, and devoid of policy implications. To be sure, these criticisms apply to some types of critical criminology. Today, however, numerous empirically situated, policy-relevant, theoretically cogent critical analyses of crime exist (see Lynch, Michalowski & Groves, 2000).

Critical criminology is an umbrella term that includes a variety of theoretical styles or subdivisions. Included under the umbrella "critical criminology" are: critical-race theories, social-feminist theories, left realism, several varieties of postmodern explanation (semiotics, constitutive criminology, chaos theory, catastrophe theory), peacemaking criminology, newsmaking criminology, anarchist criminology, and radical criminology. Although these approaches focus on different issues and employ distinctive methods, they are united by a commitment to policies that generate social and economic changes that reduce social injustice (see chapters in Arrigo, 1999).

This paper, originally titled "Towards a Radical Ecology of Urban Violence: Integrating Medical, Epidemiological, Environmental and Criminological Research on Class, Race, Lead (Pb) and Crime," was prepared for the National Institute of Justice's Violence Workshop, held December 10-11, 2002, in Washington, DC. I would like to thank Margaret Zahn and Henry Brownstein for inviting me to represent conflict criminology at this meeting, and Paul Stretesky and Richard Rosenfeld for their comments and suggestions.

Each of the critical theories noted above addresses issues pertinent to understanding violence. Left-realists, for example, have performed the important task of surveying members of working-class communities (Crawford, Jones, Woodhouse & Young, 1990) and women (DeKeseredy, 1996) about their victimization experiences and perceptions of crime and violence in their communities, including corporate crime (DeKeseredy & Goff, 1992; Wonders & Michalowski, 1996). Newsmaking criminology has devoted attention to depictions of violence in the media (Barak, 1996), pointing out that these depictions are stereotypical to the extent that they focus on street crime and exclude corporate crime, and tend to feature minority offenders. Peacemaking theories seek alternatives to traditional criminal justice–style interventions for controlling crime and violence including but not limited to mediation (Pepinsky, 1999). An example of the feminist approach is found in Chapter 8. Each of these views provides some answers concerning the causes and cures for crime and violence. Each also emerged from a broader theoretical orientation that provided the groundwork for the numerous critical criminologies that exist today: radical criminology. This chapter draws its insight from radical criminology.

Radical criminology focuses on class structures and political economy as the primary, but not the sole theoretical anchoring point for explanations of crime and justice (Lynch, Michalowski & Groves, 2000). To demonstrate the relevance of a radical position for understanding and responding to urban violence, this chapter offers an integrated view of interpersonal violence that draws upon social disorganization, medical, epidemiological, and environmental research. Specifically, this paper examines the overlap between: (1) the urban ecology of race and class; (2) the ecology of urban violence; (3) the ecological distribution of lead (Pb) pollution; and (4) the behavioral consequences of exposure to lead. In a radical view, these factors contribute to explanations of interpersonal violence because each is affected by the political economy of contemporary American capitalism.

Background: Persistent Crime Correlates

Criminological literature is replete with divergent theoretical and empirical studies of the etiology of ordinary crime and violence (e.g., street crimes). Empirically, there is little agreement concerning the *primary causes* of these behaviors. Extant empirical research, however, yields some agreement concerning several persistent *correlates* of crime and violence: (1) an ecological distribution associated with specific neighborhood characteristics such as economic resource deprivation, (2) gender—males are more likely to be involved in crime compared to females, (3) low educational attainment, and (4) age. In addition, research has also identified race and class as correlates of crime and violence, though results for these variables are dependent on several factors (e.g., kind of data, type of crime). Consequently, a good theory of crime ought to address these crime correlates. Before proceeding, it is important to recognize the limitations of criminological research on crime correlates. While specific studies may contain methodological limitations that restrict the generalizability of research findings, one criticism that connects these studies is the definition and the specific types of violence criminologists are most likely to study. Most criminological studies focus on street or ordinary violence (e.g., homicide, rape, robbery, and gang violence). This focus excludes corporate, environmental and white-collar crime offenders—or persons with characteristics opposite of those possessed by the typical street criminal. When the latter crimes are studied, none of the aforementioned crime correlates, with the exception of male gender, would emerge. Thus, when criminologists identify the correlates of crime, it is clear that this finding has limited rather than universal applicability (i.e., the correlates apply only to street violence).

Major Principles and Assumptions

Traditionally, radical models examined the role of class relationships and economic structures on the production of crime. Radicals employ the term "production of crime" to emphasize that crime is not merely illicit behavior; rather, crime must be understood in relation to the process of law-making and law enforcement. Crime, in short, is a behavior identified in criminal law that elicits a reaction from agents in the criminal justice system who are granted authority to respond to crime. Not all harmful behaviors, however, are defined as crimes, and many harmful behaviors are omitted from criminal law. Some become the subject of noncriminal rules (e.g., regulatory), while others completely escape regulation. For radicals, the fact that a behavior is not found in criminal law is not a valid reason to exclude that behavior from criminological investigation. In fact, for radicals, it is necessary to investigate noncriminal harms to test the assertion that class relationships and economic structures impact which behaviors receive the label "crime." Taking these definitional issues into account, radicals discuss crime as a political or social construction. As a social or political construction, crime represents interpretations of behavior rather than any quality of the harmful act. The radical focus on class has been used to reveal the interplay of class and economic structures on the process of defining crime, and has led to numerous descriptions of the class biases contained in the political process of defining crime.

In addition to definitional biases, radicals also examine criminal processing biases. Anyone who has studied criminal justice decisionmaking understands that criminal justice agents do not react similarly to all behaviors labeled as crime. There is, however, disagreement as to why this outcome occurs. Radicals interpret patterns in criminal justice outcomes as supporting their contention that economic, social, and political structures, as well as offender statuses such as race or social class, influence or bias processing outcomes. An extensive body of research details how structures and statuses, including race, income, and gender, determine who will be charged, prosecuted, or convicted of a crime.

Given biases in processing and lawmaking, radical criminologists argue that official crime data is likely to present a biased image of crime, one that overrepresents the harmful behaviors of the lower classes and minorities. While radicals take this view, they also recognize that nonofficial sources of data confirm some differences in street crime across race and class groups. Because they recognize the existence of these kinds of biases, radicals proceed with caution when employing official sources of crime data.

While radical models traditionally emphasize the impact of class on crime production, this view has been extended to include a focus on gender and race (Lynch, Michalowski & Groves, 2000). Over the past two decades and in response to persistent findings in criminological research, radical interpretations of crime have expanded to include a broader theoretical base capable of explaining a wider array of crimes. With this broadened theoretical focus, few radical analyses of crime maintain the traditional, unidimensional focus on class. Nevertheless, in the radical view, class relationships and economic structures remain the primary determinants of social and political processes. Thus, radical examinations of crime seek to explain how class and economic context influence the commission, distribution, level, and response to crime in a specific society.

Explaining the pattern of violent street crime. In the radical view, class and race structures are particularly important for understanding violence, especially the ecology or distribution of violent crime. For example, class and race power structures found in American society produce conditions conducive to violence. These conditions, which concentrate forms of resource deprivation and other economic difficulties (e.g., underdevelopment, a lack of quality employment, etc.) in low-income and minority communities, are of particular importance for understanding violence in urbanized areas. There is no singular radical explanation concerning the impact of race- and class-linked resource deprivation on violent crime. Resource deprivation may impact levels of interpersonal violence through a variety of intervening mechanisms. For example, in resource-deprived environments, violence may become a means of gaining status, creating an identity, or simply coping with adverse economic and social conditions (Hagan, 1994; Lynch, Michalowski & Groves, 2000). Given the existence of resource deprivation, violence may also result as a response to the daily frustrations of living, including finding a decent job, racial discrimination, a lack of social capital, poor schools, inadequate recreational programs for youths, and securing adequate housing in a safe community (Hagan, 1994). It should also be emphasized that America's race and class hierarchy impacts the ecology of violence through the type of race and class segregation that characterized America's social and economic systems (Hagan, 1994; Lynch, Michalowski & Groves, 2000; Massey & Denton, 1993). In other words, because economically deprived groups are segregated, forms of violence that result from and are a response to economic and social deprivations will exhibit an ecological pattern that maps onto the location of low-income and minority communities.

No radical explanation of violence would be complete without reference to the creation and enforcement of criminal law. Radicals argue that economic structures influence both processes. Crimes are behaviors that not only are harmful, but may be either more prevalent among less powerful class and race groups or pursued more forcefully in areas these groups inhabit. Police agencies charged with enforcing criminal laws devoted a greater amount of their resources to discovering crime in lower-class and minority communities. The structure of law, and law enforcement activities, helps produce an image that crime is primarily the work of the poor and racial and ethnic minorities (Reiman, 2001).

Neglected Forms of Violence: Corporate and Environmental Violence

While radical criminology can contribute to a discussion of violent street crime, one of its major contributions has been to draw attention to corporate and environmental violence (Lynch, Michalowski & Groves, 2000). Discussions of corporate and environmental violence—which we can define as avoidable physical harms caused by unsafe products and workplace conditions, and the routine production, treatment, and storage of toxic waste in lower, working-class, and minority communities—is typically absent from traditional criminological examination of violent crime in American society. Traditional criminology has yet to address the widespread, violent forms of victimization inflicted by corporate and environmental crime on urban working and lower classes and African-American and Hispanic communities. Of particular importance is the range of toxic crimes to which members of these communities are exposed (Lynch & Stretesky, 2001b). The negative health consequences associated with toxic crimes—increased rates of disease, illness, cancer, and death—are well documented in medical and epidemiological research, and have extensive detrimental impacts on the least powerful groups in society (Lynch & Stretesky, 2001b). The neglect of corporate violence in traditional criminological analyses of violent crime, as well as by criminal justice agencies, marginalizes its victims by excluding them as academic subjects—and by excluding them from the protective mechanisms society has established to control crime. Indeed, marginalized groups find that corporate victimization is not defined or treated as criminal violence, and that enfeebled regulatory agencies charged with protecting public health "normalize" and ignore corporate violence. For radicals, however, corporate and environmental violence are an important dimension of urban violence.

To be sure, radical criminologists have addressed numerous issues relevant to the problem of urban violence, and have expanded the notion of violence to include corporate offenders and victims. It is not possible to examine the specifics of radical views on corporate violence within the scope of the present analysis. It is nevertheless necessary to call attention to these issues and problems (Lynch, Michalowski & Groves, 2000).

Redirection: Integrating Radical and Medical Approaches to Explain Interpersonal Violence

Earlier in this chapter, some general guiding principles of radical explanations of violence were reviewed. Capturing the opportunity presented by this book, the remainder of this chapter will focus on integrating radical explanations with evidence concerning another persistent correlate of ordinary crimes of violence, which has been neglected by criminologists: exposure to lead.

The relationship between lead exposure, aggression, crime, and violent behavior bas been well documented in medical and epidemiological literature (see below). The process by which lead affects human behavior, though less understood, is biologically based. This emphasis appears inconsistent with the kinds of macro-level explanations radicals prefer (Lynch & Stretesky, 2001a). While radical explanations do not incorporate biological theories of crime, the radical perspective can incorporate this kind of explanation at the structural level by focusing on the ecological relationship between race, class, and the distribution of lead and crime in urban environments in America. In turn, the ecology of these relationships can be related to America's economic structure. In other words, while lead affects behavior through biological pathways, exposure to lead is influenced by race and class structures that characterized the urban ecology of American cities. In turn, the urban ecology of cities has been affected by economic development processes generated by American capitalism (see Lynch, Michalowski & Groves, 2000).

Drawing attention to the ecology of class, race, and lead, the remainder of this chapter explores a radical explanation of "traditional" forms of interpersonal, urban street violence in America. To illustrate this view, attention is drawn to one particular urban waste hazard, the distribution of lead (Pb), and the medical literature on lead's behavioral impacts. This discussion emphasizes the need to address the spatial distribution of environmental hazards from a theoretical vantage point sensitive to class and race power differentials and patterns of segregation associated with the structure of the American economic system.

Toward a Political Ecology of Urban Areas and Crime

Radical theories of crime are derived from a diverse literature, much of which is empirical in nature (e.g., see the journal, *The Review of Radical Political Economy*). It is not possible to review this extensive literature here. Nevertheless, radical economists, environmentalists, historians, and political scientists have long been interested in explaining the connection between the economy, urban structures, and other dimensions of urban life. In so doing, they have produced radical urban histories, class-based urban development models, economic and social capital allocation models, and class-race linked models of industrial hazards and pollution, all capable of contributing to discussions of violence and crime.

A persistent feature of violence is its concentration within resource-deprived urban areas. Within criminology, a long-standing tradition that grounded theoretical explanations of crime in relation to the characteristics of urban neighborhoods was established in the Chicago School. Today, those working in the Chicago tradition continue the search for the etiology of crime in various urban networks.

The Distribution of Environmental Harms and Crime

Modern methods of analysis allow researchers to map the physical connections between ecological hazards (e.g., locations of toxic waste sites, polluting industries, and chemical accidents), community race and class characteristics, and negative social outcomes such as the distribution of health problems or crime. A portion of this literature has connected the concentration, presence, proximity, and exposure to noxious chemical pollutants to negative human health outcomes (e.g., Jacobs, Clickner, Zhou, Viet, Marker, Rogers, Zeldin, Broene & Friedman, 2002; Kraft & Scheberle, 1995; Reed, 1992). Some of these outcomes, which relate to the incidence of disease, illness, and death rates, have little bearing on the subject of violence and crime causation for the traditional criminologist, though they are subject matter for those interested in the consequences of environmental corporate crime, and in social justice issues (Burns & Lynch, 2004; Lynch & Stretesky, 2001a). A subset of these health outcomes, however, includes impacts on IQ, school achievement, hyperactivity, impulsivity, and learning disabilities, to name but a few. For their part, criminologists have studied these outcomes as both causes and correlates of crime and violence. Indeed, many of the correlates and causes of crime that criminologists have studied result from lead exposure.

Background on Lead

General information. Lead is prevalent in urban environments and is found in air, soil, water, and dust. Once ingested,[1] lead has a half-life as long as five to 30 years in bone.[2] Lead's persistence in bone helps explain cross-generational sources of lead exposure without the need for direct exposure. For example, hormonal changes in pregnant women liberate lead stored in bones and may cause significant increases in maternal blood lead levels and fetal exposure (Silbergeld, 1991; Silbergeld, Schwartz & Mahaffey, 1988). Direct exposure to environmental sources of lead, while important, is not the only potential source of elevated lead concentrations in young children.

Lead and health. Lead exposure has been associated with a variety of health and behavioral problems.[3] From the perspective of crime causation, central nervous system, cognitive, and neurobehavioral damage are the most important. Extant research indicates that lead's health impacts are greater among the lower and working classes and African Americans, and are also a neglected source of urban violence among these groups.

Numerous cognitive and neurobehavioral outcomes associated with lead are irreversible.[4] In criminological terms, children exposed to lead may suffer cognitive and neurobehavioral impacts that affect their behavior and life course. When coupled with negative social circumstances, it has been suggested that early childhood lead exposure enhances the probability of delinquent and criminal behavior (see below).

Young children are particularly vulnerable to the deleterious effects of lead. Children, more so than adults, are likely to suffer cognitive and neurobehavioral disorders from low-level lead exposure because of differences in lead intake–weight ratios, and because children are at a stage of development at which lead has a greater disruptive potential on human development. Estimates indicate that as many as one million preschool age children have elevated lead levels, meaning that the potential social disruptive effects of lead exposure are extensive (Markowitz, 2000). It is important to keep in mind that exposure to lead, especially among young children, can be connected to class and race segregation, which in turn can be connected to the political economic system.

Lead exposure trends and correlates. Because lead is a major health concern, lead exposure patterns in the U.S. population have been tracked by the National Health and Nutrition Examination Survey (NHANES) since 1976 (Brody, Pirkle, Kramer, Flegal, Matte, Gunter & Paschal, 1994; Pirkle, Brody, Gunter, Kramer, Paschal, Flegal & Matte, 1994). NHANES studies reveal that while average blood lead levels have fallen since 1976, urban poor, African-American, Hispanic, and Mexican-American children continue to exhibit higher blood lead levels than white, suburban, or rural children.[5] There are also gender differences, which range from insignificant to rather substantial differences (Anderson, Pueschel & Linakis, 1996; Dye, Hirsch & Brody, 2002), with males having higher average blood lead levels than females.

In short, race, class, gender, age, and residential location impact lead exposure, which, in turn, is associated with adverse health consequences and negative behavioral outcomes. This evidence suggests that structural features of social organization, including race and class segregation patterns that have economic origins, translate into proximity to locations associated with lead exposure (Reed, 1992).

Although lead exposure trends indicate long-term declines in blood lead levels (since the mid-1970s), a substantial portion of young children (under age six) still have blood lead levels above those associated with negative behavioral outcomes.[6] Thus, despite reductions in environmental lead and blood lead levels, "Exposure to lead remains an international public health problem, despite major reductions in its use in industrial processes in developed countries" (Hayes, McElvaine, Orbach, Fernandez, Lyne & Matte, 1994:1017) due to the small quantity of lead required to cause adverse human health and behavioral consequences.

The urban ecology of lead. Though lead remains widely disbursed in human environments, lead remains more highly concentrated in urban as opposed to suburban and rural locations. The distribution of lead in the environment is associated with: older homes (through lead-based paint hazards) (Jacobs, Clickner, Zhou, Viet, Marker, Rogers, Zeldin, Broene & Friedman, 2002), roadways, lead smelters, plumbing, dust, hazardous waste, and Superfund sites, as well as industries that recycle or employ lead in production processes. Studies indicate that the ecology of lead has class and race dimensions (Kraft & Scheberle, 1995; Stretesky, 2002) and that minorities are more likely to live in housing proximate to sources of lead contamination.

Empirical Evidence: Lead Outcomes Associated with Crime and Delinquency

Medical and epidemiological studies on the impact of lead on human behavior have examined a diverse array of topics. A portion of this literature has revealed that lead exposure is associated with numerous crime correlates including: low birth weight, attention deficit disorder, patterns of aggression, mental retardation, learning disabilities, hyperactivity, impulsivity, low frustration tolerance, self-control, antisocial behavior, neurological dysfunction, increased rates of school failure, behavioral problems in school, poor academic achievement, dropping out, IQ deficiencies, and developmental delays (Bellinger, 1996; also see this chapter's Appendix). Specific studies of the impact of lead exposure on criminal and delinquent behavior have been undertaken at the individual and geographic levels, and over time.

Crime, delinquency, and lead: Individual-level studies. Studies of the relationship between lead exposure and delinquent and antisocial behavior demonstrate a persistent effect of lead on behavior, especially among children. Needleman, McFarland, Ness, Fienberg, and Tobin (2002) found that bone lead levels were four time higher in youths (ages 12-18) adjudicated delinquent when compared to controls. In fact, bone lead level was the second strongest predictor of delinquency, and only the subject's race had a greater influence on delinquent adjudication.

The results of the study by Needleman and associates support previous research. Thomson, Raab, Hepburn, Hunter, Fulton, and Laxan (1989) discovered an association between lead exposure and teacher ratings of aggressive and antisocial behavior. Likewise, Needleman, Riess, Tobin, Biesecker, and Greenhouse (1996) demonstrated a relationship between bone lead concentrations and teachers', parents', and juveniles' self-reported delinquent and antisocial behavior.

Wasserman, Liu, Pine, and Graziano (2001) also discovered an association between lead and delinquency. This result was strengthened by research by Dietrich, Ris, Succop, Berger, and Bornschein (2001) into early lead exposure and the emergence of delinquent behavior. Using a longitudinal birth cohort (1979-1985) of inner-city youths, Dietrich and associates discovered an association between prenatal and postnatal exposure to lead measured by blood lead levels, and parent- and self-reported antisocial and delinquent behavior.

Few studies have examined the lead-crime connection using adults, though these studies also detect a lead effect. Using data from the Collaborative Perinatal Project in Philadelphia, Denno (1990) found that lead poisoning was the best predictor of male criminality. Pihl and Ervin (1990) discovered lead concentration differences comparing violent and nonviolent adult offenders using hair assays.

In short, the effect of lead on criminal and delinquent behavior in individual-level studies is strikingly consistent. These studies are supported by research showing an association between lead and aggression more generally (Sciarillo, Alexander & Farrell, 1992; Huesmann, Eron, Lefkowitz & Walder, 1984).

Crime and lead: Time-series associations. A recent study by Nevin (2000) extended individual-level research findings on lead exposure and crime to time-series analyses. Nevin found an association between the amount of lead used in the production of gasoline and paint and violent crime rates in the United States from 1900 to 1998. By demonstrating the strength of this relationship over time, Nevin added a layer of evidence supporting the connection between lead exposure and criminal behavior outcomes.

Crime and lead across geographic units. Two recent ecological studies lend support to the individual-level relationship found between lead exposure and crime. Stretesky and Lynch (2001) found a relationship between air lead concentrations and homicide rates across 3,111 U.S. counties controlling for more than 20 crime correlates and pollution confounders. Results of this study were confirmed using air lead measures and violent and property crime rates (Stretesky & Lynch, 2004).

In sum, recent sociologically grounded studies illustrate that individual-level findings produced by medical researchers have a persistent and regular spatial and time dimension strong enough to be evident at the ecological and historical levels, and that the ecology of lead and violent crime are similar. These studies support the lead–crime/delinquency relationship discovered at the individual level by demonstrating that the relationship between lead exposure and criminal involvement is not washed out at higher levels of aggregation.

To date, social scientists interested in explaining crime and violence have neglected medical and epidemiological evidence that environmental hazards may alter behavior. Findings related to lead were reviewed above. Extant research, however, has yet to address whether lead is associated with particular kinds of violent crime, or violence in general. Research results on the association between aggression and lead exposure, however, indicate that measures of body lead concentrations are associated with a general tendency toward aggression. This research does not specify the situational conditions that may contribute to aggression in general or to specific violent outcomes.

Other Environmental Suspects

The effort to understand the connection between exposure to environmental contaminants and human behavior is relatively recent. Lead is not the only environmental contaminant linked to neurobehavioral, criminal, violent, or delinquent outcomes. Among other elements classified as heavy metals (Cadmium, for example) is also a suspected potential source of aggression, violence, and crime (Pihl & Ervin, 1990). Little research, however, exists on the behavioral effects of heavy metals other than lead. Likewise, it has long been recognized that overexposure to pesticides, hazardous wastes, and chemicals such as dioxin and PCBs (polychlorinated biphenyls), which mimic human hormones and act as endocrine disruptors, can have neurobehavioral impacts that generate violent behavior (Colborn, Dumanoski & Myers, 1996; on experiments in mice see, Vom Saal, 1989; Vom Saal, Nagel, Palanza, Boechler, Parmigiani & Welshons, 1995). For example, in recent decades, the prevalence of childhood neurological conditions, including cancers of the brain, has risen dramatically. This outcome has been linked to exposure to environmental contaminants that act as hormone mimics. The amount of synthetic pesticides used today, nearly nine pounds per capita, is 30 times higher than in the mid-1940s. And while exposure to these chemical has increased by 30 times, potency has increased by a factor of 10 (Colborn, Dumanoski & Myers, 1996:138). Viewed in this way, exposure to environmental contaminants are seen not only as important behavior modifiers, but as pathways of violent victimization. Yet, these issues are neglected in criminological discussions of violent behavior (Lynch & Stretesky, 2001b). It is also likely that exposure to these potential behavioral influences have an economic explanation consistent with radical criminological theory similar to the explanation offered for lead exposure.

Theoretical Summary

Research derived from social disorganization theory revealed an important fact about crime: crime has an ecological distribution. Beneath this well-known distribution lie neglected factors associated with the ecological distribution of crime and violence. Among these factors is the distribution of environmental contaminants such as lead, which is an antecedent to a number of variables criminologists employ in etiology explanations of crime. Numerous studies on the relationship between lead exposure, aggression, crime, and violence suggest that lead plays at least some role in the etiology of crime and violence. To be sure, however, lead is not the entire answer.

It is not enough to know that lead may impact behavior. Lead exposure has ecological dimensions, meaning that lead is more likely to be found in specific environments, and thus more likely to impact certain segments of the population. From a radical perspective, the ecology of lead (and crime) is explicable with reference to the influence of race and class structures in America. Communities with elevated lead levels are characterized by a high proportion of minority and low-income families. For these less powerful, marginalized groups, the production or disposal of lead in or near their communities not only increases health risks associated with lead exposure, but may also alter the life course of individuals exposed to lead. In some sense, then, low-income and minority communities are victims of prevailing forms of economic organization that make their communities acceptable sites for lead pollution. The economic deprivation that also characterizes these communities means local residents are less likely to be able to respond to this situation, either collectively or individually. Economically deprived communities lack the resources needed to remedy lead exposure, and poor families may not seek medical help for exposed children.

Conclusion

This chapter has demonstrated ways in which radical explanations of crime are consistent with major empirical findings on the etiology and distribution of crime and violence, as well as with studies of human health made in other disciplines. This review has also illustrated that critical theories need not be anti-empirical or theoretically abstract to explain crime.

It should be made clear that the view of violence offered here takes research findings from several disciplines, integrates them, and radicalizes them by paying close attention to ecological and structural issues stemming from the type of race and class hierarchy, urban ecological structures, and forms of economic production that characterize American cities. The prime determinants of exposure to lead, for instance, are urban residence, race, and class. In short, one cannot discuss the impact of lead on human behavior in general, or crime in particular, without acknowledging the role political economic factors such as class and race segregation have on the probability that people of different race and class groups will be exposed to lead. This lesson can be extended to many other factors that have been suggested as causes of crime and violence. Taking such an approach is important because behind the apparent disarray of the numerous individual-level factors that correlate with crime and violence are broader social and economic structures that influence the mass of human behavior.

Endnotes

[1]   A positive lead balance occurs when daily ingestion exceeds five micrograms per kilogram of body weight (Graef, 1992). Lead is primarily absorbed in the gastrointestinal tract and lungs (70-90%) (Anderson, Pueschel & Linakis, 1996). Once ingested, lead is disbursed in the blood, soft tissue, and bone. Under conditions of steady lead intake, approximately 5 to 10 percent of lead is found in blood, 10 to 20 percent in soft tissue and as much as 90 percent in bone (Graef, 1992).

[2]   The persistence of lead in the human body depends on where it is stored. Lead has a half-life of 35 days in blood (Ellenhorn & Barceloux, 1988), 50 days in soft tissue, and five to 30 years in bone (Anderson, Pueschel & Linakis, 1996:77). Lead found in the blood will be transported to soft tissue and bones, meaning that some percentage of circulating lead will be stored for much longer periods than blood half-lives indicate.

[3]   Certain lead compounds are known animal carcinogens. Lead is also a known teratogen and mutagen, and has also been associated with central nervous system damage, enzyme system effects (Piomelli, Seaman, Zullow, Curran & Davidow, 1982), and cognitive and neurobehavioral damage (Berney, 1996:15-16).

[4]   Prior to the 1970s, lead was perceived as an acute poison, while its other effects, such as those on behavior, were not sufficiently recognized or studied. Due to improvement in scientific equipment and research methodology, estimates of the critical cognitive and neurobehavioral disruption attributable to lead has fallen from 80 micrograms of lead per deciliter of blood in 1950 to one-eighth of that amount today. Some studies indicate behavior effects at subclinical concentrations (Staudinger & Roth, 1998).

5   For example, the percentage of nonHispanic black children ages one to five living in large cities (greater than one million in population) with elevated blood lead levels (greater than 10 micrograms per deciliter of blood) was seven times higher than the percentage of nonHispanic white children. In cities with populations under one million, the difference was a factor of three (see Brody, Pirkle, Flegal, Matte, Gunter & Paschal, 1994). As noted by Berney (1996:23), "Black children have higher blood lead levels in all age, urban status, income, and educational categories. Racial disparities between blacks and whites are greatest among the poor." Recent studies continue to indicate race and class differences in blood lead concentrations despite general reductions in blood lead levels (Bernard & McGeehin, 2003; Malcoe, Lynch, Keger & Skaggs, 2002).

6   The geometric mean blood lead (mg/dL) level for children ages four to five declined from 10.9 between 1982-1984, to 3.5 by 1988-1991 (Pirkle et al., 1994). It should be noted, however, that children in the 1988-91 sample who were above the seventy-fifth blood mean percentile had a blood lead level greater than 5.9 mg/dL (Pirkle, Brody, Gunter, Kramer, Paschal, Flegal & Matte, 1994).

Discussion Questions

1.   Criminological research has isolated several persistent correlates of crime. Identify these correlates and discuss ways in which you might tie these correlates together to explain violent crime.

2.   What do radicals mean when they use the term "production of crime"? How is this idea different than a simpler view that seeks to identify the causes of crime?

3.   This chapter points out that most criminological discussions of violence exclude an analysis of corporate violence. Think about the world around you, and come up with some examples of corporate violence. Discuss whether you think these activities ought to be treated as crimes, and what could be done about these acts of violence.

4.   Exposure to the element lead (Pb) has a number of health and behavioral consequences. Describe the behavioral consequences of lead exposure and explain how these consequences may be related to violent criminal behavior.

5.   How are persistent crime correlates, lead exposure, and violent behavior connected?

References

Anderson, A.C., S.M. Pueschel, and J.G. Linakis (1996). "Pathophysiology of Lead Poisoning." In S.M. Pueschel, J.G. Linakis, and AC. Anderson (eds.), *Lead Poisoning in Childhood*. Baltimore: Paul H. Brookes.

Arrigo, B. (ed.) (1999). *Social Justice/Criminal Justice*. Belmont, CA: Wadsworth.

Barak, G. (1996). "Mass-Mediated Regimes of Truth: Race, Gender and Class in Crime 'News' Themes." In M. Schwartz and D. Milovanovic (eds.), *Race, Gender and Class in Criminology*. New York: Garland.

Bellinger, D. (1996). "Learning and Behavioral Sequele of Lead Poisoning." In S.M. Pueschel, J.G. Linakis, and A.C. Anderson (eds.), *Lead Poisoning in Childhood*. Baltimore: Paul H. Brookes.

Bernard, S.M., and M.A. McGeehin (2003). "Prevalence of Blood Lead Levels > or = 5 micro g/dl among U.S. Children 1 to 5 years of Age and Socioeconomic and Demographic Factors Associated with Blood Leads Levels 5 to 10 micro g/dl, Third National Health and Nutrition Examination Survey, 1988-1994." *Pediatrics*, 112, 6:1308-1313.

Berney, B. (1996). "Epidemiology of Childhood Lead Poisoning." In S.M. Pueschel, J.G. Linakis, and A.C. Anderson (eds.), *Lead Poisoning in Childhood*. Baltimore: Paul H. Brookes.

Brody, D.J., J.L. Pirkle, R.A. Kramer, K.M. Flegal, T.D. Matte, E.W. Gunter, and D.C. Paschal (1994). "Blood Lead Levels in the U.S. Population: Phase 1 of the Third National Health and Nutrition Examination Survey (NHANES III, 1988-1991)." *Journal of the American Medical Association*, 272:277-283.

Burns, R.G., and M.J. Lynch (2004). *Environmental Crime: A Sourcebook*. New York: LFB Scholarly.

Colborn, T., D. Dumanoski, and J.P. Myers (1996). *Our Stolen Future*. NY: Penguin.

Crawford, A., T. Jones, T. Woodhouse, and J. Young (1990). *Second Islington Crime Survey*. London: Middlesex Polytechnic Centre for Criminology.

DeKeseredy, W. (1996). "The Canadian National Survey on Women Abuse in University/College Dating Relationships." *Canadian Journal of Criminology*, 38(1):81-104.

DeKeresedy, W., and C. Goff (1992). "Corporate Violence Against Canadian Women." *The Journal of Human Justice*, 4:55-70.

Denno, D.W. (1990). *From Birth to Adulthood*. Cambridge, UK: Cambridge University Press.

Dietrich, K.N., M.D. Ris, P.A. Succop, U.G. Berger, and R.L. Bornschein (2001). "Early Exposure to Lead and Juvenile Delinquency." *Neurotoxicology and Teratology*, 23:511-518.

Dye, B.A, R. Hirsch, and D.J. Brody (2002). The Relationship between Blood Lead Levels and Periodontal Bone Loss in the United States, 1988-94." *Environmental Health Perspectives*, 10(10):997-1002.

Ellenhorn, M., and D. Barceloux (eds.) (1988). *Medical Toxicology*. New York: Elsevier.

Graef, J. (1992). "Lead Poisoning." *Clinical Toxicology Review*, 14:1-6.

Hagan, J. (1994). *Crime and Disrepute*. Thousand Oaks, CA: Pine Forge.

Hayes, D.B, M.D. McElvaine, H.G. Orbach, A.M. Fernandez, S. Lyne, and T.D. Matte (1994). "Long Term Trends in Blood Lead Levels Among Children in Chicago: Relationship to Air Lead Levels." *Pediatrics*, 93:195-200.

Huesmann, L.R., L.D. Eron, M.M. Lefkowitz, and L.O. Walder (1984). "Stability and Aggression over Time and Generations." *Developmental Psychology*, 20:1120-1134.

Jacobs, D.E., R.P. Clickner, J.Y. Zhou, S.M. Viet, D.M. Marker, J.W. Rogers, D.C. Zeldin, P. Broene, and W. Friedman (2002). "The Prevalence of Lead-Based Paint Hazards in U.S. Housing." *Environmental Health Perspectives*, 110, 10:599A-606A.

Kraft, M., and D. Scheberle (1995). "Environmental Justice and the Allocation of Risk: The Case of Lead and Public Health." *Policy Studies Journal*, 23:113-123.

Lynch, M.J., R.J.Michalowski, and W.B. Groves (2000). *The New Primer in RadicalCriminology: Critical Perspectives on Crime, Power and Identity*. Monsey, NY: Criminal Justice Press.

Lynch, M.J., and P.B. Stretesky (2001a). "Radical Criminology." In R. Paternoster and R. Bachman (eds.), *Explaining Crime and Criminal: Essays in Criminological Theory*. Los Angeles: Roxbury.

Lynch, M.J., and P.B. Stretesky (2001b). "Toxic Crimes." *Critical Criminology*, 10:153-172.

Malcoe, L.H., R.A. Lynch, M.C. Keger, and V.J. Skaggs (2002). "Lead Sources, Behaviors and Socioeconomic Factors in Relation to Blood Lead of Native American and White Children." *Environmental Health Perspectives*, 110 (S2):221-231.

Markowitz, M. (2000). "Lead Poisoning: A Disease for the Next Millennium." *Current Problems in Pediatrics*, 30:62-70.

Massey, D., and S. Denton (1993). *American Apartheid: Segregation and the Making of the Underclass*. Cambridge, MA: Harvard University Press.

Needleman, H.L., R.A. Riess, M.J. Tobin, G.E. Biesecker, and J.B. Greenhouse (1996). "Bone Lead Levels and Delinquent Behavior." *Journal of the American Medical Association*, 275:363-369.

Needleman, H.L., C. McFarland, R.B. Ness, S.E. Fienberg, and M.J. Tobin (2002). "Bone Lead Levels in Adjudicated Delinquents: A Case Control Study." *Neurotoxicology and Teratology*, 24:711-717.

Nevin, R. (2000). "How Lead Exposure Relates to Temporal Changes in IQ, Violent Crime, and Unwed Pregnancy." *Environmental Research Section*, A83:1-22.

Pepinsky, H. (1999). "Peacemaking Criminology and Social Justice." In B. Arrigo (ed.), *Social Justice/Criminal Justice*. Belmont, CA: Wadsworth.

Pihl, R.O., and F. Ervin (1990). "Lead and Cadmium in Violent Criminals." *Psychological Report*, 66(3):839-844.

Piomelli, S., C. Seaman, D. Zullow, A. Curran, and B. Davidow (1982). "Childhood Lead Poisoning in the '90s." *Pediatrics*, 93:508-510.

Pirkle, R.A., D.J. Brody, E.W. Gunter, R.A. Kramer, D.C. Paschal, K.M. Flegal, and T.D. Matte (1994). "The Decline in Blood Lead Levels in the United States: The National Health and Nutrition Examination Surveys (NHANES)." *Journal of the American Medical Association*, 272:284-291.

Reed, W. (1992). "Lead Poisoning: A Modern Plague Among African-American Children." In R. Braithwaite and S. Taylor (eds.), *Health Issues in the Black Community*. San Francisco: Jossey-Bass.

Reiman, J. (2001). *The Rich Get Richer and the Poor Get Prison*. Boston: Allyn & Bacon.

Sciarillo, W.G., G. Alexander, and K.D. Farrell (1992). "Lead Exposure and Child Behavior." *American Journal of Public Health*, 82:1356-1360.

Silbergeld, E.K. (1991). "Lead in Bone: Implications for Toxicology During Pregnancy and Lactation." *Environmental Health Perspectives*, 91:63-70.

Silbergeld, E.K., J. Schwartz, and K. Mahaffey (1988). "Lead and Osteoporosis." *Environmental Health Perspectives*, 47:79-94.

Staudinger, K.C., and V.S. Roth (1998). "Occupational Lead Exposure." *American Family Physician*, February:719-734.

Stretesky, P.B., and M.J. Lynch (2004). "The Distribution of Lead, Violent and Property Crime Rates Across U.S. Counties." *Journal of Health and Social Behavior*, 45,2.

Stretesky, P.B., and M.J. Lynch (2001). "The Relationship Between Lead Exposure and Homicide." *The Archives of Pediatric and Adolescent Medicine*, 155 (May):579-582.

Thomson, G.O., G.M. Raab, W.S. Hepburn, R. Hunter, M. Fulton, and D.P. Laxan (1989). "Blood-Lead Levels and Children's Behavior." *Journal of Child Psychology and Psychiatry*, 30 (4):515-528.

Vom Saal, F. (1989). "Perinatal Testerone Exposure has Opposite Effects on Intermale Aggression and Infanticide in Mice." In P. Brain, D. Mainardi, and S. Parmigiani (eds.), *House Mouse Aggression: A Model for Understanding the Evolution of Social Behaviour*. New York: Harwood Academic.

Vom Saal, F.S., S.C. Nagel, P. Palanza, M. Boechler, S. Parmigiani, and W.V. Welshons (1995). "Estrogenic Pesticides: Binding Relative to Estradiol in MCF-7 Cells and Effects of Exposure During Fetal Life on Subsequent Territorial Behaviour in Male Mice." *Mechanisms of Toxicity and Biomarkers to Assess Adverse Effects of Chemicals*, 77 (1-3):343-350.

Wasserman, G.A., X. Liu, N.S. Pine, and J.H. Graziano (2001). "Contributions of Maternal Smoking During Pregnancy and Lead Exposure to Early Childhood Behavior Problems." *Neurotoxicology and Teratology*, 23:13-21.

Wonders, N., and R.J. Michalowski (1996). *Arizona Crime Survey*. Flagstaff, AZ: Northern Arizona University Social Research Laboratory.

Appendix: Brief Medical Research, Lead Exposure Outcome Bibliography

Banks, E., L. Ferretti, and D. Shucard (1997). "Effects of Low-Level Lead Exposure on Cognitive Function in Children." *Neurotoxicology*, 18:237-282.

Bellinger, D., K. Stiles, and H.L. Needleman (1992). "Low Level Lead Exposure, Intelligence and Academic Achievement." *Pediatrics*, 90:855-861.

Bellinger, D., H.L. Needleman, R. Broomfield, and M. Mintz (1984). "A Follow-up Study of the Academic Achievement and Classroom Behavior of Children with Elevated Dentine Lead Levels." *Biological Trace Element Research*, 6:207-223.

Fergusson, D.M., J.E. Fergusson, L.J. Horwood, and N.G. Kinzett (1988). "A Longitudinal Study of Dentine Lead Levels, Intelligence, School Performance and Behavior." *Journal of Child Psychology and Psychiatry*, 29:781-792.

Fulton, M., G. Raab, G. Thomas, D. Laxen, R. Hunter and W. Hepburn (1987). "Influence of Blood Lead on the Ability and Attainment of Children in Edinburgh." *Lancet*, 1:1221-1225.

Gittleman, R., and B. Eskenazi (1983). "Lead and Hyperactivity Revisited." *Archives of General Psychology*, 40:827-833.

Needleman, H.L., and C. Gatsonis (1990). "Low Level Lead Exposure and the IQ of Children." *Journal of the American Medical Association*, 263:673-678.

Needleman, H.L., C. Gunnoe, A. Leviton, H. Peresie, C. Maher, and P. Barret (1979). "Deficits in Psychological and Classroom Performance of Children with Elevated Dentine Lead Levels." *New England Journal of Medicine*, 300:659-695.

Needleman, H.L., A. Schell, D. Bellinger, A. Leviton, and E.N. Allred (1990). "The Long-Term Effects of Exposure to Low Doses of Lead in Childhood." *New England Journal of Medicine*, 322.

Oliver, D., J. Clark, and K. Voeller (1972). "Lead and Hyperactivity." *Lancet*, 2:900-903.

Oliver, D., S. Hoffman, J. Scerd, and J. Clark (1977). "Lead and Hyperactivity." *Journal of Abnormal Psychology*, 5:405-416.

Pocock, S., M. Smith, and P. Baghurst (1994). "Environmental Lead and Children's Intelligence: A Systematic Review of the Epidemiological Evidence." *British Medical Journal*, 309:1189-1197.

Silva, P., L. Hughes, S. Williams, and J. Faed (1988). "Blood Lead, Intelligence, Reading Attainment and Behavior in Eleven Year Old Children in Dunedin, New Zealand." *Journal of Child Psychology and Psychiatry and Allied Disciplines*, 29:43-52

Stiles, K., and D. Bellinger (1993). "Neuropsychological Correlates of Low-Level Lead Exposure in School Aged Children." *Neurotoxicology and Teratology*, 15:27-35.

Winneke, G., U. Kramer, A. Brockhaus, U. Ewers, G. Kujanek, H. Lechner, and W. Janke (1983). "Neuropsychological Studies in Children with Elevated Tooth-Lead Concentrations." *International Archives of Occupational and Environmental Health*, 51:231-252.

Yule, W., R. Lansdown, I. Millar, and M. Urbanowicz (1981). "The Relationship between Blood Lead Concentrations, Intelligence and Attainment in a School Population: A Pilot Study." *Dev Med Child Neurol.*, 23:567-576.

CHAPTER 7

The Basic Routine Activity Approach to Crime Analysis

Marcus Felson

Since the *routine activity approach* was presented in 1979, it has been applied to many fields of crime. It has been extended and elaborated, but the most basic statement of the approach has yet to be published in a single place. The routine activity approach works at all scales, from the immediate crime setting to the global level of product manufacturing. This paper offers those basics, elaborating step by step, including applications of the routine activity approach to violent acts.

The routine activity approach to crime rate analysis was presented one quarter-century ago (Cohen & Felson, 1979; Felson & Cohen, 1981). This approach has since been elaborated and applied much more broadly (Felson, 2002; Felson & Clarke, 1998.) The approach is sometimes presented too simply and sometimes with too many complications. This chapter seeks to find a balance so that anyone new to the topic will learn the fundamentals of the routine activity approach. This chapter also shows that the approach clearly applies to violent criminal acts. The strategy of the chapter is to begin with the simplest model and complicate it step by step until the reader has an absolutely clear notion of the approach. Then the approach will be applied to violent crime. Not all wrinkles are considered nor is the literature of the past 25 years reviewed, but the reader should have no question at the end what the routine activity approach is and what it can do for understanding criminal behavior in general and violent acts in particular.

The routine activity approach orients itself to the criminal event, not the offender (see also Brantingham & Brantingham, 1999). Its initial focus was predatory crimes—those criminal events in which one person takes or damages the person or property of at least one other. It began by further narrowing its focus to offenses involving physical contact. The original routine activity approach sought to explain the occurrence of direct-contact predatory offenses—nothing more and nothing less. The approach clearly emphasizes mundane offenses and dissuades readers from giving undue attention to unusual criminal acts. Since that time, however, some scholars have applied it even to bizarre offenses and found them to have surprisingly routine elements (Rossmo, 2000).

The routine activity approach works at all scales, from the immediate crime setting to the global level of product manufacturing. It is therefore both a micro and macro theory of crime. The approach applies to many types of crime, including violent acts. The approach helps us escape defining the study of violence in terms of violent *persons.* Criminologists have not been able to isolate a separate and distinct category of persons that only commits violent offenses, neglecting all other offenses. This is not to deny disproportionate participation of some persons in violence, but to recognize that such correspondence is *not a definition.* Imagine a population in which almost everybody has the chickenpox, but some have more pox than others. One could not then *define* that condition by a group of persons. One would have to turn to something more direct.

Some scholars emphasize or even define a violent *environment,* a broad community or society that has greater violence (or at least measures it better). Again, it does not make sense to define violence in terms of where it is more common. Something should be defined only in terms of itself, and a proper definition of violence can only be behavioral. Indeed, the word "violence" is really a shortcut for *acts of violence.* These include acts that are legal and those that are illegal.

The routine activity approach is a framework for studying criminal acts and how they are carried out. This approach is ideally suited to analyzing illegal violent acts as well as how they occur despite society's banning them, but it also fits violence within a larger set of illegal acts as they occur in the context of everyday life.

Routine Features of Crime in Very Local Settings

The routine activity approach builds upon the immediate crime setting. An illegal act has minimal and tangible elements, each clearly stated. This is a "what you see is what you get" theory, based on features of crime and society that are close to daily life and can be recognized and perceived by any observer. Translating this theory into broader and vaguer terms defeats the purpose entirely.

Minimal Elements

The routine activity approach names three minimal elements of crime: (1) a likely offender, (2) a suitable target of crime, and (3) the absence of a capable guardian against crime. These three minimal elements must converge in space and crime for an ordinary crime to occur. Thus, the routine activity approach was not designed to explain crime over the Internet, telephone threats, or daring offenses with guardians present. It was designed for ordinary crimes, when an offender finds an easy target unsupervised by guardians.

Likely offenders. The routine activity approach does not state that all persons are equally likely to be offenders, but it does allow that anybody might commit at least some criminal act. It recognizes that analyses of crime often exaggerate the differences in criminality among individuals and groups. Moreover, it shifts the focus away from offenders and toward the other elements of crime. The routine activity approach does not deny the role of people, but it shifts them to the background and move events in the sociophysical world into center stage.

Targets, not victims. One of the main points of the routine activity approach is to shift attention toward the targets of crime. The word "target" is chosen over "victim" for a reason. Immediate victims of crime are often absent. The word "victim" can reach broadly to family or even society, but the routine activity approach seeks a tangible focus in studying crime. The concept of "victim" draws attention away from the criminal act and hence undermines the ability to analyze it in practical terms. Moreover, many offenders are impersonal toward their targets. Perhaps a majority of crimes are carried out without grudges. Even when offenders do have a personal grudge, they normally inflict tangible harm on their enemy, now their target of specific illegal action.

Guardians, not guards. A guardian is somebody whose presence or proximity serves to prevent crime. A guardian is not usually a guard or police officer. Ordinary citizens going about their lives might be guardians against crime. Indeed, many people serve to dissuade offenders without knowing they are doing so. The owners of property might serve as the best guardians if they are close enough to interfere with a crime, but their absence makes them ineffective in this role.

Specific Convergences, Not General Environments

The routine activity approach avoids general and vague terms about environs or environments. It speaks instead of specific convergences that make crime possible, likely, unlikely, or impossible.

Target's Value to the Offender

A target is suitable or unsuitable for crime. Although some unsuitable targets are occasionally attacked, they should be treated as anomalies. Targets are more suitable if they are valuable, inert, visible, or accessible. The acronym VIVA sums these four.[1] The value of the target must reflect the viewpoint of the offender. Thus, a young offender is more likely to steal a recording of the latest popular entertainer and less likely to steal a recording of Beethoven or Vivaldi. The concept of value also applies to targets of violence. Targets are highly unequal in their values to the violent offender. Offender preferences about whom to assault might be guided by pursuit of property, sexual gratification, power, a desire to redress grievances, or any other goal of a violent offense.

Target's Visibility and Access

A target that is highly visible attracts the offender's attention more frequently. Conversely, few offenders go out of their way to discern crime opportunities compared to those encountering such opportunities as they go about their daily routines.

Easy access makes a target more suitable as well. Most offenders avoid complex entry and difficult access to crime targets. Offenders also pay attention to their exits so they can escape safely or remove their targets if they wish to do so.

Inertia Makes a Target Less Suitable

Inertia is the tendency of a body to stay where it is. The offender must overcome inertia to take control of the crime target for his or her own uses. The reason why washing machines, despite high value, are seldom stolen is because they are too high in inertia. However, two offenders with a truck available and sufficient time can still steal one. Inertia must also take into account whether immediate targets of property crime are attached to something heavier. Inertia also applies to targets of violence, but in a more interesting way. Human targets who are low in inertia are either smaller or less muscular and thus easier upon which to gain physical advantage.

Tools and Weapons

From the outset, the routine activity approach has considered human artifacts, including tools and weapons, because they affect the opportunity to carry out illegal activities. The general strategy of the routine activity approach is to begin with the simplest and most basic elements of crime, then to elaborate from there. Such elaboration leads to a complex interplay among offenders, targets, and guardians. The target's features—value, inertia, visibility, and access—also interact with tools and weapons to produce a vast variety of illegal possibilities. The convergences and divergences of the minimal elements of crime are greatly affected by local routines that go well beyond the individual offender or crime incident.

Community Routines Affecting Violent Acts and Other Crimes

The routines of daily life serve to assemble offenders and targets with guardians absent. These routines are the key to crime-rate presences and absences.

Transport Routines

Automobiles and public transit are significant for crime opportunities and crime rates. Autos provide a plethora of crime targets—not only the cars themselves but also their contents and parts. Autos become targets of vandalism and theft as well as vehicles for carrying out illegal attacks against persons and property. Parking lots and structures become important locales for property crime, as well as for occasional violent offenses.

Public transit provides another large source of crime opportunity, with attacks occurring en route, in stations, or inside transit cars. Vandalism against public transit is significant, and these systems are part of the trip-to-crime process. Offenders tend to commit crimes along or near the routes with which they are familiar.

Residential Routines

The styling and spacing of housing has tremendous impact on its vulnerability to various types of crime. Stand-alone houses are more vulnerable to burglary. Areas of low ownership or high mobility are more at risk of a variety of crimes. The design of houses has a major impact on crimes there or on the streets outside. Crime prevention through environmental design, as well as environmental criminology, are increasingly fusing with the routine activity approach to provide a single view of how home and street generate crime opportunities to a larger or smaller extent (see Crowe & Zahm, 1994; Smith & Clarke, 2000).[2]

Work Routines

Work schedules are important for exposing persons and property to crime risk. Homes are vulnerable when residents and neighbors are away at work. Cars are more at risk parked away from home for work purposes. Businesses are likely to become victims of burglary or vandalism after employees are gone for the day or the weekend. The business cycle shows up in crime rates. The time period leading toward Christmas has higher crime rates generally, despite increasing cold in many parts of the United States. During the daytime, absence from residential areas makes the areas easy targets for burglary and household crimes. By removing guardians from the area on workdays, offenders have easy access and low risk of apprehension. Several homes in a row are likely to be unsupervised, making offender jobs all the easier.

School Routines

Youths are most likely to commit crimes or to fall victim to them at the time school is closing and they are making their way home in the afternoon. School days and school terms have a great impact on the crime patterns of young people. In general, school youths get in less trouble on weekend days than weekdays. In the United States, the progression of the school term can lead to more control, at least until the approach of Christmas in the winter and the movement toward spring.

Night Activities

The routine activity approach emphasizes that activities away from family and household settings produce more crime vulnerabilities. This works in different ways for daytime and nighttime activities. At night, risks are more likely to involve drinking alcohol, as well as acts of violence. Some property offenses also increase. Autos are very likely to be stolen from parking areas in entertainment districts. Many people who have been drinking alcohol in these areas make excellent targets for robbery as well. Those businesses and residences located near nighttime bars or fast food restaurants are also highly vulnerable to attack.

Weather and Climate

Weather and climate have a major impact on everyday routines, thus affecting offending and victimization. In the northern tier of the United States and other nations, seasonality is more dramatic and crime rates respond accordingly. For example, Sweden's crime rates are dramatically higher in the season of long days and lower in the darkened winter. However, in the southeastern United States, seasonality of crime is reduced and reflects mainly school and business cycles.

One Thing Leads to Another

Students of crime increasingly realize that one illegal act or shady behavior can lead a person deeper into risk, whether as an offender or a target of crime. The disinhibition of alcohol is the easiest example. In addition, minor drug abuse can lead to more serious abuse and other criminal acts. The routine inter-relationships among illegal acts are an area of increasing interest.

National and Multinational Routines

Routine activities vary not only locally but also at the national and multinational levels.

Consumer Trends

The best example is the mass production and dissemination of lightweight consumer electronics from the 1960s on. This occurred in the United States, Europe, and many nations. In most of the Western world, this helped produce a massive crime wave in the 1960s and 1970s.

Labor Costs

In addition, the higher cost of labor permeated Western societies, with related reductions in the number of store clerks watching goods and preventing their theft. Retail establishments provide increasing crime opportunities to both shoplifters and employees. Wholesale establishments have fewer employees watching more valuable goods, some of which are easily stolen.

Female Labor Force

The expansion of female labor force participation rates in the Western world has left residential areas largely depleted of adults during the daytime. That makes it more difficult to supervise youths, who might then become offenders or targets of crime. It also makes it more difficult to supervise residential streets and homes, enhancing their vulnerabilities.

Violent Routines

It is a mistake to think that the routine activity approach applies mainly to property crimes.

Robbery Routines

Robberies of many types respond to routine opportunities. During the approximate period 1960-1980, bank-related robberies responded to the spread of branch banking, then to the proliferation of automatic teller machines (ATMs). The spread of small convenience stores provided additional robbery targets. Street robberies responded to remote parking lots and the declining street population, leaving stragglers as targets with no proximate guardians.

More recently, ATMs have moved inside or adjacent to the stores where the cash is spent, with less time exposed to risk of carrying cash. In addition, more point-of-sale plastic transactions reduce the amount of cash in home drawers, pockets, purses, and cash registers, to the detriment of robbers. In addition, credit cards, checks, and check cards speed up noncash transactions, reducing risk to all parties. The parallel increase in plastic fraud is also a routine activity consequence, although this increased risk is perhaps not as great as the decline in risk of robbery and theft related to cash.

Nonviolent Routines Leading to Violent Acts

Nonviolent crimes beget violent crimes. On occasion, residents surprise a burglar in the act, and a violent encounter might ensue. On occasion, a robbery does not go smoothly and results in an assault. Even a shoplifting incident can lead to violent acts if the offender is challenged. As nonviolent incidents reach millions in number, a noteworthy minority can lead to a violent event. Moreover, an offender who intends a threat without injury—such as a quiet robbery—can easily end up with more than what he or she expected.

Nonpredatory Acts of Violence

The routine activity approach can be extended to include nonpredatory acts of violence, especially fights that have no innocent party. Although these are not predatory offenses, combatants must converge in space and time. A fight is most likely to occur when peacemakers are absent and instigators are present. Insults in proximity to an audience are more likely to be answered and to escalate into violent acts. Thus, nonpredatory acts of violence can result from certain types of routine activity. Small groups of young males drinking in proximity to one another present that risk, especially if some of the groups have no ongoing friendly ties to one another.

Diversified Motives for Assault

Assaults are very diverse in motive. Some are committed for reasons of power or dominance. Others are retribution for grievances, or to restore one's self image after a perceived insult. There is reason to question the existence of "expressive violence" and "irrational violence," given new understanding of diverse assault motives.

Routine Activities and Crime Prevention

When the routine activity approach was first presented, it was not linked to crime prevention at all. Since that time, this approach has been linked to situational crime prevention, crime prevention through environmental design, and problem-oriented policing. These methods of crime prevention overlap with one another and with alcohol management. If crime can increase in response to new opportunities, it can therefore decrease in response to their removal.

Endnotes

[1]   The VIVA elements have been elaborated by Professor Ronald V. Clarke (see Clarke, 1999).

[2]   See these four web sites for more on crime prevention: Center for Problem Oriented Policing at www. popcenter.org; Australian Institute of Criminology at www. aic.gov.au; Jill Dando Insititute at www. jdi.ucl.ac.uk; and Rutgers University Crime Prevention Service at crimeprevention.rutgers.edu.

Discussion Questions

1. What are the three minimal elements for direct-contact predatory crime?

2. What does VIVA stand for, and exactly how does it help us predict crime?

3. Does the routine activity approach focus more on offenders or more on criminal acts?

4. How does legal work relate to illegal activity?

5. Does the routine activity approach apply to violence, violent environments, or violent acts?

References

Brantingham, P.L., and P.J. Brantingham (1999). "A Theoretical Model of Crime Hot Spot Generation." *Studies on Crime and Crime Prevention*, 8(1):7-26

Clarke, R.V. (1999). *Hot Products: Understanding, Anticipating, and Reducing Demand for Stolen Goods*. Paper 112. Police Research Series. London: British Home Office Research Series. Availabe at: www.homeoffice.gov.uk/rds/prgpdfs/fprs112.pdf

Cohen, L.E., and M. Felson (1979). "Social Change and Crime Rate Trends: A Routine Activity Approach." *American Sociological Review*, 44:588-608.

Crowe, T.D., and D. Zahm (1994). "Crime Prevention Through Environmental Design." *Land Management* 7(1):22-27.

Felson, M. (2002). *Crime and Everyday Life*, 3rd ed. Thousand Oaks, CA: Sage.

Felson, M., and L.E. Cohen (1981). "Modeling Crime Rate Trends—A Criminal Opportunity Approach." *Journal of Research in Crime and Delinquency*, 18:138-164. (As corrected, 1982, 19,1.)

Felson, M., and R.V. Clarke (1998). *Opportunity Makes the Thief*. Paper 98. Police Research Series. London: British Home Office Research Series. Available at: www.homeoffice.gov.uk/rds/prgpdfs/fprs98.pdf

Rossmo, K. (2000). *Geographic Profiling*. Boca Raton, FL: CRC Press.

Smith, M., and R.V. Clarke (2000). "Crime and Public Transport." *Crime and Justice: A Review of Research*, 27:169-233.

CHAPTER 8

Feminist Theories of Violent Behavior

Claire M. Renzetti

Introduction

Feminist theory is relatively new in criminology. It is one of the outcomes of the resurgence of feminism as a social movement during the 1970s. Feminists were critical of virtually all academic disciplines for having excluded women from research and theorizing or, if women were included, for reinforcing sexist stereotypes. Criminology was no exception. "Beginning in the mid-1970s, feminist-inspired analyses drew attention to the neglect of women and the bias in male-centered theories of crime and criminal justice" (Jurik, 1999:34), and feminist criminologists set out to rectify these oversights and errors.

It is important to state at the outset that feminist criminology is not a single, unified theoretical perspective, but rather a group of related theories. There are various feminist criminological theories whose proponents often disagree with one another as much as with "mainstream" criminologists. Popular feminist theoretical perspectives include socialist feminism, standpoint feminism, multicultural feminism, and postmodern feminism (Jurik, 1999; Lorber, 1998; Wonders, 1999). However, there are several principles that feminist criminologists hold (more or less) in common. This chapter, therefore, begins by outlining these principles. The chapter then turns to feminist definitions of violence and some of the early feminist theorizing on violence, highlighting its progressive contributions to understanding violent behavior as well as its limitations in this area. Finally, the chapter examines some of the recent developments in feminist theorizing on violence that may be considered most promising and explores how they may be applied to various forms of violent behavior, including those that feminist criminologists have largely neglected to study.

Principles of Feminist Criminology

Despite the diversity in feminist criminology, there is a set of assumptions that underlies these feminist perspectives. At the core of feminist criminology is the recognition that *gender*—the socially constructed expectations, attitudes, and behaviors associated with females and males, typically organized dichotomously as *femininity* and *masculinity*—is a central organizing component of social life. This means that in studying any aspect of social life, including violence, one must consider in what ways it is gendered—that is, in what ways gender influences its frequency and manifestations—because "gender and gender relations order social life and social institutions in fundamental ways" (Daly & Chesney-Lind, 1988:108).

Embedded in this principle is another assumption: that gender is "not a natural fact but a complex social, historical, and cultural product" (Daly & Chesney-Lind, 1988:108). Feminists acknowledge the complex interactions between biology and culture that produce gender, but conceptualize gender as a *process* that is shaped by and that shapes social action, opportunities, and experiences.

Saying that gender shapes and is shaped by social action, opportunities, and experiences is not meant to imply that the genders or gender relations are symmetrical in our society or most others. Rather, another core principle of feminist criminology is that our society, both on a macro (structural/institutional) level and a micro (interpersonal) level, is characterized by *sexism*, the differential valuing of one gender over the other. In our society, sexism takes place within the context of *patriarchy*, a social system in which men dominate women and that which is considered masculine is more highly valued or is regarded as more important than that which is considered feminine (Curran & Renzetti, 2001).

Male voices and experiences have historically been privileged over female voices and experiences in our society. However, feminists also point out that while all men benefit from patriarchy, not all men are equally privileged—and not all women are equally disadvantaged. In other words, there is no "universal 'women's experience' or 'men's experience' that can be described independently of other facets of experience such as race, ethnicity, and class" as well as age, sexual orientation, and physical ability (Flavin, 2003:232). Further, the intersection of these social locating factors does not simply produce more disadvantage or more privilege in people's lives. Rather, from a feminist perspective, these intersections produce *qualitatively different* life experiences and opportunities that must be studied in their own right. This attention to *intersectionality* is a relatively recent development in feminism, the product of critiques by feminists of color who demonstrated how "mainstream" feminism inappropriately generalized the experiences of white, middle-class, and working-class women to *all* women (Crenshaw, 1994; King, 1988).

Finally, because feminist criminology grew out of the feminist movement, it has as a fundamental component collective social action to address sexism and promote gender equity. The means and goals of this social action remain contentious issues among feminists, but *social activism* is nonetheless a core principle of feminist criminology that has produced concrete results, such as revisions of rape laws, the establishment of shelters for battered women, and the adoption in many jurisdictions of mandatory or preferred arrest policies in domestic violence cases.[1]

Defining Violence

Before discussing early feminist theorizing on violence, it is necessary to state how violence is defined by feminist theorists. Traditionally, violent behavior has been defined rather narrowly to include acts of physical assault such as beating, punching, kicking, threatening with a weapon, or using a weapon against another person. These narrow definitions rely heavily on legalistic criteria. One of the major contributions of feminist research and theorizing on violence has been to broaden the definition of violent behavior to include sexual, psychological, and economic violence and, following the lead of radical or critical criminologists, to distinguish interpersonal violence and structural violence (Barak, 2003; DeKeseredy, 2000). Structural violence is perpetrated by institutions, such as the healthcare system, which historically used women, especially poor women, for medical experiments and labeled women who rejected traditional gender roles as mentally ill (Ehrenreich & English, 1973; Gilbert & Scher, 1999; see also Rynbrandt & Kramer, 2001, for a discussion of violence perpetrated by corporations).

In broadening the definition of violence, feminists have emphasized *victims'* perceptions and experiences as well as the consequences of particular actions, instead of solely using legal criteria specified in jurisdictions' criminal codes. They point out that an individual may be severely injured by behavior that does not involve physical assault. For example, individuals who are stalked or who are constantly berated and insulted suffer serious and long-term psychological harm as a result (Crowell & Burgess, 1996; DeKeseredy, 2000). Feminists, therefore, conceptualize violence in terms of a "continuum of unsafety" (Stanko, 1990). Violence is defined by feminists as any act—physical, sexual, or verbal—that is experienced by an individual as a threat, invasion, or assault and that has the effect of hurting or degrading that individual and/or of depriving that individual of her or his ability to control contact with another individual (Koss, Goodman, Browne, Fitzgerald, Keita & Russo, 1994). Although such a broad definition has raised concerns, particularly with regard to measurement, feminists seek to encompass a wide range of behaviors in their theorizing and research, arguing that narrow definitions do not adequately capture violent victimization experiences, especially those of women (DeKeseredy, 2000; Desai & Saltzman, 2001).

Early Feminist Theorizing on Violence

In 1975, Freda Adler sounded the alarm that women were not only committing more crimes, but that their crimes were becoming more *masculine* in character: Based on her analysis of the Uniform Crime Reports between 1960 and 1972, she concluded that women were committing more serious and more violent crimes (Adler, 1975). Adler attributed these changes to the women's movement, which she saw as opening previously closed legitimate and illegitimate opportunities to women: "Is it any wonder that once women were armed with male opportunities they should strive for status, criminal as well as civil, through established male hierarchical channels?" (Adler, 1975:10). Consequently, much early feminist criminological research and theorizing was an attempt to put out the fire that Adler had started. This work took a decidedly critical and defensive stance: offering a litany of problems with Adler's methodology, reanalyzing her data to show that women's violent crime had *not* changed in either frequency or severity, and presenting labor force and other statistics to show that the women's movement had not succeeded in "liberating" women and that sexism was alive and well.

A major contribution of this early feminist work was its emphasis on the importance of gender in understanding crime. Gender is the strongest predictor of criminal involvement; males consistently perpetrate more crime, and more serious crime, including violent crime, than females do. However, apart from these "corrective" responses to Adler's research, violence *by* women was left largely unexamined, a point that will be addressed later in this chapter.

Instead, feminist criminologists turned their attention to crimes of violence that they felt mainstream criminology had neglected: men's violence against women, including sexual assault, incest, sexual harassment, and battering. The feminist movement encouraged women to voice publicly what traditionally had been regarded as private experiences. A popular slogan of the movement was "the personal is political." In small consciousness-raising groups as well as large "speak-outs," women were empowered to reveal—some for the first time in their lives—their victimization at the hands of men, often men they knew and who claimed to love them. It became clear that men's violence against women was not as rare as many of us would have liked to think, and that actual or even potential victimization had serious personal and social consequences for women's everyday lives. Although some criminologists have criticized feminists for referring to men's violence against women as an "epidemic" (see, for example, Felson, 2002), empirical documentation of the frequency and severity of this violence spurred feminists to develop a theoretical model for explaining it.

At the risk of oversimplifying the theory, feminist criminology sees men's violence against women as a means of preserving and reinforcing men's dominance and women's subordination in a patriarchal society (Yllo, 1993). Men's violence against women is an outgrowth of gender inequality. In patriarchal societies, men have greater access to resources (e.g., income) than women do, and greater resources translate into greater power—that is, the ability to control others and get them to comply with one's wishes. Women's economic dependence on men is one control tactic men can use to preserve their dominance; violence (or the threat of violence) may be seen as the ultimate control tactic to ensure women's subordination. Gender norms shore up these unequal gender relations to such an extent that men's superiority is taken for granted by many people, male and female. It is also hardly surprising to feminists that women are more likely to be violently victimized by men they know, because gender norms bestow a sense of entitlement on men—entitlement to women's bodies, services, and deference (especially the bodies, services, and deference of "their" women). A substantial body of research with male perpetrators documents their sense of entitlement as well as their motives for using violence to punish and control women (see, for example, Barnett, Lee & Thelan, 1997; Scully & Marolla, 1985).

Critics of feminist theory have argued that in patriarchal societies, and particularly among men who adhere to "traditional" gender norms such as "men are superior to women" and "women are weak," there is strong support for chivalry, which serves to protect women from violence, not make them more vulnerable to it (Felson, 2002). The overwhelming majority of people, they claim, abhor the idea of a man behaving violently toward a woman, which helps to explain why when men do violently victimize women, "they prefer to do it when no one is watching" (Felson, 2002:73). While this argument has some common-sense appeal as well as some empirical research to support it, feminists respond that it overlooks a critical caveat: Chivalry protects women against men's violence *only if* the women conform to patriarchal standards of "true womanhood." Research consistently shows that a sizable minority of women and men believe that it is acceptable for a man to hit a woman or force her to have sex under "certain circumstances," which typically can be subsumed under the heading, "She did something to deserve it"; for example, she was promiscuous, she used alcohol or other drugs, she was unfaithful to him, she is a lesbian. Research documents the elevated risk of violent victimization among women who "deviate" from the norms of "true womanhood" (see, for example, Crenshaw, 1994; Perry, 2001).

Nevertheless, feminists have recognized limitations in their theory of male violence. For instance, despite the shocking frequency of male violence against women, it is the case that relatively few men actually batter, rape, or in other ways violently victimize women. As Yllo (1993) asks, "Why is a subordinate, cowering wife pleasing [or rewarding] to some men, but not others?" (p. 57). More recently, in response to research on violence in lesbian relationships as well as increasing arrests of heterosexual women for domestic violence, feminist criminologists have begun to expand their theoretical perspectives to account for women's use of violence in intimate relationships as well as other social contexts (das Dasgupta, 2002; Girshick, 2002; Renzetti, 1992, 1999). Although this work has taken a number of directions, we will examine what may be considered some of the most promising theoretical developments.

Doing Gender and Violence

Sociologist Candace West and her colleagues (West & Fenstermaker, 1995; West & Zimmerman, 1987) borrow the ethnomethodological concept of *situated action* or *situated accomplishment* to reframe gender as something men and women *do* in response to contextualized norms of masculinity and femininity, rather than as a static social role. In other words, males and females "do gender" in various situations, making choices—albeit choices constrained by structural conditions and normative expectations—of how they will establish their masculinity and femininity, respectively. Thus, gender changes over time and varies from situation to situation, depending on normative demands as well as an individual's resources and perceptions of others' evaluations of him or her. Moreover, doing gender intersects with doing race/ethnicity, class, sexual orientation, and age, producing "a multitude of masculinities and femininities—each shaped by structural positioning—rather than one static set of gender roles" (Miller, 2002:435).

Drawing on these ideas, some feminist criminologists theorize that violence constitutes a means for accomplishing gender in certain contexts. For example, Messerschmidt (1993, 2000), through secondary analysis and analysis of in-depth life history narratives of young men, focuses on males' conscious decisions to use certain actions in specific situations and the meanings they give to these actions. His data show that violent crime, such as robbery and fighting, are a means for young, urban, poor and working-class males to construct a type of masculinity, which he calls the "hardman." In the social settings in which these young men live their everyday lives, many other resources for accomplishing masculinity are blocked; violent crime is an available option. Similarly, Bufkin (1999) and Perry (2001) apply the notion of gender as situated accomplishment in their analyses of hate crime. In considering the characteristics of typical hate crime perpetrators and their victims, as well as the characteristics of the crimes themselves (e.g., language used by perpetrators, the group nature of many hate crimes, the use of alcohol by perpetrators), both Bufkin and Perry theorize that committing hate crimes is a means of accomplishing a particular type of masculinity, *hegemonic masculinity*—that is, white, Christian, able-bodied, heterosexual masculinity. Although feminist theorists have to date neglected to study terrorist violence, the concept of hegemonic masculinity may be helpful in explaining why there appear to be so few women in terrorist organizations, particularly those tied to fundamentalist religious or conservative political groups, which tend to adhere strongly to norms of gender segregation and inequality.

As the foregoing examples indicate, this perspective, known as *structured action theory* (see Messerschmidt,1997), has been applied primarily to violence by men and boys. Very recently, several criminologists have begun extending it as an explanation of women's and girls' violence. For instance, Messerschmidt (1995, 1997, 2002) has examined girl gang members' violent behavior in terms of structured action theory. Messerschmidt reports that when girl gang members engage in violence, such as when they fight with rival gang members to protect the "hood," they are not behaving like boys, but rather are engaging in normatively appropriate femininity—that is, femininity positively sanctioned by gang members, femininity that intersects with racial, class, sexual, and generational norms in the social context of the gang. He refers to this normative gang femininity as "bad girl femininity," and he emphasizes that the gang girls, in bragging about their violence, do not describe themselves as masculine, but as "bad."

Miller (2002), who has also applied structured action theory to gang girls' violence, argues for more nuanced analyses of doing gender through violence, avoiding, in particular, a dualistic conception of gender (masculine *or* feminine). She urges theorists to account for the complexity and flexibility of social actors' agency coupled with the structural, institutional, and intersubjective constraints on their behavior. She shows, for example, how in some violent situations gang girls may see themselves as behaving "like boys": "embracing a *masculine* identity that they view as contradicting their bodily sex category (that is female)" (p. 443). This does not mean, of course, that this self-identity construction is permanent or holds in other situations. She also highlights situations, such as robbery, whereby crime is not a resource for women to accomplish gender, but rather gender is used as a resource for women to accomplish crime.[2] Finally, she notes situations in which other social locating factors, such as race, can have primacy over gender. For instance, she points out that whereas the African-American gang girls she studied saw violence as normative and status-enhancing, research with Asian-American gang girls indicates that violence is not "celebrated and normative" but rather a "consequence of and response to the abuse . . . that characterizes their lives at home" (Joe & Chesney-Lind, 1995:428).

Victimization as a Pathway to Offending by Girls and Women

Although criminological research on girls and women continues to lag behind research on boys and men, females are getting more attention because their arrest and incarceration rates have increased in recent years. Today, as in the past, females' involvement in the criminal justice system is primarily as property offenders. The percentage of women, particularly women of color, arrested for drug offenses has increased substantially during the past two decades (Bush-Baskette, 1998), but these women appear to be at greater risk of being violently victimized than of committing violent offenses (Mancuso & Miller, 2001; Steffensmeier, 2001). Women's overall rate of violent offending has remained relatively constant since the 1960s (Kruttschnitt, 2001), although women's rates of arrest for assault have risen, perhaps as a result of police making more dual arrests when responding to domestic violence calls. Nevertheless, public concern about the perceived increase in violence by girls and women has helped to promote more research and theorizing (including feminist research and theorizing) on gender and violence.

One significant contribution of feminist criminologists in this area has been the connection between victimization and offending among girls and women. As the research by Joe and Chesney-Lind (1995) shows, feminist criminologists have found a correlation between females' violent victimization, especially during childhood, and their subsequent involvement in crime, including crimes of violence. For example, recent research shows a significant increase in arrest for violent crime among girls who have been neglected and abused, compared with girls who were not neglected and abused, but this relationship does not hold for boys (Widom & Maxfield, 2001). In a study of dating violence among college students, Monson and Langhinrichsen-Rohling (2002) found that female students were less likely than male students to sexually victimize their dating partners, but they were more likely to perpetrate nonsexual violence against them, although it was less severe than the nonsexual violence perpetrated by male students against their dating partners. The female perpetrators in this study were more likely than the male perpetrators to have been sexually abused as children. Additional research shows that girls who were sexually abused are nearly three times more likely than girls who were not sexually abused to run away from home and to be arrested for violent offenses (Siegel & Williams, 2003).

This pattern continues in adulthood. Women who were abused and neglected as children are more likely than women who were not abused or neglected during childhood to be arrested as adults for violent crimes, but this is not the case for men (English, Widom & Brandford, 2001; Widom & Maxfield, 2001). Abuse as an adult can also lead to violent offending by women. When women do commit violent offenses, they most often victimize someone close to them (e.g., an intimate partner, their children, another relative); men, on the other hand, are as likely to violently victimize someone close to them as they are a stranger, particularly during the commission of another felony (Kruttschnitt, 2001). However, homicide research indicates that women who kill their intimate partners rarely have a criminal record of violent offending, but do have a long history of being physically and sexually abused by those intimate partners (O'Keefe, 1997; Osthoff, 2001).

Conclusion

This review of feminist theories of violence has highlighted the strengths of this theorectical perspective on violence. However, implicit in the discussion are several limitations of the theory—and the empirical research that tests it—to date. Missing, for example, are empirical analyses of men's *and* women's narrative accounts of why they engage in specific acts of violence, how they justify their behavior, and what these acts mean to them in general but more specifically in terms of gender and other social locating factors (e.g., social class, race/ethnicity, sexuality, age, physical ability, religion). Without such analyses, the similarities and differences in males' and females' violent behavior—including whether males and females engage in violence under similar or different circumstances, and in what situations gender "matters" to them relative to other factors of identity construction—cannot be determined. Moreover, the feminist perspective has been criticized for overemphasizing men's violence, particularly men's violence against women, while overlooking women's use of violence. As previously noted, more women are being arrested for intimate partner violence. It is critically important, therefore, that this phenomenon not be too quickly dismissed as an artifact of mandatory arrest laws in which officers are failing to identify the primary aggressor. Instead, feminist criminologists must look carefully at those situations in which women and girls *as women and girls* engage in violence (see Messerschmidt, 2002). This means seriously exploring the possibility that women may use violence in situations *other than* as a direct or indirect response to violent victimization at some point in their lives. Some feminist criminologists, psychologists, social workers, practitioners, and advocates are taking on this challenging task (see, for example, Bible, das Dasgupta & Osthoff, 2002a; 2002b; 2003). As noted elsewhere (Renzetti, 1999), research *frames* a problem in the political and public consciousness, which in turn influences public policy and criminal justice responses. In developing a feminist theory of women's *and* men's uses of violence—a theory that places gender at the center of the analysis—feminist criminologists can contribute to the development of public policy and criminal justice interventions that are not gender-neutral, but rather gender-equitable.

Endnotes

[1]   For a discussion of some of the feminist debates surrounding these issues, see Buzawa and Buzawa (2002); Donnelly, Cook, and Wilson (1999); Ferarro (2003); and Ford (2003).

[2]   In her study of robbery, Miller (1998) found that men typically use guns, physical contact, and violence in male-on-male robberies—"clearly a reflection of the masculine ideologies shaping men's robberies" (p. 50). Women, on the other hand, usually rob other women, whom they perceive as vulnerable and easy to intimidate. If women do rob men, they play on gender stereotypes of women as weak and sexually available in order to manipulate their targets into situations in which the robbery is more easily accomplished.

Discussion Questions

1.   What are the primary assumptions of feminist criminology?

2.   What was the major focus of early feminist theorizing on violence and how has this focus changed in recent years?

3.   How does one "do gender," particularly with regard to violence?

4.   How does violent victimization intersect with violent offending for girls and women?

5.   How might the current limitations of feminist theorizing on violence be overcome?

References

Adler, F. (1975). *Sisters in Crime*. New York: McGraw-Hill.

Barak, G. (2003). *Violence and Nonviolence: Pathways to Understanding*. Thousand Oaks, CA: Sage.

Barnett, O.W., C.Y. Lee, and R. Thelan (1997). "Gender Differences in Attributions of Self-Defense and Control in Interpartner Aggression." *Violence Against Women*, 3(5):462-481.

Bible, A., S. das Dasgupta, and S. Osthoff (eds.) (2002a). "Women's Use of Violence in Intimate Relationships: Part I." *Violence Against Women*, (Special Issue), 8(11).

Bible, A., S. das Dasgupta, and S. Osthoff (eds.) (2002b). "Women's Use of Violence in Intimate Relationships: Part II." *Violence Against Women* (Special Issue), 8(12).

Bible, A., S. das Dasgupta, S., and S. Osthoff (eds.) (2003). "Women's Use of Violence in Intimate Relationships: Part III." *Violence Against Women* (Special Issue), 9(1).

Bufkin, J. (1999). "Bias Crime as Gendered Behavior." *Social Justice*, 26:155-176.

Bush-Baskette, S. (1998). "The War on Drugs as a War Against Black Women." In S.L. Miller (ed.), *Crime Control and Women*, pp. 113-129. Thousand Oaks, CA: Sage.

Buzawa, E.S., and C.G. Buzawa (2002). *Domestic Violence: The Criminal Justice Response.* Thousand Oaks, CA: Sage.

Crenshaw, K.W. (1994). "Mapping the Margins: Intersectionality, Identity Politics, and Violence against Women of Color." In M.A. Fineman and R. Mykitiuk (eds.), *The Public Nature of Private Violence*, pp. 93-119. New York: Routledge.

Crowell, N.A., and A.W. Burgess (eds.) (1996). *Understanding Violence against Women.* Washington, DC: National Academy Press.

Curran, D.J., and C.M. Renzetti (2001). *Theories of Crime.* Boston: Allyn & Bacon.

Daly, K., and M. Chesney-Lind (1988). "Feminism and Criminology." *Justice Quarterly*, 5:497-538.

das Dasgupta, S. (2002). "A Framework for Understanding Women's Use of Nonlethal Violence in Intimate Heterosexual Relationships." *Violence Against Women*, 8(11):1364-1389.

DeKeseredy, W.S. (2000). "Current Controversies on Defining Nonlethal Violence Against Women in Intimate Heterosexual Relationships." *Violence Against Women*, 6(7):728-746.

Desai, S., and L.E. Saltzman (2001). "Measurement Issues of Violence Against Women." In C.M. Renzetti, J.L. Edleson, and R.K. Bergen (eds.), *Sourcebook on Violence against Women*, pp. 35-52. Thousand Oaks, CA: Sage.

Donnelly, D.A., K.J. Cook, and L.A. Wilson (1999). "Provision and Exclusion: The Dual Face of Services to Battered Women in Three Deep South States." *Violence Against Women*, 5(7):710-741.

Ehrenreich, B., and D. English (1973). *Witches, Nurses, and Midwives: A History of Women Healers.* Old Westbury, NY: Feminist Press.

English, D.J., C.S. Widom, and C.B. Brandford (2001). *Childhood Victimization and Delinquency, Adult Criminality, and Violent Criminal Behavior: A Replication and Extension. Final Report.* Washington, DC: U.S. Department of Justice, National Institute of Justice.

Felson, R.B. (2002). *Gender and Violence Reexamined.* Washington, DC: American Psychological Association.

Ferraro, K.J. (2003). "The Words Change, But the Melody Lingers: The Persistence of the Battered Woman Syndrome in Criminal Cases Involving Battered Women." *Violence Against Women*, 9(1):110-129.

Flavin, J. (2003). "Feminism for the Mainstream Criminologist: An Invitation." In C.M. Renzetti, D.J. Curran, and P.J. Carr (eds.), *Theories of Crime: A Reader*, pp. 223-245. Boston: Allyn & Bacon.

Ford, D.A. (2003). "Coercing Victim Participation in Domestic Violence Prosecutions." *Journal of Interpersonal Violence*, 18(6):669-684.

Gilbert, L.A., and M. Scher (1999). *Gender and Sex in Counseling and Psychotherapy.* Boston: Allyn & Bacon.

Girshick, L.B. (2002). *Woman-to-Woman Sexual Violence: Does She Call It Rape?* Boston: Northeastern University Press.

Joe, K.A., and M. Chesney-Lind (1995). "'Just Every Mother's Angel': An Analysis of Gender and Ethnic Variation in Youth Gang Membership." *Gender & Society*, 9:408-430.

Jurik, N.C. (1999). "Socialist Feminist Criminology and Social Justice." In B.A. Arrigo (ed.), *Social Justice, Criminal Justice*, pp. 30-50. Belmont, CA: Wadsworth.

King, D.R. (1988). "Multiple Jeopardy, Multiple Consciousness: The Context of Black Feminist Ideology." *Signs*, 14:42-72.

Koss, M.P., L. Goodman, A. Browne, L. Fitzgerald, G.P. Keita, and N.F. Russo (1994). *No Safe Haven*. Washington, DC: American Psychological Association.

Kruttschnitt, C. (2001). "Gender and Violence." In C.M. Renzetti and L. Goodstein (eds.), *Women, Crime, and Criminal Justice*, pp. 77-92. Los Angeles: Roxbury.

Lorber, J. (1998). *Gender Inequality: Feminist Theories and Politics*. Los Angeles: Roxbury.

Mancuso, R.F., and B.A. Miller (2001). "Crime and Punishment in the Lives of Women Alcohol and Other Drug (AOD) Users: Exploring the Gender, Lifestyle, and Legal Issues." In C.M. Renzetti and L. Goodstein (eds.), *Women, Crime, and Criminal Justice*, pp. 93-110. Los Angeles: Roxbury.

Messerschmidt, J.W. (2002). "On Gang Girls and a Structured Action Theory: A Reply to Miller." *Theoretical Criminology*, 6(4):461-475.

Messerschmidt, J.W. (2000). *Nine Lives: Adolescent Masculinities, the Body, and Violence*. Boulder, CO: Westview.

Messerschmidt, J.W. (1997). *Crime as Structured Action: Gender, Race, Class and Crime in the Making*. Thousand Oaks, CA: Sage.

Messerschmidt, J.W. (1995). "From Patriarchy to Gender: Feminist Theory, Criminology, and the Challenge of Diversity." In N.H. Rafter and F. Heidensohn (eds.), *International Feminist Perspectives in Criminology*, pp. 167-188. Philadelphia: Open University Press.

Messerschmidt, J.W. (1993). *Masculinities and Crime*. Lanham, MD: Rowman & Littlefield.

Miller, J. (2002). "The Strengths and Limits of 'Doing Gender' for Understanding Street Crime." *Theoretical Criminology*, 6(4):433-460.

Miller, J. (1998). "Up It Up: Gender and the Accomplishment of Street Robbery. *Criminology*, 36(1):37-66.

Monson, C.M., and J. Langhinrichsen-Rohling (2002). "Sexual and Nonsexual Dating Violence Perpetration: Testing an Integrated Perpetrator Typology." *Violence and Victims*, 17:403-428.

O'Keefe, M. (1997). "Incarcerated Battered Women: A Comparison of Battered Women who Killed Their Abusers and Those Incarcerated for Other Offenses." *Journal of Family Violence*, 12(1):1-19.

Osthoff, S. (2001). "When Victims Become Defendants: Battered Women Charged with Crimes." In C.M. Renzetti and L. Goodstein (eds.), *Women, Crime, and Criminal Justice*, pp. 232-242.

Perry, B. (2001). *In the Name of Hate: Understanding Hate Crime*. New York: Routledge.

Renzetti, C.M. (1999). "The Challenge to Feminism Posed by Women's Use of Violence in Intimate Relationships." In S. Lamb (ed.), *New Versions of Victims: Feminists Struggle with the Concept*, pp. 42-56. New York: New York University Press.

Renzetti, C.M. (1992). *Violent Betrayal: Partner Abuse in Lesbian Relationships*. Newbury Park, CA: Sage.

Rynbrandt, L., and R.C. Kramer (2001). "Corporate Violence Against Women." In C.M. Renzetti and L. Goodstein (eds.), *Women, Crime, and Criminal Justice*, pp. 165-175. Los Angeles: Roxbury.

Scully, D., and J. Marolla (1985). "'Riding the Bull at Gilley's: Convicted Rapists Describe the Rewards of Rape. *Social Problems*, 32:251-263.

Siegel, J.A., and L.M. Williams (2003). "The Relationship Between Child Sexual Abuse and Female Delinquency and Crime: A Prospective Study." *Journal of Research in Crime and Delinquency*, 40(1):71-94.

Stanko, E.A. (1990). *Everyday Violence: How Women and Men Experience Sexual and Physical Danger*. London: Pandora.

Steffensmeier, D. (2001). "Female Crime Trends, 1960-1995." In C.M. Renzetti and L. Goodstein (eds.), *Women, Crime, and Criminal Justice*, pp. 191-211. Los Angeles: Roxbury.

West, C., and S. Fenstermaker (1995). "Doing Difference." *Gender & Society*, 9(1):8-37.

West, C., and D.H. Zimmerman (1987). "Doing Gender." *Gender & Society*, 1(1):125-151.

Widom, C.S., and M.G. Maxfield (2001). *An Update on the "Cycle of Violence."* Washington, DC: U.S. Department of Justice, National Institute of Justice.

Wonders, N.A. (1999). "Postmodern Feminist Criminology and Social Justice." In B.A. Arrigo (ed.), *Social Justice, Criminal Justice*, pp. 109-128. Belmont, CA: Wadsworth.

Yllo, K.A. (1993). "Through a Feminist Lens: Gender, Power, and Violence. In R.J. Gelles and D.R. Loseke (eds.), *Current Controversies on Family Violence*, pp. 47-62. Newbury Park, CA: Sage.

CHAPTER 9

Violent Structures

Donald Black

Pure Sociology

Pure sociology is a new kind of sociological theory that excludes several features of virtually all other explanations of human behavior: (1) psychology (a concern with the human mind), (2) teleology (a concern with human action as a means to an end), and (3) anthropocentrism (a concern with humans rather than social life in the strictest sense). It includes none of the assumptions or claims common to other theories, such as those about the subjective experience or goals of the people whose behavior they explain. Its logic also differs from both microscopic explanations (based on the characteristics of individuals) and macroscopic explanations (based on the characteristics of groups or aggregates). Instead, *pure sociology explains each form of social life with its social geometry*—its multidimensional location and direction in social space. The geometry of a social phenomenon includes the various social distances it spans, the social directions it travels, and the social elevations it inhabits. This geometry explains why it occurs (e.g., Baumgartner, 2002; Black, 1995, 1998, 2000a, 2000c, 2002; see also Horwitz, 2002b).

This paper was prepared for a Workshop on Theories of Violence, organized by Margaret A. Zahn and Anna Jordan, and sponsored by the National Institute of Justice, Violence and Victimization Division, Washington, DC, December 10-11, 2002. The chapter partly derives from my lectures entitled "Dangerous Structures" and "Violent Structures," presented at the Department of Sociology, University of Pennsylvania, Philadelphia, April 7, 2000, and a symposium entitled "Hidden Structures of Social Reality: Five Innovative Theories," at the University of Virginia, Charlottesville, April 18, 2000. I thank Mark Cooney, Marcus Mahmood, and Roberta Senechal de la Roche for comments on an earlier draft.

Violence

The focus of this chapter is moralistic violence. Violence is the use of physical force against people or property, including threats and attempts. Although most violence is moralistic, some is predatory, recreational, or ritualistic. *Predatory violence* is the use of force in the acquisition of wealth or other resources, such as in a robbery or rape. *Recreational violence* arises for its own sake, such as for sport or amusement. *Ritualistic violence* is ceremonial, such as a beating during an initiation into a gang or a human sacrifice during a religious event. *Moralistic violence* is a form of social control[1]—a process that defines and responds to deviant behavior, such as when a man kills his wife's lover or a teenager attacks a peer for insulting him (see Black, 1983; 1998:xv; Cooney & Phillips, 2002). Most such violence is self-help: the handling of a grievance with aggression (see Black, 1990:74-79). Violent self-help includes beatings, killings, fights, and other physical attacks between individuals, as well as collective forms such as feuds, lynchings, riots, terrorism, genocide, and warfare. Although governments and legal officials may use aggression against those they define as deviant, the following pages address only violent self-help by individuals and groups acting on their own.

Violence is a prominent mode of conflict management in nearly all known societies, but it appears unevenly across the social locations of each society where it arises. Some locations in social space have a great deal of violence, others have little or none. And the means by which violence occurs and its degree of severity differ greatly from one social location to another. How, then, do we explain the variable nature of violence, including its incidence, form, and magnitude?

The Law-like Nature of Violence

First we must recognize that moralistic violence partly resembles law, a process commonly regarded as the very opposite of violence. Both belong to the same sociological family—social control. Although modern law defines and responds to most violence as crime, a form of deviant behavior, most violence defines and responds to deviant behavior as well (see Black, 1983). Most violence is explicitly or implicitly a form of justice—punishment, retaliation, resistance, or revenge. It rights a wrong. In modern life, then, most violence is both crime and social control at once. Yet because moralistic violence differs substantially from most other crime (such as robbery, burglary, or pornography), its criminal nature is theoretically incidental. Instead, the primary theoretical challenge is to understand it as a phenomenon similar to law itself.

Violence not only resembles law in its moralistic nature but also in the highly precise manner of its application. It is not an all-or-nothing phenomenon, like an explosion with unpredictable consequences. Rather, just as each case of conflict within the jurisdiction of law attracts a particular style and quantity of legal consequences (such as a specific fine or payment of damages), so each case within the jurisdiction of self-help attracts a particular form and quantity of violence (such as a specific weapon or degree of injury). The social geometry of each conflict predicts whether violence occurs at all and, if so, its nature and extent.

The Geometry of Violence

Earlier theories of violence focus on the characteristics of individuals or collectivities (for an overview, see, e.g., Smith & Zahn, 1999). However, a shortcoming of individualistic theories (such as those attributing violence to learning or frustration) is that no individuals are violent in all their conflicts. A shortcoming of collectivistic theories (such as those attributing violence to cultural traditions or social inequality) is that no collectivities are violent in all their conflicts. Individualistic theories are thus badly nearsighted, unable to see beyond the individual to each conflict where violence actually occurs, and collectivistic theories are badly farsighted, unable to see within the collectivity to each conflict where violence actually occurs. In other words, individualistic theories *overindividualize* violence (as if individuals alone explain violence), while collectivistic theories *overcollectivize* violence (as if collectivities such as societies or communities alone explain violence). Because both ignore the conflict structures that generate violence—the violent structures—both *understructuralize* the explanation of violence. They therefore fail to predict and explain precisely when and how violence takes place—who is violent in a particular way, toward whom, and on what occasion.

Pure sociology focuses on the social geometry of each conflict that might arise, including the various social distances between the parties, their social elevation, and the social direction of the grievance. It specifies how particular conflict structures attract particular forms and quantities of violence (see, e.g., Black, 1995, especially pp. 852-858). Pure sociology thus transcends both individualism and collectivism—microcosms and macrocosms—and explains violence better than either. Violent structures explain any and all cases of violence, whether scuffling between children, fighting between husband and wife, feuding between gangs, rioting between ethnic groups, or warfare between tribes, nations, or groups of nations. Structures are violent, not individuals or collectivities. Structures kill, not guns or people. Consider, for example, when and how weapons enter conflicts.

The Behavior of Weapons

The social geometry of a conflict—the conflict structure—predicts and explains whether a weapon enters a conflict and, if so, its nature and use. For instance, all else constant (such as the nature of the conflict and other elements of the conflict structure), the role of weapons increases with the relational and cultural distance[2] between the parties (see Black, 1998:154):

> *The lethality of weapons is a direct function of social distance.*

This principle predicts and explains numerous observations from diverse societies. For example:

(1) Anthropological evidence shows that lethal weapons more readily enter distant conflicts (such as between members of different tribes or communities) than closer conflicts (such as between family members, friends, or neighbors in the same tribe). The Nuer of the Sudan thus use their spears only beyond the village: "Men of the same village or camp fight with clubs, for it is a convention that spears must not be used between close neighbors lest one of them be killed. . . . [But] when a fight starts between persons of different villages, it is with the spear" (Evans-Pritchard, 1940:151, punctuation edited). The Ik of Uganda have spears as well, but use nothing more lethal than a club or stick within the tribe: "The Ik say they never use spears in fights among themselves, which I believe to be true" (Turnbull, 1972:163).

   In many tribal and other earlier societies, all adult men carry at least one weapon such as a knife, spear, or rifle at all times, yet rarely if ever use it against fellow villagers or other close associates. For that matter, potentially dangerous parts of the human body (such as fists, fingernails, and teeth) and everyday objects (such as cooking implements and furniture) are always available to everyone, but people seldom use them against friends or relatives.

(2) When weapons enter closer conflicts, their use is relatively restrained. For instance, the Mbuti pygmies of the Congo are careful not to draw blood within the band, a small group of families who live together as a unit: "The rules of self-help among the Mbuti are quite simple. It is perfectly proper to hit someone with anything wooden; it is not at all proper to draw blood, nor to hit anyone on the forehead, which is considered a dangerous spot" (Turnbull, 1965:188-189). Although Mbuti men have bows and poison arrows, spears, knives, and machetes close at hand, they virtually never use them in close relationships. An anthropologist once saw a man throw a spear in his brother-in-law's direction, but he apparently aimed it into the ground (Turnbull, 1961:122).

Men of the Hadza tribe of Tanzania also have bows and highly lethal poison arrows, and can kill one another with ease, but they apparently never do so in their camps. Instead, their violence is limited mainly to "duels" with wooden staves (often bow staves), in which "head injuries are common but deaths are very rare" (Woodburn, 1979:252).

(3) In eastern Indonesia, men of the Dou Donggo tribe are quick to confront and threaten one another, possibly with a knife (called a *kris*) that every man wears in the front waistband of his sarong. Their associates always restrain them, however, and they apparently never use their knives or otherwise inflict personal injuries on anyone who lives in their own village (Justice, 1991:295, 302-305). Married couples do not injure one another either, though one spouse might attack jointly owned possessions, such as when one man "took out his bush knife and hacked to pieces several chairs" (p. 302).

When Irishmen square off and threaten to kill one another on Tory Island (off the coast of Ireland), their relatives and friends—like the Dou Donggo above—restrain the adversaries before anyone takes a swing or inflicts any injury more serious than a bloody nose. But fights with more distant adversaries in other parts of Ireland or elsewhere (such as London or Glasgow), might become "very nasty," with "broken bottles, boots, and gore" (Fox, 1977:144-145; see also pp. 138-143).

(4) In nineteenth-century Ireland, ritualized fights between so-called factions—usually large groups of men from adjoining rural localities—were fought with long sticks, usually of blackthorn or oak, held and used in such a way that serious injuries were unlikely: "The blackthorn was held by the middle, and only one half of it could give a blow. If it were held by the end, it would be indeed a deadly weapon, but held half-way it was more a weapon to defend its user than to hurt an opponent. Hence, the faction fight was rather a fencing competition—not a deadly combat" (O'Donnell, 1975:186, punctuation edited). Against the British, however, the weapons were more lethal—earlier swords and pikes, later guns and bombs.

Aborigine men in modern Australia sometimes brandish lethal weapons such as guns, spears, and knives in conflicts with others, but seldom do they inflict serious injuries or death unless the adversary is a stranger who speaks a different language. Although women likewise have violent conflicts with other women in their own village, the only weapon ever used is a three- or four-foot long eucalyptus stick (called a *nulla nulla*). And they avoid hitting the head and soft body parts in favor of legs, arms, or hands (Burbank, 1994:35-36, 74, 93-94).

(5) Finnish Gypsies traditionally fought duels with weapons such as clubs, whips, or knives, but carefully avoided fatalities. They used knives only to slash rather than stab, and "the winner would do anything in his power in order to prevent the loser from dying of his wounds"—sometimes taking the loser to his own home where his wife could tend his adversary's wounds to assure his recovery (Grönfors, 1986:108-109). But the urbanization of modern Finland has widened the social distance between fellow Gypsies, and the ancient rules of the duel have withered away. Guns now enter the more distant conflicts, and sudden death is replacing the lesser injuries of the past (p. 109).

(6) In some tribal societies, male neighbors or other acquaintances may handle a conflict with a ritualized duel using only fists or hands. For example, the Yanomamö of Brazil and Venezuela exchange blows to the chest with closed fists or slaps to the side with the open hand until one falls or withdraws. Occasionally they exchange blows with long sticks, eight to 10 feet in length, but wield them only in a fashion that inflicts injuries no worse than lacerations of the scalp (Chagnon, 1977:113-119). The Eskimo of the American Arctic may have a head butting (during a song duel, a ritual exchange of insults similar to "the dozens" among some African-American young men), a buffeting (an exchange of "straight-armed blows on the side of the head, until one is felled and thereby vanquished"), or a wrestling match (Hoebel, 1954:92-99). Only more distant adversaries of these tribal people are likely to face a spear, ax, knife, arrow, or, if available, a gun (see, e.g., Chagnon, 1977:122-137).

(7) In medieval Europe, knights in armor and on horseback might duel to the death in a "trial by battle" with matched lances, axes, and swords, possibly ending with the loser's mutilated body dragged away to hang in disgrace from a gibbet—a hybrid of violent self-help and law inconceivable between friends or close relatives (e.g., Vale, 2000; see also Kaeuper, 1999, e.g., pp. 159-160). In the American South until the last half of the nineteenth century and in parts of Europe until the twentieth century, gentlemen such as military officers and large landowners might handle conflicts in highly ritualized duels with swords or pistols. Though acquainted at least by name, the duelists were seldom if ever closely connected (see, e.g., McAleer, 1994; Williams, 1980). Fighting in the rural South between strangers and distant acquaintances of lesser standing normally involved no bladed weapons or guns, but only fist-fighting and possibly biting, scratching, and the gouging of eyes (Gorn, 1985).

(8) Nonhuman violence also varies with the social geometry of conflict. Teeth provide chimpanzees with a potentially lethal weapon, for instance, but their biting varies inversely with the closeness

of their conflicts: Although wild chimpanzees who forage and sleep together "rarely" bite each other, they readily use their teeth to mutilate and kill a chimpanzee stranger who trespasses on their territory. Chimpanzees in zoos are somewhat intimate with all the others in their enclosure, and usually limit the use of their teeth to minor biting of an adversary's extremities, typically a finger or a foot (for references, see Black, 2000b:115).

Violence obeys geometrical principles not only in tribal and other traditional settings but throughout the social universe, including modern societies such as the United States. In low-income African-American neighborhoods of Philadelphia (where weapons are readily available and lethal violence is comparatively frequent), for instance, weapons such as knives and guns rarely enter conflicts between closely-connected young men, such as fictive kin (those "goin' for brothers" or "cousins") or members of the same gang. Instead, close adversaries typically fight only with their fists and avoid striking the head, kicking, or biting. Getting help from friends is also taboo: "The fights are characterized by elaborate rules, including 'no hitting in the face,' 'you got to use just your hands,' and 'no double-teaming'" (Anderson, 1999:89; see also pp. 90-91; Jankowski, 1991:144-145). In one small Georgia town, some African-American young men limit their fighting with friends to "30-second bouts" without weapons or help, encircled by other friends who loudly count to 30 before screaming "stop" (Phillips, 2003:700). African-American men elsewhere in Georgia and in Texas (interviewed in prison) say they would use weapons against close associates only to threaten—"as a scare tactic"—rather than to injure or kill: "Restraint is, in part, a product of relational ties. . . . Intimates brandish a weapon, but strangers shoot" (Phillips, 2003:700-701).

Whether fighting erupts at all reflects relational distance as well, including not only friendship but who lives in what neighborhood. In the small town of Clarksville, Georgia, for instance, the "east side" and "west side" are "rival neighborhoods" whose African-American young men will fight "over almost nothing." As one remarked, "The slightest little thing can start a fight between east and west" (p. 701). Note also that while more than 40 percent of modern American households have at least one gun (see Cook & Moore, 1999:278), household shootings are extremely rare compared to the frequency of household conflicts. Even the chronic but mild violence of children in an American day care center conforms to the closeness of their conflicts (Baumgartner, 1992b).

It is possible to discover the multidimensional structure of every kind of violence—whether a beating structure, fighting structure, dueling structure, vengeance structure, lynching structure, riot structure, terrorism structure, or warfare structure—each refined to predict and explain the various forms and degrees of violence that might occur (see, e.g., Baumgartner, 1992a; Black, 1990:74-79, 2004; Cooney, 1998; Senechal de la Roche, 1996; 2001; 2004b). The social geometry of violence in tribal and other earlier societies is easier to identify than that in a modern society such as the United States, but this is partly because the structure of modern conflict is so diverse—relationally, culturally, vertically, organizationally, and otherwise (for an overview of the dimensions of social space, see Black, 1976). The identification of violent structures in modern life is also difficult because social scientists seldom describe in detail the particular conflict structures where various degrees and forms of violence arise or do not arise at all (but see, e.g., Anderson, 1999; Baumgartner, 1988; Phillips, 2003). Strangely enough, therefore, we know more about the violent structures of the remote societies studied by anthropologists and historians than about those of the more familiar and accessible societies studied by sociologists and criminologists.

The Multidimensionality of Violent Structures

My earlier examples illustrate how relational and cultural distance increase violence in conflict structures. However, relational and cultural distance are not the only dimensions of conflict structures that predict and explain whether and how violence arises. For example, every conflict structure also has a vertical dimension. Each grievance has a social elevation (defined by the social status of the parties) and a social direction, whether downward (from a social superior), lateral (between equals), upward (from a social inferior), or both downward and upward at once.[3]

The illustrations of weapon use above largely pertain to lateral conflicts, but many conflict structures are stratified, one side above the other. For instance, the beating of women and children typically has a downward direction in a patriarchal family where the oldest male rules the household. Slave discipline likewise has a downward direction but, because it normally spans a greater vertical, relational, and cultural distance than family discipline, slaves face more severe forms of beating (such as whipping and caning) and possibly mutilation (such as amputation of ears or testicles) and crippling (such as cutting of the Achilles tendon) (for references and more examples, see Black, 1998:152). And some violence is upward, against superiors. Terrorism is an extreme form of upward and distant violence that might include mass killings with guns or explosives and conceivably chemical, biological, or nuclear weapons (see Black, 2004; Senechal de la Roche, 1996:101-122; 2004b).

Conflict structures also have an organizational dimension: Is the grievance between individuals on their own, or is it partly or wholly collective?[4] A riot always involves a crowd, for instance, and possibly one crowd against another. A group might lynch an individual, carry out a series of executions, or engage in terrorism (see Senechal de la Roche, 1996:102-105:2001; see also Black, 1990:75-78). If a group participates, what is its level of organization, resources, and degree of solidarity? If two groups have a conflict, what social distances separate them? Every conflict thus arises in a multidimensional structure, and the central theoretical problem is to specify the particular structure conducive to each form and degree of violence. Consider, for example, the social structure of the blood feud.

Blood Feuds and Gang Violence

The classic blood feud is a precise, extended, and open exchange of killings, usually one death at a time. Such feuds have long arisen in many traditional societies throughout the world and across history, including the Mediterranean region, the jungles of South America, and medieval Europe (for references, see Black, 1998:75; for examples of detailed studies, see Boehm, 1984; Miller, 1990; Wilson, 1988). They also appeared in rural America in earlier times—the Hatfield and McCoy feud of nineteenth-century Appalachia being the most famous example (e.g., Waller, 1988). Classic feuds typically entail the killing of adult men from different clans or clan-like units such as large homesteads that might include nonfamily members. The classic feud nonetheless remains relevant in the modern world, partly because youth gangs in the United States (and probably elsewhere) engage in significantly similar forms of violence.

The classic blood feud is distributed widely in physical space, but its distribution in social space is quite narrow. Everywhere it arises in a distinctive configuration of social distance and social closeness with the following characteristics: The participants are *groups* largely *equal* in size and other resources; *homogeneous* in ethnicity; functionally *similar* in their activities; mutually *independent* economically and otherwise; highly *solidary* in their internal relations; and isolated from one another by an *intermediate* degree of *relational distance*, close enough only for mutual recognition (Black, 1995:855, note 130). No classic blood feud anywhere in the world has had a conflict structure without these elements, which together comprise a *stable agglomeration of social islands* (see Black, 1990:75-78).[5]

Notably feud-like is the violence (known as gang warfare) of African-American and Hispanic groups in American cities such as Los Angeles, San Francisco, Chicago, and New York City (see, e.g., Cooney, 1998:74-83; Decker & Van Winkle, 1996:20-26, 179, 186; Klein, 1995; Sanders, 1994; Shakur, 1993). Gang violence is particularly frequent and destructive in Los Angeles, where police officials estimate that gangs account for between one-fourth and one-half of all intentional homicides (Booth, 2002; see also Maxson, 1999). Gang wars do not perfectly match classic blood feuds, partly because they sometimes deviate from the precise and open exchange of one life for another, and partly because the attacks are sometimes preemptive rather than reciprocal (for detailed examples of gang violence, see, e.g., Shakur, 1993). Even so, gang wars and classic blood feuds arise in significantly similar conflict structures.

The more a feud-like conflict deviates from the multidimensional structure outlined above, the less its violence will follow the classic pattern of a precise, extended, and open exchange of killings. Replace groups with individuals, for instance, and the conflict structure will produce only violent confrontations such as duels and fights in the name of honor. Narrow the social distances between the groups by increasing their interdependence and relational closeness, and violence will decline in its continuity and severity, shifting to unreciprocated vengeance, nonlethal fighting, or even peaceful forms of settlement. Increase the social distances, however, such as the relational, cultural, and vertical distance between the groups, and violence will become more indiscriminate and warlike. Such is true of the modern gang war, with its sometimes uneven and secretive exchange of killings and preemptive strikes reflecting a greater degree of social distance than separates the groups in a classic blood feud. The automobile, for example, extends gang conflicts across greater social distances by allowing contact with gang members identifiable only by their clothing, location in enemy territory, or other outward indicators. A plurality of gangs, including gangs of strangers who are enemies of allies, also increases the social distance among and between the gangs of a large city (see, generally, Decker & Van Winkle, 1996; Shakur, 1993). Yet gangs are still comparatively close in various respects, such as culturally, economically, and functionally. Greater social distances bring true warfare and other massacres, including the mass killings sometimes seen in inter-ethnic conflicts between unequal groups of total strangers.

Conclusion

We can specify the social geometry of every kind of violence with the same predictive and explanatory power as the multidimensional model of the classic blood feud. This broader inquiry has already begun, but its progress requires considerably more information about the conflict structures that have produced violence in the past, and that will do so in the future. How, for example, do violent structures differ from nonviolent structures? Which structures produce which kinds of violence, whether collective or individual, unilateral or bilateral, open or secretive, deadly or mild? Explore the social structure of conflict, and discover the answers. Violence obeys sociological laws, and those laws are geometrical.

Endnotes

[1]   This chapter employs the concepts of social control and conflict management interchangeably. Both refer to any process that defines or responds to deviant behavior or that handles a grievance. Neither, however, implies a process of influence, such as a change of conduct by the person or group subjected to the violence (see, e.g., Black, 1984).

[2]   Relational distance refers to the degree of participation in someone's or something's existence, including the frequency and scope of contact and the amount of information communicated (see Black, 1976:40-41). Cultural distance pertains to a difference in culture, such as differences in language, religion, and modes of dress (pp. 73-74).

[3]   The vertical dimension refers to the distribution of social status, such as wealth, integration, conventionality, authority, or respectability (see generally, Black, 1976).

[4]   The organizational dimension refers to a capacity for collective action (see Black, 1976:85). Any group has a degree of organization.

[5]   One author refers to American youth gangs as "islands in the street" (Jankowski, 1991). They are islands not only in relation to one another, but also in relation to other groups and institutions in their community, including their families (see, e.g., Decker & Van Winkle, 1996: Chapters 7-8; Shakur, 1993:69, 118).

Discussion Questions

1. Give an example of moralistic violence, and describe how it differs from violence that is not moralistic.

2. How does a pure sociology of violence differ from other explanations of violence?

3. Describe the social geometry of a conflict.

4. When is someone more likely to use a weapon?

5. How is gang violence similar to a blood feud?

References

Anderson, E. (1999). *Code of the Street: Decency, Violence, and the Moral Life of the Inner City*. New York: W.W. Norton.

Baumgartner, M.P. (2002). "*The Behavior of Law*, or How to Sociologize with a Hammer." Pp. 644-649 in A.V. Horwitz (ed.), "A Continuities Symposium on *The Behavior of Law*." In *Contemporary Sociology*, 31(November).

Baumgartner, M.P. (1992a). "Violent Networks: The Origins and Management of Domestic Conflict." In R.B. Felson and J. Tedeschi (eds.), *Violence and Aggression: The Social Interactionist Perspective*, pp. 209-231. Washington, DC: American Psychological Association.

Baumgartner, M.P. (1992b). "War and Peace in Early Childhood." In J. Tucker (ed.), *Virginia Review of Sociology*, Volume 1: *Law and Conflict Management*, pp. 1-38. Greenwich, CT: JAI.

Baumgartner, M.P. (1988). *The Moral Order of a Suburb*. New York: Oxford University Press.

Black, D. (2004). "The Geometry of Terrorism." Pp. 14-25 in R. Senechal de la Roche (ed.), "Theories of Terrorism: A Symposium" In *Sociological Theory*, 22(March).

Black, D. (2002). "Pure Sociology and the Geometry of Discovery." Pp. 668-674 in A.V. Horwitz (ed.), "A Continuities Symposium on *The Behavior of Law*." In *Contemporary Sociology*, 31(November).

Black, D. (2000a). "Dreams of Pure Sociology." *Sociological Theory*, 18:343-367.

Black, D. (2000b). "On the Origin of Morality." *Journal of Consciousness Studies*, 7:107-119.

Black, D. (2000c). "The Purification of Sociology." *Contemporary Sociology*, 29:704-709.

Black, D. (1998). *The Social Structure of Right and Wrong*, rev. ed. San Diego: Academic Press.

Black, D. (1995). "The Epistemology of Pure Sociology." In H.S. Erlanger (ed.), "Donald Black and the Sociology of Law," pp. 829-870. *Law & Social Inquiry* 20 (Summer).

Black, D. (1990). "The Elementary Forms of Conflict Management." In D. Black, *The Social Structure of Right and Wrong*, rev. ed., pp. 74-94. San Diego: Academic Press.

Black, D. (1984). "Social Control as a Dependent Variable." In D. Black, *The Social Structure of Right and Wrong*, rev. ed., pp. 1-26. San Diego: Academic Press.

Black, D. (1983). "Crime as Social Control." *American Sociological Review*, 48:34-45. Longer version reprinted in Black, 1998.

Black, D. (1976). *The Behavior of Law*. New York: Academic Press.

Boehm, C. (1987). *Blood Revenge: The Enactment and Management of Conflict in Montenegro and Other Tribal Societies*. Philadelphia: University of Pennsylvania Press.

Booth, W. (2002). "In the Streets of L.A., 14 Killings in Five Days." *Washington Post*, November 21:A2. Available at: www.washingtonpost.com/wp-dyn/articles/A17595-2002Nov20.html (November 25, 2002).

Burbank, V.K. (1994). *Fighting Women: Anger and Aggression in Aboriginal Australia*. Berkeley, CA: University of California Press.

Chagnon, N. A. (1977). *Yanomamö: The Fierce People*, 2nd ed. New York: Holt, Rinehart, and Winston.

Cook, P.J., and M.H. Moore (1999). "Guns, Gun Control, and Homicide." In M.D. Smith and M.A. Zahn (eds.), *Homicide: A Sourcebook of Social Research*, pp. 277-296. Thousand Oaks, CA: Sage.

Cooney, M. (1998). *Warriors and Peacemakers: How Third Parties Shape Violence*. New York: New York University Press.

Cooney, M., and S. Phillips. (2002)."Typologizing Violence: A Blackian Perspective." *International Journal of Sociology and Social Policy,* 22:75-108.

Decker, S.H., and B. Van Winkle (1996). *Life in the Gang: Family, Friends, and Violence*. Cambridge, UK: Cambridge University Press.

Evans-Pritchard, E.E. (1940). *The Nuer: A Description of the Modes of Livelihood and Political Institutions of a Nilotic People*. New York: Oxford University Press.

Fox, R. (1977). "The Inherent Rules of Violence." In P. Collett (ed.), *Social Rules and Social Behaviour*, pp. 132-149. Oxford: Basil Blackwell.

Gorn, E.J. (1985). "'Gouge and Bite, Pull Hair and Scratch': The Social Significance of Fighting in the Southern Backcountry." *American Historical Review*, 90:18-43.

Grönfors, M. (1986). "Social Control and Law in the Finnish Gypsy Community: Blood Feuding as a System of Justice." *Journal of Legal Pluralism and Unofficial Law*, 24:101-125.

Hoebel, E.A. (1954). *The Law of Primitive Man: A Study in Comparative Legal Dynamics*. Cambridge: Harvard University Press.

Horwitz, A.V. (ed.) (2002a). "A Continuities Symposium on *The Behavior of Law*." In *Contemporary Sociology*, 31(November).

Horwitz, A.V. (2002b). "Toward a New Science of Social Life: A Retrospective Examination of *The Behavior of Law*." Pp. 641-644 in A.V. Horwitz (ed.), "A Continuities Symposium on *The Behavior of Law*." In *Contemporary Sociology*, 31(November).

Jankowski, M.S. (1991). *Islands in the Street: Gangs and American Urban Society*. Berkeley: University of California Press.

Justice, P. (1991). "Going Through the Emotions: Passion, Violence, and 'Other-Control' among the Dou Donggo." *Ethos*, 19:288-312.

Kaeuper, R.W. (1999). *Chivalry and Violence in Medieval Europe*. Oxford, UK: Oxford University Press.

Klein, M.W. (1995). *The American Street Gang: Its Nature, Prevalence, and Control*. New York: Oxford University Press.

Maxson, C.L. (1999). "Gang Homicide: A Review and Extension of the Literature." In M.D. Smith and M.A. Zahn (eds.), *Homicide: A Sourcebook of Social Research*, pp. 239-254. Thousand Oaks, CA: Sage.

McAleer, K. (1994). *Dueling: The Cult of Honor in Fin-de-Siécle Germany*. Princeton, NJ: Princeton University Press.

Miller, W.I. (1990). *Bloodtaking and Peacemaking: Feud, Law, and Society in Saga Iceland*. Chicago: University of Chicago Press.

O'Donnell, P.D. (1975). *The Irish Faction Fighters of the 19th Century*. Dublin: Anvil Books.

Phillips, S. (2003). "The Social Structure of Vengeance: A Test of Black's Model." *Criminology*, 41:673-708.

Sanders, W. B. (1994). *Gangbangs and Drive-bys: Grounded Culture and Juvenile Gang Violence*. New York: Aldine de Gruyter.

Senechal de la Roche, R. (ed.) (2004a). "Theories of Terrorism: A Symposium." *Sociological Theory*, 22(March).

Senechal de la Roche, R. (2004b). "Toward a Scientific Theory of Terrorism." Pp. 1-4 in Senechal de la Roche (ed.), "Theories of Terrorism: A Symposium." In *Sociological Theory*, 22(March).

Senechal de la Roche, R. (2001). "Why Is Collective Violence Collective?" *Sociological Theory*, 19:126-144.

Senechal de la Roche, R. (1996). "Collective Violence as Social Control." *Sociological Forum*, 11:97-128.

Shakur, S. (AKA Monster Kody Scott) (1993). *Monster: The Autobiography of an L.A. Gang Member*. New York: Atlantic Monthly Press.

Smith, M.D., and M.A. Zahn (eds.) (1999). *Homicide: A Sourcebook of Social Research*. Thousand Oaks, CA: Sage.

Turnbull, C.M. (1972). *The Mountain People*. New York: Simon and Schuster.

Turnbull, C.M. (1965). *Wayward Servants: The Two Worlds of the African Pygmies*. Westport, CT: Greenwood Press, 1976.

Turnbull, C.M. (1961). *The Forest People*. New York: Simon and Schuster.

Vale, M. (2000). "Aristocratic Violence: Trial by Battle in the Later Middle Ages." In R.W. Kaeuper (ed.), *Violence in Medieval Society*, pp. 159-181. Woodbridge, UK: Boydell Press.

Waller, A.L. (1988). *Feud: Hatfields, McCoys, and Social Change in Appalachia, 1860-1900*. Chapel Hill, NC: University of North Carolina Press.

Williams, J.K. (1980). *Dueling in the Old South: Vignettes of Social History*. College Station, TX: Texas A & M University Press.

Wilson, S. (1988). *Feuding, Conflict and Banditry in Nineteenth-Century Corsica*. Cambridge, UK: Cambridge University Press.

Woodburn, J. (1979). "Minimal Politics: The Political Organization of the Hadza of North Tanzania." In W. Shack, A., and P.S Cohen (eds.), *Politics in Leadership: A Comparative Perspective*, pp. 244-266. Oxford, UK: Clarendon Press.

PART III

Applying Theory to Substance

Violence is violence, and we know it when we see. However, in social life it takes on a number of different forms. Graeme Newman tried to define violence and ended up instead identifying a number of common forms that it could take, "from political violence, through the violence of occupations, criminal violence, violence in the home, to the violence of those who are sick, and many other forms of violence" (1979:5). Similarly, Henry Brownstein looked at newspaper accounts of violence and found specific examples of the forms that violence could take, including "a gang killing, a natural disaster that destroyed property and lives, a collision that caused a death and destruction, an act of war, an act of terrorism, and a product being sold that is acknowledged to be responsible for death and illness" (2000:6). The point is that in social experience violence is a lot of different things.

Despite the fact that violence presents itself to us in a variety of ways, each of those ways includes certain characteristics that make it recognizable to us as violence. Therefore, it is possible to think about violence as a particular social phenomenon. That being the case, it is possible for a particular theory to explain violence adequately. It is also possible that different theories each contribute in part to our understanding of violence in one or more of its forms.

In the chapters in Part III of this book, researchers who have studied violence in general or in terms of one or more of its forms were asked to write about a particular form of violence. In each case, they were asked to apply the various theories of violence to the form of violence about which they were writing. For example, do the same theories that explain terrorism also explain hate violence? If we can explain lynchings, do we then have an explanation of youth violence? Are drugs related to violence in the same way intimate relationships are related to violence?

In the introductory chapter to this book we talked about the conceptual meaning of violence. In the chapters that follow we look at violence in more concrete terms. All of these chapters are about violence in the broadest sense, but each is about a particular social manifestation of violence. For the sake of clarity and comprehension, they are presented in a logical order. First are those that are primarily about interpersonal violence. Last are those that are primarily about collective violence, such as terrorism and hate crime. That is, they are presented as a continuum from examples of interpersonal violence to examples of collective violence.

The researchers who wrote about the application of theory to substantive areas of violence for this book were asked to include particular sections in their chapter. In each case, they were asked to include: a definition of the type of violence discussed in the chapter; a description of the state of the knowledge about that type of violence; which theory or theories best explain (or are most often used to explain) this type of violence; and how he or she personally explains this type of violence.

References

Brownstein, H.H. (2000). *The Social Reality of Violence and Violent Crime*. Boston: Allyn & Bacon.

Newman, G. (1979). *Understanding Violence*. New York: J.P. Lippincott.

CHAPTER 10

Intimate Partner Violence and Sexual Assault

Mary Ann Dutton

Violence violates basic human rights and results in increasing physical, emotional, social, and economic burdens for victims, their families, and society around the world. Violence victimization is also a major public health problem, as well as a criminal justice problem. This chapter addresses intimate partner violence (IPV) and sexual violence, prevalent forms of violence victimization. While both of these forms of violence also involve children as both direct and indirect victims, the focus of this chapter is primarily on intimate partner and sexual violence in adulthood. This chapter includes a discussion of definitions of intimate partner violence and sexual violence, current knowledge, existing theories, and a personal conceptual framework for understanding intimate partner violence and sexual assault.

Definition of the Types of Violence Discussed in This Chapter

Standard definitions of sexual violence and intimate partner violence have been adopted by the Etiology and Surveillance Branch, Division of Violence Prevention, National Center for Injury Prevention and Control at the Centers for Disease Control and Prevention.

> *Sexual violence* is a sex act completed or attempted against a victim's will or when a victim is unable to consent due to age, illness, disability, or the influence of alcohol or other drugs. It may involve actual or threatened physical force, use of guns or other weapons, coercion, intimidation, or pressure. Sexual violence also

includes intentional touching of the genitals, anus, groin, or breast against a victim's will or when a victim is unable to consent; and voyeurism, exposure to exhibitionism, or undesired exposure to pornography. The perpetrator of sexual violence may be a stranger, friend, family member, or intimate partner. (Basile & Saltzman, 2002).

Other terms used to describe sexual violence can include rape by a stranger, acquaintance rape, date rape, childhood sexual abuse, sexual molestation, marital rape, or rape by an intimate partner. Sexual violence is perpetrated against women, men, and children. Rape is committed against heterosexual, gay, lesbian, transgendered, and bisexual individuals. Rape occurs in the context of places that are recognized as risky (e.g., bars, unsafe neighborhoods), as well as those that are considered safe (e.g., dorm rooms, homes). Sexual violence is used against adults, older people, children, and infants. Sexual violence is also a tool of war and has recently been recognized as a war crime, as evidenced by recent convictions by an international tribunal at the Hague of three Bosnia Serbs of "crimes against humanity" for using "rape as an instrument of terror."

Intimate partner violence is a term that is specific to intimate relationships and is preferred to other terms, such as domestic violence or family violence, because the latter terms can refer to violence against elders or between other family members, including children.

> *Intimate partner violence*—or IPV—is actual or threatened physical or sexual violence or psychological and emotional abuse directed toward a spouse, ex-spouse, current or former boyfriend or girlfriend, or current or former dating partner. Intimate partners may be heterosexual or of the same sex. Some of the common terms used to describe intimate partner violence are domestic abuse, spouse abuse, courtship violence, battering, marital rape, and date rape (Saltzman, Fanslow, McMahon & Shelley, 1999; 2002).

The Centers for Disease Control and Prevention in *Intimate Partner Violence Surveillance: Uniform Definitions and Recommended Data Elements* (Saltzman, McMahon & Shelley, 1999, 2002) identified physical violence, sexual violence, threats of physical or sexual violence, stalking, and psychological/emotional abuse as five key forms of IPV. There is an overlap between intimate partner violence and sexual violence when the perpetrator/victim relationship is an intimate partner relationship. Sexual violence includes sexual victimization against an intimate partner, and intimate partner violence includes sexual assault.

Both sexual violence and intimate partner violence occur within a social, political, and economic context. Gender and race discrimination and economic poverty increase the risk for sexual and intimate partner violence victimization for women and reduce resources necessary for effective coping (United Nations, Office of the High Commissioner for Human Rights, 2001).

Description of the State of the Knowledge

This section reviews the current knowledge related to selected salient issues pertaining to intimate partner violence and sexual assault. These include: (1) prevalence, (2) social stigma, (3) a gender analysis, (4) the role of coercion, (5) adverse health and mental health outcomes, (6) profiles of victims and offenders, and (7) the role of childhood abuse.

Prevalence

Violence against women is a common occurrence. The National Violence Against Women Survey (Tjaden & Thoennes, 2000b) provides the most current and comprehensive data concerning intimate partner violence and sexual assault. This research found that each year, approximately 1.5 million women and 834,700 men experience sexual or physical assault from an intimate partner. Indeed, almost two-thirds of women who are raped, physically assaulted, or stalked in adulthood were victimized by a current or former intimate partner. Approximately one in five adolescent females 14 to 18 years of age reported an experience of physical or sexual violence by a dating partner (Silverman, Raj, Mucci & Hathaway, 2001). In a cross-national study of gay males and lesbians in Venezuela and the United States (Burke, Jordan & Owen, 2002), nearly two-thirds in each country reported experiencing some form of domestic violence.

One in six women and one in 33 men reported an attempted or completed rape during their lifetime. Among college women, 2.8 percent report experiencing either a completed or an attempted rape during the previous year (Fisher, Cullen & Turner, 2000), a figure that escalates to at least 12 percent over the course of a four-year college education. Sexual assault against women begins at an early age. Approximately 22 percent of women who are raped are victimized prior to the age of 12 years (Tjaden & Thoennes, 2000a).

Intimate partner homicide has declined in recent years for male victims, but not for female victims. Women comprise 62 percent of intimate partner homicide victims in the United States (Rennison & Welchans, 2000). The *Family Violence in Canada: Statistical Report 2001* (Trainor & Mihorean, 2001) reported that 28 percent of female domestic homicides are committed by ex-intimate partners, compared to 10 percent for male victims. Sexual homicides constitute less than one percent of the murders committed in the United States (Meloy, 2000).

IPV and Sexual Assault are Especially Stigmatizing Forms of Victimization

Violence victimization often involves a response to the victim from others, such as when a rape victim or battered woman obtains medical treatment from an emergency department, seeks support from her minister or rabbi, or talks to a friend. When others validate the atrocity of a rape or a beating, the victim can feel supported. However, others' responses are not always helpful. When others suggest that the victim may have been implicated in the assault, for example, because of her behavior (e.g., was intoxicated, dressed provocatively, started an argument), the victim can be left with feelings of blame—feeding her own doubts about what she could have done to avoid or stop the violence. Victim-blame (Cowan, 2000; Morry & Winkler, 2001; Nayak, 2000; Smith & Welchans, 2000; West & Wandrei, 2002) likely contributes to the feelings of stigma that many sexual assault and intimate partner violence victims feel. The stigma associated with being the victim of IPV or sexual assault (Mackey, Sereika, Weissfeld & Hacker, 1992), especially among some cultural groups (Preisser, 1999), adds to the complexity of the experience of violence victimization. It is more than enough to be beaten or raped; to be held responsible for its occurrence is adding insult to injury.

Victim blame can also contribute to healthcare providers' hesitancy to inquire about both victims' victimization (Nayak, 2000) and psychological well-being (Campbell, Sefl, Barnes, Ahrens, Wasco & Zaragoza-Diesfeld, 1999). When a healthcare professional averts his or her eyes instead of addressing the sexual assault or battering directly, the nonverbal communication can convey a negative meaning to the victim. Further, stigma may partially contribute to low rates of disclosure to legal authorities. Fewer than one-half of all rapes are reported to police, according to the National Crime Victimization Survey (U.S. Department of Justice, 2002).

Finally, victim-blaming and stigmatizing women also can contribute to problems in community efforts to hold offenders accountable. Portraying victims as provocative (in the case of intimate partner violence) or seductive (in the case of sexual assault) is commonly used by defense attorneys as a strategy in the trials of those charged with these crimes to persuade judges that the accused are not responsible for having committed a crime by having beaten or raped their victims. Even young girls and murdered wives have been blamed by judges for their role in their own victimization as a rationale for lenient sentencing decisions against their alleged perpetrators.

Gender is Important for Understanding IPV and Sexual Assault

A gender analysis is required to understand both IPV and sexual assault. Such an analysis elucidates gender differences in terms of the occurrence, patterns, and dynamics of both IPV and sexual assault. While some research indicates that men and women use IPV at similar rates (Straus & Gelles, 1990), other data suggests that IPV occurs more often against women (Tjaden & Thoennes, 2000b), suggesting complex gendered patterns of IPV. A recent meta-analysis found that while women use some forms of violence (e.g., hitting, slapping, shoving) more often, men reported greater use of more severe types (e.g., choke or strangle, beat up) (Archer, 2002). Indeed, females comprised three-fourths of the intimate partner homicide victims during 1998 (Rennison & Welchans, 2000).

A gender analysis of prevalence rates between men and women requires an analysis of the context in which violence or aggression is used. Several studies have demonstrated different motivations between men and women for the use of violence and aggression in intimate relationships. Motivations for women using violence against their intimate partner have been reported as predominately self-defense and retaliation, whereas the motivations of men have been reported as primarily for purposes of punishing their partners (Hamberger, Lohr, Bonge & Tolin, 1997; Jacobson, 1994; Jacobson, Gottman, Waltz & Rushe, 1994). Only women's violence was shown to escalate in response to their partners' violence, and only women reported fear during violent and nonviolent arguments (Jacobson, Gottman, Waltz & Rushe, 1994).

Gender plays a crucial role in understanding sexual assault and rape as well as IPV. Gender differences have been found in terms of attitudes toward both rape and victims of rape (Brown & King, 1998; Fischer, 1997; Pino & Meier, 1999; Schutte & Hosch, 1997); one meta-analysis found women overall more likely to vote for conviction of alleged rapists (Schutte & Hosch, 1997). Gender also plays a role in reporting and reasons for failing to report sexual assault and rape (Pino & Meier, 1999). Women report being raped more often than men (Pino & Meier, 1999; Tjaden & Thoennes, 2000b), as well as having more associated negative outcomes following a rape (Tjaden & Thoennes, 2000b).

The Dynamic of Coercion Plays a Pivotal Role in Understanding IPV and Sexual Assault

Some forms of IPV are distinct events that signal discrete episodes (e.g., beating or rape) while other types of IPV (e.g., verbal abuse or humiliation, controlling behavior) occur as more ongoing or continuous behaviors. Identifying these discrete episodes of isolated violent incidents, while important, fails to capture the totality of the IPV experience, including the coercive control that pervades the couples relationship (Dutton, Goodman & Bennett, 1999; Jacobson, Gottman, Gortner, Berns & Shortt, 1996; Marshall, 1996; Sackett & Saunders, 1999).

It is generally accepted that coercive control defines the dynamic of IPV (Johnson & Ferraro, 2000; Pence, 2002; Pence & Paymar, 1993). It is impossible to appreciate the complexity of IPV without understanding that coercive control is the glue that connects discrete episodes of violence. Indeed, coercion is a process in which abusers both rely on prior violence to set the stage for the opportunity to coerce and use acute incidents of abuse to punctuate their retaliation for noncompliance with their demands (Dutton & Goodman, in press).

Adverse Health and Mental Health Outcomes Result from Violence Exposure

A significant body of research has documented the prevalence and extent of adverse outcomes associated with exposure to IPV, especially health and mental health problems (Brush, 2000; Campbell & Soeken, 1999a; 1999b; Dutton, Goodman & Bennett, 1999; Huth-Bocks, Levendosky & Bogat, 2002; Levendosky, 1995; Levendosky & Graham-Bermann, 2000; 2001; Street & Arias, 2001; Sullivan, Bybee & Allen, 2002; Sutherland, Bybee & Sullivan, 2002; Thompson, Kaslow & Kingree, 2002; Torres & Han, 2000; Woods, 2000). Similarly, adverse health and mental health outcomes have been associated with rape (Dunmore, Clark & Ehlers, 2001; Kalichman, Sikkema, DiFonzo, Luke & Austin, 2002; Koss, Figueredo & Prince, 2002; Nishith, Resick & Mueser, 2001; Ullman & Brecklin, 2002a; 2002b). Multiple assaults, life threatening during the assault, prior history of victimization, and lack of social support are consistent predictors of worse outcomes—given victimization exposure.

There is No Single Profile of Victims or Perpetrators

There is no single profile of an IPV victim, notwithstanding the construct of "battered woman syndrome" and "rape trauma syndrome," which has proliferated in the courtroom (U.S. Department of Justice and U.S. Department of Health and Human Services, 1996). Researchers have begun to identify differences in patterns of strategic (Burke, Gielen, McDonnell, O'Campo & Maman, 2001; Goodman, Dutton, Weinfurt & Cook, 2003) and traumatic response to IPV, in part based on differences in the configurations of IPV (Dutton, Kaltman & Goodman, 2002). Further, multiple factors—including attachment, economic resources, social support, and fear—have been used to explain IPV victims' remaining in and returning to abusive relationships (Barnett, 2001; Burke, Gielen, McDonnell, O'Campo & Maman, 2001; Choice & Lamke, 1997; Fleury, Sullivan & Bybee, 2000; Griffing, Ragin, Sage, Madry, Bingham & Primm, 2002; Johnson, 1992; Patzel, 2001; Rhodes & McKenzie, 1998; Tan, Basta, Sullivan & Davidson, 1995; Truman-Schram, Cann, Calhoun & Vanwallendael, 2000; Wuest & Merritt-Gray, 1999).

There is also no single profile of an IPV perpetrator. Numerous researchers have identified typologies of male IPV perpetrators based on a wide range of factors, including personality, patterns of violence, childhood characteristics, mental health, and substance use (Hamberger, Lohr, Bonge & Tolin, 1996; 1997; Holtzworth-Munroe, 2000; Holtzworth-Munroe, Meehan, Herron, Rehman & Stuart, 2000; Jacobson, Gottman & Shortt, 1995; Waltz, Babcock, Jacobson & Gottman, 2000). Although specific factors may be associated with an increased prevalence or risk of recurrent IPV, IPV occurs among a wide range of types of men. Holtzworth-Munroe's typology suggests at least two continua relevant for characterizing male abusers: antisocial and borderline, a finding similar to earlier research (Gondolf, 1988). No similar typologies have been offered for female IPV perpetrators.

Childhood Abuse Increases the Risk for Adulthood IPV and Sexual Assault

A prior history of childhood abuse has important implications for intimate partner violence and sexual assault in later life. A history of childhood abuse increases the risk for adult perpetration of domestic violence and sexual assault (Kunitz, Levy, McCloskey & Gabriel, 1998; Widom & Ames, 1994). This perpetuation of violence and abuse from generation to generation suggests the critical importance of violence prevention and early intervention. Childhood sexual abuse also increases the risk for sexual revictimization during adulthood (Cloitre, 1998; Nelson, Heath, Madden, Cooper, Dinwiddie, Bucholz, Glowinski, McLaughlin, Dunne, Statham & Martin, 2002). The risk of intimate partner violence victimization also increases when the individual has been exposed to childhood abuse, either as a victim directly or by witnessing abuse toward the child's mother (Ehrensaft, Cohen, Brown, Smailes, Chen & Johnson, 2003; Whitfield, Anda, Dube & Felitti, 2003). These findings clearly point to the need for prevention that would reduce not only the risk of childhood abuse and exposure to intimate partner violence, but also the risk of subsequent adolescent and adulthood revictimization given such exposure.

Which Theory or Theories Best Explain this Type of Violence

There is an abundance of theories that have been developed to describe both intimate partner violence and sexual assault. These theories span the gamut and include those that focus on factors at the individual, family, and social/cultural levels (McQuestion, 2003). However, no theory that focuses on a single cause adequately explains either sexual assault or domestic violence (Koss, 2003). Thus, the most adequate theoretical perspective is one that integrates the many risk factors for violent offending. This approach has been referred to as an ecological perspective (Bronfenbrenner, 1986, 1992). An ecological model of intimate partner violence or sexual assault is not a theory *per se*, but a framework within which to organize risk factors, most of which are associated with a specific theoretical foundation. Generally, an ecological model can be described as a collection of risk factors, imbedded in concentric spheres, that exert influence on the outcome of violent offending (see Figure 10.1). Each of these domains exerts influence directly, and in combination with each other. One advantage of an ecological framework as a perspective from which to derive an understanding of intimate partner and sexual violence is that this approach allows for an integration of multiple influences on behavior (Bronfenbrenner, 1992), each derived from its own theoretical construction, thus avoiding simplistic, single-factor explanations.

Figure 10.1
General Ecological Model of Factors Explaining
Intimate Partner Violence and Sexual Assault

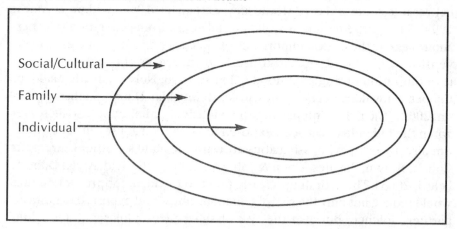

Factors referred to as the social or cultural level of the ecological model fall within a social sanctioning of violence against women, referred to as feminist theories of intimate partner and sexual violence (Dobash & Dobash, 1998; Schechter, 1996; Schechter & Gary, 1988). Family-level factors in the social ecology have emphasized the influence of dysfunctional family systems that involve exposing children to violence (Ehrensaft, Cohen, Brown, Smailes, Chen & Johnson, 2003; Whitfield, Anda, Dube & Felitti, 2003), childhood physical and sexual abuse and neglect (Widom & Ames, 1994), and parental alcoholism or other substance abuse. Individual factors that have been incorporated into an ecological model of intimate partner and sexual violence include "sexual proprietariness" or entitlement as a motivational explanation for male violence against women (Wilson & Daly, 1995, 1998), substance abuse (Flett & Hewitt, 2002; White, Gondolf, Robertson, Goodwin & Caraveo, 2002), and psychopathology, including personality disorder or traumatic sequelae of childhood abuse (Dutton, 1998; Dutton & Holtzworth-Munroe, 1997; White, Gondolf, Robertson, Goodwin & Caraveo, 2002). Current debate about theories of "abusive personality" for intimate partner violence perpetrators exists (Dutton, 2003; Gondolf, 1999; 2003).

In sum, an ecological model offers the most comprehensive and sophisticated integrative theoretical approach to understanding intimate partner and sexual violence. It provides for the inclusion of factors at all levels of the ecology (social, family, individual), and thus offers a more adequate characterization of the many influences that account for the use of violence.

Personal Perspective on Theories of Intimate Partner Violence and Sexual Assault

Notwithstanding the usefulness of the ecological model of intimate partner and sexual violence, there are current limitations to this approach. The most important of these shortcomings is the lack of theoretical integration of the levels within the social ecology in terms of how the interaction between factors across or within levels influences violence perpetration. The factors described within an ecological model of intimate partner or sexual violence are routinely studied in isolation, without consideration of the moderating or mediating effects of the other factors in the model. The complexity of the ecological model makes this task a methodological and statistical challenge. Nevertheless, there is a need to understand not only how ecological factors operate individually, but how they operate in the context of other factors. For example, is the effect merely additive (i.e., more factors leads to more risk of engaging in intimate partner or sexual violence), or perhaps, is it synergistic (i.e., the presence of one factor enhances the effect of another factor)?

A second limitation of current ecological models of intimate partner and sexual violence models is that they tend to focus solely on risk factors and exclude protective influences. An even more sophisticated approach to disentangling the influences that contribute to perpetration would be to include protective factors that may minimize the effects of identified risk factors. Such an approach is particularly important for understanding why some individuals with many risk factors present nonetheless do not emerge as violent perpetrators. Further, such information would provide valuable insights for the development of effective prevention and intervention strategies.

While the ecological model of intimate partner and sexual violence offers a perspective that can accommodate the complexities of the social context in which such violence is perpetrated, there remains a need for further theoretical development in this area. More complete theoretical model building followed by empirical testing and then theoretical refinement is needed to propel the field of intimate partner violence and sexual assault forward toward more effective solutions.

Discussion Questions

1. According to the Centers for Disease Control and Prevention, does sexual violence include attempts to touch someone's breast or groin against their will?

2. What is the prevalence of physical or sexual assault from a dating partner?

3. Which risk factors predict worse adverse health outcomes?

4. A childhood history of abuse increases the risk for what behavior? Is there a single psychological profile?

References

Archer, J. (2002). "Sex Differences in Physically Aggressive Acts between Heterosexual Partners: A Meta-Analytic Review." *Aggression & Violent Behavior,* 7(4):313-351.

Barnett, O.W. (2001). "Why Battered Women Do Not Leave, Part 2: External Inhibiting Factors—Social Support and Internal Inhibiting Factors." *Trauma Violence & Abuse,* 2(1):3-35.

Basile, K.C., and L.E. Saltzman (2002). *Sexual Violence Surveillance: Uniform Definitions and Recommended Data Elements.* Atlanta: Centers for Disease Control and Prevention.

Bronfenbrenner, U. (1992). "Ecological Systems Theory." In *Six Theories of Child Development: Revised Formulations and Current Issues,* pp. 187-249. London, UK: Jessica Kingsley.

Bronfenbrenner, U. (1986). "Ecology of the Family as a Context for Human Development: Research Perspectives." *Developmental Psychology,* 22(6):723-742.

Brown, J., and J. King (1998). "Gender Differences in Police Officers Attitudes Towards Rape; Results of an Exploratory Study." *Psychology, Crime and Law,* 4(4):265-279.

Brush, L.D. (2000). "Battering, Traumatic Stress, and Welfare-to-Work Transition." *Violence Against Women,* 6(10):1039-1065.

Burke, J.G., A.C. Gielen, K.A. McDonnell, P. O'Campo, and S. Maman (2001). "The Process of Ending Abuse in Intimate Relationships: A Qualitative Exploration of the Transtheoretical Model." *Violence Against Women,* 7(10):1144-1163.

Burke, T.W., M.L. Jordan, and S.S. Owen (2002). "Cross-National Comparison of Gay and Lesbian Domestic Violence." *Journal of Contemporary Criminal Justice,* 18(3):231-257.

Campbell, J.C., and K.L. Soeken (1999a). "Forced Sex and Intimate Partner Violence: Effects on Women's Risk and Women's Health." *Violence Against Women,* 5(9):1017-1035.

Campbell, J.C., and K.L Soeken. (1999b). "Women's Responses to Battering: A Test of the Model." *Research in Nursing & Health,* 22(1):49-58.

Campbell, R., T. Sefl, H.E. Barnes, C.E. Ahrens, S.M. Wasco, and Y. Zaragoza-Diesfeld (1999). "Community Services for Rape Survivors: Enhancing Psychological Well-Being or Increasing Trauma?" *Journal of Consulting & Clinical Psychology,* 67(6):847-858.

Choice, P., and L.K. Lamke (1997). "A Conceptual Approach to Understanding Abused Women's Stay/Leave Decisions." *Journal of Family Issues,* 18(3):290-314.

Cloitre, M. (1998). Sexual Revictimization: Risk Factors and Prevention. In *Cognitive-Behavioral Therapies for Trauma,* pp. 278-304. New York: Guilford Press.

Cowan, G. (2000). "Women's Hostility Toward Women and Rape and Sexual Harassment Myths." *Violence Against Women,* 6(3):238-246.

Dobash, R.E., and R.P. Dobash (1998). *Rethinking Violence Against Women.* Thousand Oaks, CA: Sage.

Dunmore, E., D.M. Clark, and A. Ehlers (2001). "A Prospective Investigation of the Role of Cognitive Factors in Persistent Posttraumatic Stress Disorder (PTSD) after Physical or Sexual Assault." *Behaviour Research & Therapy,* 39(9):1063-1084.

Dutton, D. (2003). "MCMI Results for Batterers: A Response to Gondolf." *Journal of Family Violence,* 18(4):253-255.

Dutton, D.G. (1998). *The Abusive Personality.* New York: Guilford Press.

Dutton, D.G., and A. Holtzworth-Munroe (1997). "The Role of Early Trauma in Males Who Assault Their Wives." In *Developmental Perspectives on Trauma: Theory, Research, and Intervention,* pp. 379-401. Rochester, NY: University of Rochester Press.

Dutton, M.A., and L.A. Goodman (forthcoming). "Coercive Control in Intimate Partner Relationships." *Psychology of Women Quarterly.*

Dutton, M.A., L.A. Goodman, and L. Bennett (1999). "Court-Involved Battered Women's Responses to Violence: The Role of Psychological, Physical, and Sexual Abuse." *Violence & Victims,* 14(1):89-104.

Dutton, M.A., S. Kaltman, and L.A. Goodman (2002). *Configuration of Types of Intimate Partner Violence (IPV).* Paper presented at the annual meeting of the International Society for Traumatic Stress Studies, Baltimore, MD.

Ehrensaft, M.K., P. Cohen, J. Brown, E. Smailes, H. Chen, and J.G. Johnson (2003). "Intergenerational Transmission of Partner Violence: A 20-Year Prospective Study." *Journal of Consulting & Clinical Psychology,* 71(4):741-753.

Fischer, G.J. (1997). "Gender Effects on Individual Verdicts and on Mock Jury Verdicts in a Simulated Acquaintance Rape Trial." *Sex Roles,* 36(7-8):491-501.

Fisher, B., F.T. Cullen, and M.G. Turner (2000). *The Sexual Victimization of College Women* (No. NIJ 182369). Washington, DC: National Institute of Justice, U.S. Department of Justice.

Flett, G.L., and P.L. Hewitt (2002). "Personality Factors and Substance Abuse in Relationship Violence and Child Abuse: A Review and Theoretical Analysis." In *The Violence and Addiction Equation: Theoretical and Clinical Issues in Substance Abuse and Relationship Violence,* pp. 64-97. New York: Brunner-Routledge.

Fleury, R.E., C.M. Sullivan, and D.I. Bybee (2000). "When Ending the Relationship Does Not End the Violence: Women's Experiences of Violence by Former Partners." *Violence Against Women,* 6(12):1363-1383.

Gondolf, E.W. (2003). "MCMI Results for Batterers: Gondolf Replies to Dutton's Response." *Journal of Family Violence,* 18(6):387-389.

Gondolf, E.W. (1999). "MCMI-III Results for Batterer Program Participants in Four Cities: Less 'Pathological' than Expected." *Journal of Family Violence,* 14(1):1-17.

Gondolf, E.W. (1988). "Who Are Those Guys? Toward a Behavioral Typology of Batterers." *Violence & Victims,* 3(3):187-203.

Goodman, L.A., M.A. Dutton, K. Weinfurt, and S. Cook (2003). "The Intimate Partner Violence Strategies Index: Development and Application." *Violence Against Women,* 9(2):163-186.

Griffing, S., D.F. Ragin, R.E. Sage, L. Madry, L.E. Bingham, and B.J. Primm (2002). "Domestic Violence Survivors' Self-Identified Reasons for Returning to Abusive Relationships." *Journal of Interpersonal Violence,* 17(3):306-319.

Hamberger, L.K., J.M. Lohr, D. Bonge, and D.F. Tolin (1997). "An Empirical Classification of Motivations for Domestic Violence." *Violence Against Women,* 3(4):401-423.

Hamberger, L.K., J.M. Lohr, D. Bonge, and D.F. Tolin (1996). "A Large Sample Empirical Typology of Male Spouse Abusers and Its Relationship to Dimensions of Abuse." *Violence & Victims,* 11(4):277-292.

Holtzworth-Munroe, A. (2000). "A Typology of Men Who Are Violent Toward Their Female Partners: Making Sense of the Heterogeneity in Husband Violence." *Current Directions in Psychological Science,* 9(4):140-143.

Holtzworth-Munroe, A., J.C. Meehan, K. Herron, U. Rehman, and G.L. Stuart (2000). "Testing the Holtzworth-Munroe and Stuart (1994) Batterer Typology." *Journal of Consulting and Clinical Psychology,* 68(6):1000-1019.

Huth-Bocks, A.C., A.A. Levendosky, and G.A. Bogat (2002). "The Effects of Domestic Violence During Pregnancy on Maternal and Infant Health." *Violence & Victims,* 17(2):169-185.

Jacobson, N.S. (1994). "Contextualism Is Dead: Long Live Contextualism." *Family Process,* 33(1):97-100.

Jacobson, N.S., J.M. Gottman, E. Gortner, S. Berns, and J.W. Shortt (1996). "Psychological Factors in the Longitudinal Course of Battering: When Do the Couples Split Up? When Does the Abuse Decrease?" *Violence & Victims,* 11(4):371-392.

Jacobson, N.S., J.M. Gottman, and J.W. Shortt (1995). "The Distinction Between Type 1 and Type 2 Batterers—Further Considerations: Reply to Ornduff et al. (1995), Margolin et al. (1995), and Walker (1995)." *Journal of Family Psychology,* 9(3):272-279.

Jacobson, N.S., J.M. Gottman, J. Waltz, and R. Rushe (1994). "Affect, Verbal Content, and Psychophysiology in the Arguments of Couples with a Violent Husband." *Journal of Consulting and Clinical Psychology,* 62(5):982-988.

Johnson, I.M. (1992). "Economic, Situational, and Psychological Correlates of the Decision-Making Process of Battered Women." *Families in Society,* 73(3):168-176.

Johnson, M.P., and K.J. Ferraro (2000). "Research on Domestic Violence in the 1990s: Making Distinctions." *Journal of Marriage and the Family,* 62(4):948-963.

Kalichman, S.C., K.J. Sikkema, K. DiFonzo, W. Luke, and J. Austin (2002). "Emotional Adjustment in Survivors of Sexual Assault Living with HIV-AIDS." *Journal of Traumatic Stress,* 15(4):289-296.

Koss, M.P. (2003). "Evolutionary Models of Why Men Rape: Acknowledging the Complexities." In *Evolution, Gender, and Rape,* pp. 191-205. Cambridge, MA: MIT Press.

Koss, M.P., A.J. Figueredo, and R.J. Prince (2002). "Cognitive Mediation of Rape's Mental, Physical and Social Health Impact: Tests of Four Models in Cross-Sectional Data." *Journal of Consulting and Clinical Psychology,* 70(4):926-941.

Kunitz, S.J., J.E. Levy, J. McCloskey, and K.R. Gabriel (1998). "Alcohol Dependence and Domestic Violence as Sequelae of Abuse and Conduct Disorder in Childhood." *Child Abuse and Neglect,* 22(11):1079-1091.

Levendosky, A.A. (1995). *Parenting in Battered Women: The Effects of Domestic Violence on Women and Children.* Unpublished manuscript. University of Michigan.

Levendosky, A.A., and S.A. Graham-Bermann (2001). "Parenting in Battered Women: The Effects of Domestic Violence on Women and Their Children." *Journal of Family Violence,* 16:171-192.

Levendosky, A.A., and S.A. Graham-Bermann (2000). "Trauma and Parenting in Battered Women: An Addition to an Ecological Model of Parenting." *Journal of Aggression, Maltreatment & Trauma,* 3(1):25-35.

Mackey, T., S.M. Sereika, L.A. Weissfeld, and S.S. Hacker (1992). "Factors Associated with Long-Term Depressive Symptoms of Sexual Assault Victims." *Archives of Psychiatric Nursing,* 6(1):10-25.

Marshall, L.L. (1996). "Psychological Abuse of Women: Six Distinct Clusters." *Journal of Family Violence,* 11(4):379-409.

McQuestion, M.J. (2003). "Endogenous Social Effects on Intimate Partner Violence in Colombia." *Social Science Research,* 32(2):335-345.

Meloy, J.R. (2000). "The Nature and Dynamics of Sexual Homicide: An Integrative Review." *Aggression and Violent Behavior,* 5(1):1-22.

Morry, M.M., and E. Winkler (2001). "Student Acceptance and Expectation of Sexual Assault." *Canadian Journal of Behavioural Science,* 33(3):188-192.

Nayak, M.B. (2000). "Factors Influencing Hesitancy in Medical Students to Assess History of Victimization in Patients." *Journal of Interpersonal Violence,* 15(2):123-133.

Nelson, E.C., A.C. Heath, P.A.F. Madden, M.L. Cooper, S.H. Dinwiddie, K.K. Bucholz, A. Glowin-ski, T. McLaughlin, M.P. Dunne, D.J. Statham, and N.G. Martin (2002). "Association Between Self-Reported Childhood Sexual Abuse and Adverse Psychosocial Outcomes: Results from a Twin Study." *Archives of General Psychiatry,* 59(2):139-145.

Nishith, P., P.A. Resick, and K.T. Mueser (2001). "Sleep Difficulties and Alcohol Use Motives in Female Rape Victims with Posttraumatic Stress Disorder." *Journal of Traumatic Stress,* 14(3):469-479.

Patzel, B. (2001). "Women's Use of Resources in Leaving Abusive Relationships: A Natural-istic Inquiry." *Issues in Mental Health Nursing,* 22(8):729-747.

Pence, E. (2002). "The Duluth Domestic Abuse Intervention Project." In E. Aldarondo and F. Mederos (eds.), *Programs for Men Who Batter: Intervention and Prevention Strate-gies in a Diverse Society,* pp. 6.1–6.46. Kingston, NJ: Civic Research Institute.

Pence, E., and M. Paymar (1993). *Education Groups for Men Who Batter: The Duluth Model.* New York: Springer.

Pino, N.W., and R.F. Meier (1999). "Gender Differences in Rape Reporting." *Sex Roles,* 40(11-12):979-990.

Preisser, A.B. (1999). "Domestic Violence in South Asian Communities in America: Advocacy and Intervention." *Violence Against Women,* 5(6):684-699.

Rennison, C.M., and S. Welchans (2000). *Bureau of Justice Statistics, Special Report: Inti-mate Partner Violence.* Available at: www.ojp.usdoj.gov/bjs/

Rennison, C.M., and S. Welchans (May 2000). *Intimate Partner Violence.* Washington, DC: U.S. Department of Justice, Office of Justice Programs.

Rhodes, N.R., and E.B. McKenzie (1998). "Why Do Battered Women Stay? Three Decades of Research." *Aggression and Violent Behavior,* 3(4):391-406.

Sackett, L.A., and D.G. Saunders (1999). "The Impact of Different Forms of Psychological Abuse on Battered Women." *Violence & Victims,* 14(1):105-117.

Saltzman, L.E., J.L. Fanslow, P.M. McMahon, and G.A. Shelley (2002). *Intimate Partner Vio-lence Surveillance: Uniform Definitions and Recommended Data Elements, Ver-sion 1.* Atlanta: Centers for Disease Control and Prevention, National Center for Injury Prevention and Control, Division of Violence Prevention. First printing 1999.

Schechter, S. (1996). "The Battered Women's Movement in the United States: New Directions for Institutional Reform." In *Future Interventions with Battered Women and Their Fam-ilies,* pp. 53-66. Thousand Oaks, CA: Sage.

Schechter, S., and L.T. Gary (1988). "A Framework for Understanding and Empowering Bat-tered Women." In *Abuse and Victimization Across the Life Span,* pp. 240-253. Baltimore: Johns Hopkins University Press.

Schutte, J.W., and H.M. Hosch (1997). "Gender Differences in Sexual Assault Verdicts: A Meta-Analysis." *Journal of Social Behavior & Personality,* 12(3):759-772.

Silverman, J.G., A. Raj, L.A. Mucci, and J.E. Hathaway (2001). "Dating Violence Against Ado-lescent Girls and Associated Substance Use, Unhealthy Weight Control, Sexual Risk Behav-ior, Pregnancy, and Suicidality." *JAMA: Journal of the American Medical Association,* 286(5):572-579.

Smith, P., and S. Welchans (2000). "Peer Education: Does Focusing on Male Responsibility Change Sexual Assault Attitudes?" *Violence Against Women,* 6(11):1255-1268.

Straus, M., and R. Gelles (1990). *Violence in American Families: Risk Factors and Adaptations to Violence in 8,145 Families*. New Brunswick, NJ: Transaction.

Street, A.E., and I. Arias (2001). "Psychological Abuse and Posttraumatic Stress Disorder in Battered Women: Examining the Roles of Shame and Guilt." *Violence & Victims,* 16(1):65-78.

Sullivan, C.M., D.I. Bybee, and N.E. Allen (2002). "Findings From a Community-Based Program for Battered Women and Their Children." *Journal of Interpersonal Violence,* 17(9):915-936.

Sutherland, C.A., D.I. Bybee, and C.M. Sullivan (2002). "Beyond Bruises and Broken Bones: The Joint Effects of Stress and Injuries on Battered Women's Health." *American Journal of Community Psychology,* 30(5):609-636.

Tan, C., J. Basta, C.M. Sullivan, and W.S. Davidson (1995). "The Role of Social Support in the Lives of Women Exiting Domestic Violence Shelters: An Experimental Study." *Journal of Interpersonal Violence,* 10(4):437-451.

Thompson, M.P., N.J. Kaslow, and J.B. Kingree (2002). "Risk Factors for Suicide Attempts Among African American Women Experiencing Recent Intimate Partner Violence." *Violence & Victims,* 17(3):283-295.

Tjaden, P., and N. Thoennes (2000a). *Final Report of the Prevalence, Incidence, and Consequences of Violence Against Women*. Washington, DC: National Institute of Justice and Centers for Disease Control and Prevention.

Tjaden, P., and N. Thoennes (2000b). "Prevalence and Consequences of Male-to-Female and Female-to-Male Intimate Partner Violence as Measured by the National Violence Against Women Survey." *Violence Against Women,* 6(2):142-161.

Torres, S., and H.R. Han (2000). "Psychological Distress in Non-Hispanic White and Hispanic Abused Women." *Archives of Psychiatric Nursing,* 14(1):19-29.

Trainor, C., and K. Mihorean (2001). *Family Violence in Canada: A Statistical Profile 2001* (No. 85-224-XIE). Ottawa: Minister of Industry.

Truman-Schram, D.M., A. Cann, L. Calhoun, and L. Vanwallendael (2000). "Leaving an Abusive Dating Relationship: An Investment Model Comparison of Women Who Stay versus Women Who Leave." *Journal of Social and Clinical Psychology,* 19(2):161-183.

United Nations, Office of the High Commissioner for Human Rights (2001). *Gender Dimensions of Racial Discrimination*. Geneva: United Nations. Available at: www.unhchr.ch/pdf/wcargender.pdf

Ullman, S.E., and L.R. Brecklin (2002a). "Sexual Assault History and Suicidal Behavior in a National Sample of Women." *Suicide & Life-Threatening Behavior,* 32(2):117-130.

Ullman, S.E., and L.R. Brecklin (2002b). "Sexual Assault History, PTSD, and Mental Health Service Seeking in a National Sample of Women." *Journal of Community Psychology,* 30(3):261-279.

U.S. Department of Justice (2002). *Criminal Victimization in the United States, 2002 (NCJ 200561)*. Washington, DC: U.S. Department of Justice, Bureau of Justice Statistics.

U.S. Department of Justice and U.S. Department of Health and Human Services (1996). *The Validity and Use of Evidence Concerning Battering and Its Effects in Criminal Trials* (NCJ No. 160972). Washington, DC: U.S. Department of Justice and U.S. Department of Health and Human Services.

Waltz, J., J.C. Babcock, N.S. Jacobson, and J.M. Gottman (2000). "Testing a Typology of Batterers." *Journal of Consulting and Clinical Psychology,* 68(4):658-669.

West, A., and M.L. Wandrei (2002). "Intimate Partner Violence: A Model for Predicting Interventions by Informal Helpers." *Journal of Interpersonal Violence,* 17(9):972-986.

White, R.J., E.W. Gondolf, D.U. Robertson, B.J. Goodwin, and L.E. Caraveo (2002). "Extent and Characteristics of Woman Batterers among Federal Inmates." *International Journal of Offender Therapy and Comparative Criminology,* 46(4):412-426.

Whitfield, C.L., R.F. Anda, S.R. Dube, and V.J. Felitti (2003). "Violent Childhood Experiences and the Risk of Intimate Partner Violence in Adults: Assessment in a Large Health Maintenance Organization." *Journal of Interpersonal Violence,* 18(2):166-185.

Widom, C.S., and M.A. Ames (1994). "Criminal Consequences of Childhood Sexual Victimization." *Child Abuse and Neglect,* 18(4):303-318.

Wilson, M., and M. Daly (1995). "An Evolutionary Psychological Perspective on Male Sexual Proprietariness and Violence Against Wives." In *Interpersonal Violent Behaviors: Social and Cultural Aspects*, pp. 109-133. New York: Springer.

Wilson, M., and M. Daly (1998). "Lethal and Nonlethal Violence Against Wives and the Evolutionary Psychology of Male Sexual Proprietariness." In *Rethinking Violence Against Women*, pp. 199-230. Thousand Oaks, CA: Sage.

Woods, S.J. (2000). "Prevalence and Patterns of Posttraumatic Stress Disorder in Abused and Postabused Women." *Issues in Mental Health Nursing,* 21(3):309-324.

Wuest, J., and M. Merritt-Gray (1999). "Not Going Back: Sustaining the Separation in the Process of Leaving Abusive Relationships." *Violence Against Women,* 5(2):110-133.

CHAPTER 11

Youth Violence: An Overview

Finn-Aage Esbensen

Definition of Youth Violence

The study of American youth violence is inexorably linked with the study of youth gangs. Early research by the Chicago School, as well as theoretical statements of the 1950s and 1960s (e.g., Cloward & Ohlin, 1960; Cohen, 1955; Miller, 1958; Short & Strodtbeck, 1965), sought to explain male youth group offending. Given the well established empirical relationship between youth violence and gang membership, this chapter continues the tradition of jointly discussing these two phenomena.

It is important to place youth violence in historical and comparative perspective. Involvement of youths in violent episodes is by no means a twentieth-century invention. Youth violence, whether in the context of youth gangs or not, has been characteristic of adolescent life for centuries. It is worth noting, though, that American youth violence appears to be particularly lethal in comparison to that found in other industrialized nations (e.g., Huizinga & Schumann, 2001; U.S. Department of Health and Human Services, 2001). Media and academic attention to gangs and associated violence tends to fluctuate across time. Following a relatively prominent youth violence and gang problem in the 1950s and 1960s, the 1970s and early 1980s were relatively calm. Then, beginning in the late1980s, the United States experienced an epidemic of youth violence.

This youth violence epidemic was evident through examination of Uniform Crime Reports (UCR) and National Crime Victimization Survey (NCVS) data. Both data sources revealed rising rates of youth violence during the late 1980s and early 1990s. In their comprehensive analyses of trends in youth violence, Cook and Laub (1998, 2002) reported that violent crime arrest rates doubled between 1966 and 1975 for youths ages 13 to 17, and were static between 1975 and 1984 before doubling again from 1984 to 1994. Since 1994, the violent crime rate for youths has been on the decline, reaching its 1984 rate by 2000. By way of comparison, property crime arrest rates were relatively stable between 1975 and 1994 before declining steadily, reaching 1966 levels in 2000.

While rape and homicide in particular garner considerable attention, both from the media and researchers, they are relatively low prevalence offenses. Although, during the seven-year period between 1987 and 1994, gang homicides increased fivefold in Chicago while doubling in Los Angeles County (Howell, 1999). In spite of this increase in gang homicides, the vast amount of violent offending involves the two other offenses traditionally categorized as violent: aggravated assault and robbery. According to 2001 UCR data, for example, there were 67,002 juvenile arrests for violent offenses; 62,916 (94%) of these were for aggravated assault and robbery. Based upon the UCR data, youthful violent offenders accounted for approximately 15 percent of all violent crime arrests in the United States in 2001 (Snyder, 2003). A disproportionate number of these youth are males, living in urban areas, and members of a racial/ethnic minority. While the rate of arrests for young males historically has been significantly greater than the arrest rate for young females, girls nonetheless account for a growing number of these arrests.

State of the Knowledge

The relatively recent declines in youth arrest rates for both violent and property crime are encouraging. Recent homicide reports from the Chicago and Los Angeles Police Departments, however, suggest a resurgence in both gang and nongang homicides in those cities. Furthermore, the recent report on youth violence submitted to the U.S. Surgeon General (U.S. Department of Health and Human Services, 2001) reported trend data from the Monitoring the Future study (self-reports from high school seniors) and found a slow but steady increase from 1980 through 1998 in reported rates of robbery and assaults resulting in injuries. Thus, while homicide, robbery, and aggravated assault arrest rates may have peaked in 1993, other indicators suggest that the prevalence and incidence of youth violence in general remain at undesirably high levels.

The youth violence epidemic also brought growing awareness of the disproportionate contribution of youth gangs to violence. While violent offenses are relatively rare occurrences in the context of adolescent activities (e.g., Decker & van Winkle, 1996; Esbensen, Huizinga & Weiher, 1993; Fleisher, 1998; Klein, 1995), they appear to be less so for gang youths. For example, in their 11-city study of adolescents, Esbensen and colleagues (2001) found that, depending upon the definition of gang member used, the gang-involved youth committed from four to six times as many violent crimes as did nongang youth. Similarly, Thornberry and Burch (1997) reported that 30 percent of a school-based sample in Rochester indicated that they were gang members at some point prior to the end of high school. These gang youths, however, accounted for 86 percent of all serious offenses in that study. Even more strikingly, Huizinga (1997) found that the 14 percent of the Denver Youth Survey sample that was gang-affiliated accounted for 79 percent of serious violence during the five-year study period. In their research involving 15-year-old youths in Seattle, Battin and colleagues (1998) reported that gang members committed twice as many violent acts as did youths who were not gang members but had delinquent friends. Compared with youths who did not have delinquent friends, the gang youths reported committing seven times as many violent acts during the previous year. All three of these panel studies (Rochester, Denver, and Seattle) documented the facilitation effect of gangs on youth violence; that is, delinquency increases substantially after a youth has joined the gang (Esbensen & Huizinga, 1993; Thornberry, 1998; Thornberry, Krohn, Lizotte & Chard-Wierschem, 1993). Thus, it is imperative to study not only violent offending by juveniles, but also the group context within which it occurs. While there is some debate about a possible tautology in the measurement of self-reported delinquency and peer delinquency, Elliott and Menard (1996) examined this issue with National Youth Survey (NYS) data. They found that association with delinquent peers preceded initiation of delinquency.

Much of the current literature on youth violence relies upon arrest data from the UCR and upon self-reported offending obtained in general surveys of youth. Some comments about these data sources are in order. The Philadelphia Cohort Study (Wolfgang, Figlio & Sellin, 1972) provided vast amounts of information about serious and chronic offenders. Even within the 6 percent of chronic offenders identified in that study, only about one-third were classified as violent. Furthermore, more than 88 percent of the violent offenders had only one violent offense, and 73 percent of the aggravated assaults were committed by 32 of the 627 chronic offenders (Tolan & Gorman-Smith, 1998). With respect to self-reports of offending, Huizinga and colleagues (1996) found little correlation between arrests and self-reports. Of violent offenders in that study (those who reported committing an offense in which another person sustained a serious injury), 74 percent had been arrested in the prior year but only 6 percent had an arrest for a serious violent offense, while another 15 percent had an arrest for a minor violent offense. Concern thus arises with respect to the suitability of these data sources for the study of youth violence.

The reliance on UCR data to describe the prevalence and epidemiology of youth violence poses concerns for a number of criminologists who study youth crime. Perhaps the most serious issue is the possibility that these data, especially arrest statistics, mis-specify the extent and distribution of youth crime. Let us consider some of the issues that are raised concerning law enforcement data. First, most youth crime is committed in groups, whereas most adult crime is solitary. Thus, one offense committed by a youth may well represent multiple offenders whereas with adults, one offense often means one offender. Second, youthful offenders tend to be opportunistic and relatively unsophisticated offenders, resulting in higher rates of detection and apprehension. Furthermore, research also suggests that bias in the arrest process affects the actual probability of arrest, and this bias is related to the very characteristics in which we may be interested (i.e., age, sex, and race). A considerable body of literature has examined discretionary practices of agents of the criminal and juvenile justice systems (e.g., Walker, Spohn & DeLone, 2000; Wilbanks, 1987). In addition to discretion on the part of justice officials, several characteristics of juveniles may also result in a disproportionate arrest rate. As stated above, juveniles not only tend to commit crimes in groups, but they are also less sophisticated offenders than adults. Both of these factors may contribute to a higher arrest probability. (For a more detailed discussion of reliability and validity issues associated with the UCR measures, consult Hindelang, Hirschi & Weis, 1981; Mosher, Miethe & Phillips, 2002; O'Brien, 1985.)

Another concern with the FBI and law enforcement data is the fact that policy changes in enforcement or crime definition can greatly impact the volume of crime. For instance, Zimring (1998:1) noted that a substantial increase in aggravated assaults was attributable to "reclassifications rather than increased rates of serious violence." Underscoring the extent to which violent offending is statistically rare, Snyder (2003:4) reported that "in 2001, there were 296 arrests for Violent Crime Index offenses for every 100,000 youth between 10 and 17 years of age. If each of these arrests involved a different juvenile (which is unlikely), then no more than one in every 330 persons ages 10-17 was arrested for a Violent Crime Index offense in 2001, or about one-third of one percent of all juveniles ages 10-17 living in the U.S." Although statistically rare among the general adolescent population, violent offending nonetheless generates considerable public concern. In fact, for many years, youth violence was identified as one of the main political issues in the United States (Bernard, 1999). The perceived frequency and seriousness of youth violence has spawned a "get tough" policy movement that has resulted in a number of changes in the juvenile justice system, including lowering the age of majority, inclusion of mandatory minimums in juvenile sentencing, and blended sentences (i.e., combining juvenile and adult sentencing options). Discussion of these policy issues, while important, falls outside the domain of this current chapter. We turn next to examination of theories and explanations of youth violence.

Explaining Youth Violence

A number of theoretical perspectives, including some of the theories presented in Part II of this text, have been used to explain youth violence. It is important to reiterate that violent offending by youths, while a substantial problem, is nonetheless a statistically rare phenomenon. To explain its occurrence it is necessary to review the characteristics of those involved as offenders and victims.

Characteristics of Violent Offenders and Victims

The stereotypical violent offender (and victim) is a male who lives in the inner city and who is a member of a racial or ethnic minority. Just as gang researchers in the past 10 years have documented more female members than was previously believed, arrest statistics indicate that females account for a growing percent of violent offenders; in 1966, the ratios of both male-to-female and black-to-white violent offending was in excess of 10:1. These ratios had fallen to close to 4:1 by 2000, leading Cook and Laub to conclude that "arrests for violent offending are less concentrated demographically now than in previous decades" (2002:126). Whether these declining ratios represent behavioral changes among youths or whether they reflect policy or reporting changes by law enforcement agencies remains to be determined.

Perpetrators of violence have generally been described as males. As suggested by the arrest ratios, this world view is changing. Likewise, the presence of girls in gangs is also being acknowledged by some contemporary researchers. Recent estimates of female involvement in gangs, as measured by self-reports, range from 20 to 46 percent (Bjerregaard & Smith, 1993; Campbell, 1991; Esbensen, Huizinga & Weiher, 1993; Esbensen & Winfree, 1998; Fagan, 1990; Moore, 1991). Interestingly, while many commentators suggest that the current level of female involvement in gangs is a new phenomenon, Klein and Crawford (1995) reported that 25 percent of the Los Angeles gang members included in their 1967 study were females. These self-report estimates contrast with the figure of less than 10 percent provided by law enforcement (Curry, Ball & Fox, 1994). While homicide does appear to be the domain of males in general and male gang members in particular (e.g., Decker & Van Winkle, 1996; Miller & Decker, 2001), it appears that female gang members are active in other forms of violent offending. Gang girls commit a wide variety of offenses, similar to the pattern exhibited by gang boys, only at a slightly lower frequency.

Since the late 1980s, there has been growing concern about the emergence of a "new female offender," one that is more ruthless and violent than in the past. The gang research reported above provides fuel for this belief. Examination of trends in arrest data lend further credence to the picture of young females becoming increasingly violent. Snyder, for example, reports that "the change in the female juvenile arrest rate between 1980 and 2001 was greater than the change in the male rate for aggravated assault (113% vs. 22%), simple assault (257% vs. 109%), and weapons law violations (140% vs. 16%)" (2003:8). These observed increases in female arrest rates, however, are somewhat deceiving given the initial low base rates of female offending. That is, a small increase in the raw number of arrests produces a proportionately large increase in arrest rates. (For instance, if there were 100 female arrests and 500 male arrests in Year 1, 50 additional female arrests in Year 2 would represent a 50 percent increase in female arrests. The same absolute increase in male arrests, however, would represent a 10 percent increase.) Although the rapid increases in female juvenile arrests should not be dismissed, neither should they be cause for overreaction. In 1997, for example, one in three female arrests was for property crime, and three out of four of these were primarily for shoplifting (Snyder & Sickmund, 1999:127). Furthermore, for person offenses committed by females, the most common offense was assault, a category that consists largely of normal adolescent fighting and/or by fighting with parents. While female arrest rates have indeed been increasing, the male-to-female ratio of violent offending remains approximately 4:1, leading Chesney-Lind and Sheldon (1998) to conclude that the true nature of girls' misbehaviors is generally the same as it has always been.

Youth violence is generally portrayed as a minority problem. This image is reinforced by the fact that during the early 1990s homicide became the second leading cause of death for adolescent males ages 15 to 19 and the leading cause of death among African-American males (Huff, 2004). While African-American youths are overrepresented in violent crime arrest statistics, the majority of such arrestees, although underrepresented, are white. In 2001, white juveniles under the age of 18 accounted for 55 percent of arrests while representing 78 percent of all youths [one cautionary note with regard to UCR data is that "most Hispanics (an ethnic designation, not a race) were classified as white" (Snyder, 2003:9)]. African-American youths accounted for 45 percent of arrests while representing only 17 percent of all youths (Snyder, 2003). Although the disparity between white arrest rates and black arrest rates for violent offenses declined steadily between 1980 and 2001, African-American youths are still more likely to be both offenders and victims of violence. For murder, the white arrest rate has averaged between two and seven per 100,000 youths ages 10 to 17 since 1980. The black arrest rate for murder, however, has been above 10 per 100,000 for this entire period, exceeding 20 per 100,000 for most of this period. More telling, perhaps, is the fact that in 1993 there were 60 arrests for murder per 100,000 black youths. Arrest data reveal similar patterns for robbery and aggravated assault, with black youths exhibiting arrest rates from four to eight times higher than those for white youths. By 2001, the black-to-white ratio of arrests for violent crimes was approximately 3.6:1, significantly lower than the 6.3:1 ratio that was reported in 1980 (Snyder, 2003).

As with other forms of violence, homicides tend to be intraracial; homicide victims tend to reflect the ethnic and racial composition of the communities in which the homicides occur. Research conducted by Block (1993) confirmed the intraracial nature of gang homicides in Chicago;

Hispanic and African-American residents were more likely to be victims of gang homicides in their respective neighborhoods than were Anglos.

As a side note, it is worthwhile mentioning that early gang studies provided a rich source of information about white ethnic gangs. It was not until the late 1950s, for instance, that researchers began to identify gang members by race (Spergel, 1995). This change in gang composition is closely tied to the social disorganization of urban areas and the research focus on urban youth. Covey, Menard, and Franzese (1997:240) suggested that the scarcity of non-Hispanic, white, ethnic gangs may be attributable to the smaller proportion of non-Hispanic European Americans residing in neighborhoods characterized by social disorganization (that is, high rates of poverty, mobility, welfare dependency, and single-parent households). As research expands to more representative samples of the general population, a redefinition of the racial and ethnic composition of gang members is likely. For example, in their 11-city study, Esbensen and Lynskey (2001) reported that community-level demographics were reflected in the composition of youth gangs; that is, gang members were white in primarily white communities, and gang members tended to be African-American in predominantly African-American communities.

Stereotypical family characteristics of violent youths (i.e., family structure, parental education, and income) also have been subject to revision—gang youths, for instance, are found in intact two-parent, single-parent, and recombined families. Likewise, gang youths are not restricted to homes in which parents have low educational achievement or low incomes. Klein (1995:75-76) summarizes gang characteristics as follows (emphasis added):

> it is not sufficient to say that gang members come from lower-income areas, from minority populations, or from homes more often characterized by absent parents or reconstituted families. It is not sufficient because most youths from such areas, such groups, and such families do *not* join gangs.

Risk factors associated with youth violence. Whether we rely on meta-analyses such as that conducted by Lipsey and Derzon (1998), literature reviews such as that reported by Hawkins and colleagues (1998), or whether we conduct our own reviews, the results are quite robust if we use a "risk factor" approach. This strategy (which gained considerable popularity during the 1990s) has the advantage that factors related to (and in most instances preceding) youth violence are identified. The approach, however, is not theoretical and thus does not allow for theory testing. However, in many instances, theoretical statements are not precise enough to allow for operationalization of key concepts. Conversely, operationalizations are not distinct enough to reflect unique theoretical constructs. Agnew, Brezina, Wright, and Cullen (2002:52) acknowledge that "it is sometimes difficult to distinguish 'strain' from 'social control' measures. Grades, for example, can be taken as a measure of both strain and level of social control." The risk factor approach emphasizes the empirical reality while minimizing the theoretical rationale underlying the observed relationships. Prior to exploring theoretical explanations of youth violence, I will provide a brief review of the risk factor literature.

Youth violence cannot be explained without taking into consideration the significance of structural and community factors. However, considering that most youths who reside in areas where youth violence is prominent choose not to engage in these activities, additional factors are required to explain the prevalence and incidence of youth violence. A considerable body of research assessing risk factors associated with violence has emerged during the past decade. It has become common to examine these risk factors within the following five domains: (1) individual and family demographics, (2) peer group, (3) community, (4) school, and (5) personal attributes. The role of individual and family demographics was discussed in the preceding section, so the following discussion is limited to the remaining contexts.

The community is the domain examined most frequently in regard to both the prevalence of youth violence and the emergence of gangs. Numerous studies indicate that poverty, unemployment, the absence of meaningful jobs, and social disorganization contribute to the presence of youth violence and gangs (Anderson, 1999; Curry & Thomas, 1992; Fagan, 1990; Hagedorn, 1988; 1991; Huff, 1990; Vigil, 1988). There is little debate that gangs are more prominent in urban areas and that they are more likely to emerge in economically distressed neighborhoods. However, the 1990s have seen the proliferation of youth gangs and violence to rural and suburban communities (Egley, Howell & Major, 2004). The traditional community in which youth gangs and associated violence are found, however, continues to be characterized as urban, socially disorganized, and economically marginal. The housing projects or barrios of Los Angeles, Chicago, and New York are viewed as the stereotypical homes of youth violence. The publication of Wilson's (1987) account of the underclass—those members of society who are truly disadvantaged and affected by changes in social and economic conditions—has renewed interest in the social disorganization perspective advanced by Thrasher (1923/1967) and Shaw and McKay (1942). According to Moore (1991:137-138):

> Gangs as youth groups develop among the socially marginal adolescents for whom school and family do not work. Agencies of street socialization take on increased importance under changing economic circumstances, and have an increased impact on younger kids.

These conditions, which have resulted in a lack of education and employment and in lives of poverty without opportunities (Short, 1997), are compounded for females, who experience the additional burden of sexual discrimination and traditional role expectations. Social structural conditions alone, however, cannot account for the presence of gangs or youth violence. Fagan (1990), for instance, found that while the inner-city youths in his study lived in areas with weak social controls and limited legitimate opportunities for success, most youths avoided gang life and the associated violence.

School risk factors have received less attention than other factors (see this chapter's Appendix for some general comments on school violence). Regardless, several school-related factors consistently have been found to be associated with youth violence: "early and persistent antisocial behavior at school, academic failure beginning in elementary school, and lack of commitment to school" (Howell, 2003:114). Similar school-related risk factors have been found to be predictive of gang joining (Bjerregaard & Smith, 1993; Esbensen & Deschenes, 1998; Hill, Howell, Hawkins & Battin-Pearson, 1999; Maxson, Whitlock & Klein, 1998). Some gender differences, however, have been reported. In the Rochester study, expectations for educational attainment were predictive of gang membership for girls but not for boys (Bjerregaard & Smith, 1993). In a similar vein, Esbensen and Deschenes (1998) found that commitment to school was lower among gang-member girls than non-gang-member girls. No such differences were found for boys.

Recent surveys have contrasted gang and nongang youth's attitudes (i.e., personal attributes). In Seattle, Hill and colleagues (1999) found that gang youths held more antisocial beliefs than did nongang youths. Maxson, Whitlock, and Klein (1998), in their San Diego study, found that gang members had more delinquent self-concepts and greater tendencies to resolve conflicts by threats, and had experienced more critical stressful events. On a more generic level, both the Seattle and San Diego studies found significant differences between gang and nongang youths within multiple contexts (i.e., individual, school, peer, family, and community).

Extending this comparative approach, Esbensen, Huizinga, and Weiher (1993) examined gang youths, serious youthful offenders who were not gang members, and nondelinquent youths. The nondelinquent youths differed from the delinquent and gang youths, reporting lower levels of commitment to delinquent peers, lower levels of social isolation, lower tolerance for deviance, and higher levels of commitment to positive peers. In a replication of that study, Deschenes and Esbensen (1997) created a typology of nondelinquents, minor delinquents, serious delinquents, and gang members. Based on delinquency scores, they categorized eighth-grade students into one of these four classifications. On every measure tested, gang members were significantly different from each of the other groups but were clearly the most distinct from nondelinquents (generally at least one standard deviation above the mean). Gang members were more impulsive, engaged in more risk-seeking behavior, were less committed to school, and reported less communication with and lower levels of attachment to their parents. Nongang youths were more committed to prosocial peers and less committed to delinquent peers. Whether comparing gang youths to nongang youths, violent offenders to nonoffenders, or gang youths to violent nongang youths, there has been a consistent finding from these studies: gang youths score higher on risk factors than do the nongang offenders, who in turn score higher than the nonoffenders.

As discussed at the outset of this chapter, the most consistent finding associated with research on gangs, and for much violent offending in general, is the overarching influence of *peers* (e.g., Battin-Pearson, Thornberry, Hawkins & Krohn, 1998; Elliott & Menard, 1997; Warr, 2002; Warr & Stafford, 1991). In their comparison of stable and transient gang youths, Battin-Pearson and colleagues reported that the strongest predictors of sustained gang affiliation were a high level of interaction with antisocial peers and a low level of interaction with prosocial peers. Researchers have examined the influence of peers through a variety of measures, including exposure to delinquent peers, attachment to delinquent peers, and commitment to delinquent peers. Regardless of how this peer affiliation is measured, the results are the same; association with delinquent peers is one of the strongest predictors (that is, risk factors) of violent offending and gang membership.

Explaining Youth Violence

The risk and protective factor approach just detailed has a number of desirable attributes but at the same time fails to provide causal linkages between specific risk factors and youth violence. Why, for instance, are low levels of school commitment associated with youth violence and gang involvement? And what accounts for the finding that individuals with high levels of impulsivity appear to be associated with violent offending, while adolescents with unsupervised free time are more likely to experience violent victimization. A conceptual or theoretical framework facilitates an understanding of such observed relationships and also guides policy recommendations.

In light of the multiple risk factors for youth violence discussed above, combined with the fact that these risk factors represent several theoretical perspectives, one strategy for explaining youth violence is to propose an integrated theoretical model. There is no single cause of youth violence and, as such, multiple explanations may be required. Alternatively, an integrated perspective that identifies multiple pathways to violence might prove beneficial. A quick review of the risk factor literature reveals that various risk factors can be classified within different theoretical frameworks. For instance, the following risk factors for youth violence are indicators of *social bond/control* theory: lack of commitment to school, low levels of attachment to parents, low family involvement, low level of involvement in school, and low commitment to prosocial peers. Risk factors indicative of *self-control theory* include: low parental monitoring and supervision, and higher levels of impulsivity and risk-seeking. *Social learning theory* (see Chapter 1 of this volume) is evidenced by the presence of the following risk factors: friends who engage in problem behavior, favorable attitudes to problem behavior, early initiation of problem behavior, pro-gang attitudes, prior involvement in delinquency, low levels of guilt associated with violence, and high tolerance of physical violence. The *routine activities* (see Chapter 7 of this volume) perspective has highlighted the importance of the extent to which youths engage in unsupervised socializing (i.e., youths hanging out where no adults are present and hanging out where drugs and alcohol are available). The more time youths spend in such unsupervised settings, the more likely they are to be involved in violence—both as offenders and as victims. An integrated theoretical framework combining these perspectives may be better able to explain youth violence.

One noticeable absence from the preceding list of risk factors is any mention of community or structural variables. While there is little doubt that macro-level factors are associated with differential rates of youth offending (i.e., violent index offending rates are higher in high-density, urban, impoverished areas than in low-density, affluent suburbs), it is also an established fact that the majority of youths in areas with high violent offending do not commit violent offenses. Thus, while we must acknowledge that certain structural and demographic characteristics are correlated with violence, these "exogenous" variables, while important, do not adequately explain the variations in rates of youth violence that are found within communities or among individuals who share the same characteristics. For instance, while rates of youth violence are quite high in St. Louis, most youths living in St. Louis are not violent. Similarly, boys are more likely to be involved in violent offending than are girls. That does not, however, mean that all boys are violent. Knowing that an individual is a young man living in St. Louis does not explain or predict youth violence. Therefore, while structural and individual factors help to account for variations in rates of offending, other factors are necessary to explain why some similarly situated youths engage in violence while others do not.

During the past 25 years, integrated theoretical models have gained acceptance and appeal. These integrated models acknowledge the limitations of single theories and maintain that additional explanatory power is achieved by combining theories in a coherent model. One of the earlier integrated models proposed by Elliott and colleagues (1979) combined elements of social strain, social learning, and social control theories. Since then, others have developed integrated models incorporating a wide range of perspectives (see, for instance, the works of Colvin & Pauly, 1983; Sampson & Laub, 1993; Thornberry, 1987; Winfree, Esbensen & Osgood, 1996). It is my belief that these theoretical integrations hold the most promise for explaining and ultimately informing policies to intervene with and eventually prevent youth violence.

Appendix: A Brief Comment on School Violence

A series of high-profile shootings in American schools contributed to the perception that youth violence was becoming increasingly lethal. Following on the "epidemic" described earlier in this chapter, this wave of school violence prompted policy changes to increase the safety of schools. These policy initiatives tended to emphasize security measures: zero tolerance policies with respect to weapons (including lunch knives) were enacted; metal detectors and surveillance cameras were installed; and security officers were hired. The truth of the matter is that schools were, and continue to be, relatively safe havens for youths and the adults who work there. During the 1990s, the Centers for Disease Control and Prevention conducted two national studies of school homicides, covering the period from 1992 to 1999. The overall trend indicated a decline in the number of school homicides but an increase in the number of victims per incident. School-related homicides account for less than 1 percent of all homicides of youths (U.S. Department of Health and Human Services, 2001:31). It is important to note that 84 percent of school homicides involved firearms.

The Monitoring the Future (MTF) survey, as well as a survey conducted by the U.S. Department of Education reveal that the rate of nonfatal violence at schools has remained relatively stable throughout the 1990s. The MTF data reveal that, from 1980 through 1998, approximately 5 percent of high school seniors report being injured with a weapon at school. While quite stable for the aggregate and for white students, the rate has been less so for African-American students, varying from approximately 12 percent in 1981 to around 7 percent in 1998.

How bad is school crime? During the 1998-1999 school year there were 38 homicides at American schools. Of these, 33 involved school-aged children. These 33 homicides represent less than 1 percent of all youth homicides. During that same time period, there were 2,391 nonschool homicides involving youths between the ages of five and 19. In other words, for every youth killed on school property, there were 72 children murdered away from school (Devoe, Ruddy, Miller, Planty, Snyder, Peter, Kaufman, Duhart & Rand, 2002).

Discussion Questions

1. What did Cook and Laub mean when they wrote that violent offending is "less concentrated demographically than in previous decades"?

2. What are risk factors, and what risk factors are associated with youth violence?

3. According to the information provided in this chapter, more girls are arrested for violent offenses than ever before, and self-report studies suggest that girls comprise more than 25 percent of gang members. Are girls becoming more violent? Is there a new breed of violent female offenders?

4. What theoretical perspective do you believe best explains youth violence?

References

Agnew, R., T. Brezina, J.P. Wright, and F.T. Cullen (2002). "Strain, Personality Traits, and Delinquency: Extending General Strain Theory." *Criminology,* 40:43-72.

Anderson, E. (1999). *Code of the Street: Decency, Violence, and the Moral Life of the Inner City*. New York: Norton.

Battin, S.R., K.G. Hill, R. Abbott, R.F. Catalano, and J.D. Hawkins (1998). "The Contribution of Gang Membership to Delinquency Beyond Delinquent Friends." *Criminology*, 36:93-115.

Battin-Pearson, S.R., T.P. Thornberry, J.D. Hawkins, and M.D. Krohn (1998). *Gang Membership, Delinquent Peers, and Delinquent Behavior. Juvenile Justice Bulletin*. Washington, DC: U.S. Department of Justice.

Bernard, T.J. (1999). "Juvenile Crime and the Transformation of Juvenile Justice: Is There a Juvenile Crime Wave?" *Justice Quarterly*, 16:337-356.

Bjerregaard, B., and C. Smith (1993). "Gender Differences in Gang Participation, Delinquency, and Substance Use." *Journal of Quantitative Criminology*, 4:329-355.

Block, C.R. (1993). "Lethal Violence in the Chicago Latino Community." In A.V. Wilson (ed.), *Homicide: The Victim/Offender Connection*. Cincinnati: Anderson.

Campbell, A. (1991). *The Girls in the Gang,* 2nd ed. Cambridge, MA: Basil Blackwell.

Chesney-Lind, M., and R. Shelden (1998). *Girls, Delinquency, and Juvenile Justice*, 2nd ed. Belmont, CA: West/Wadsworth.

Cloward, R.A., and L. Ohlin (1960). *Delinquency and Opportunity*. New York: Free Press.

Cohen, A.K. (1955). *Delinquent Boys*. New York: Free Press.

Colvin, M., and J. Pauly (1983). "A Critique of Criminology: Toward an Integrated Structural-Marxist Theory of Delinquency Production." *American Journal of Sociology*, 89:513-551.

Cook, P.J., and J.H. Laub (2002). "After the Epidemic: Recent Trend in Youth Violence in the United States." In M. Tonry and M.H. Moore (eds.), *Youth Violence*. Chicago: University of Chicago Press.

Cook, P.J., and J.H. Laub (1998). "The Unprecedented Epidemic in Youth Violence." In M. Tonry and M.H. Moore (eds.), *Youth Violence*. Chicago: University of Chicago Press.

Covey, H.C., S. Menard, and R.J. Franzese (1997). *Juvenile Gangs,* 2nd ed. Springfield, IL: Charles C Thomas.

Curry, G.D., and R.W. Thomas (1992). "Community Organization and Gang Policy Response." *Journal of Quantitative Criminology*, 8(4):357-374.

Curry, G.D., R.A. Ball, and R.J. Fox (1994). *Gang Crime and Law Enforcement Record Keeping. Research in Brief.* Washington, DC: U.S. Department of Justice, Office of Justice Program, National Institute of Justice.

Decker, S.H., and B. Van Winkle (1996). *Life in the Gang: Family, Friends, and Violence.* New York: Cambridge University Press.

Deschenes, E.P., and F.-A. Esbensen (1997). "Saints, Delinquents, and Gang Members: Differences in Attitudes and Behavior." Paper presented at the annual meeting of the American Society of Criminology, San Diego, CA.

Devoe, J.F., S.A. Ruddy, A.K. Miller, M. Planty, T.D. Snyder, K. Peter, P. Kaufman, D.T. Duhart, and M.R. Rand (2002). *Indicators of School Crime and Safety 2002*. Washington, DC: U.S. Department of Education, Office of Educational Research and Improvement, and U.S. Department of Justice, Office of Justice Programs.

Egley A., Jr., J.C. Howell, and A.K. Major (2004). "Recent Patterns of Gang Problems in the United States: Results from the 1996-2002 National Youth Gang Survey." In F.-A. Esbensen, S.G. Tibbetts, and L. Gaines (eds.), *American Youth Gangs at the Millennium*. Long Grove, IL: Waveland.

Elliott, D.S., S.S. Ageton, and R.J. Canter (1979). "An Integrated Theoretical Perspective on Delinquent Behavior." *Journal of Research in Crime and Delinquency*, 16:3-27.

Elliott, D.S., and S. Menard (1996). "Delinquent Friends and Delinquent Behavior: Temporal and Developmental Patterns." In J.D. Hawkins (ed.), *Delinquency and Crime: Current Theories*. New York: Cambridge University Press.

Esbensen, F.-A., and E.P. Deschenes (1998). "A Multisite Examination of Youth Gang Membership: Does Gender Matter?" *Criminology*, 36:799-828.

Esbensen, F.-A., and D. Huizinga (1993). "Gangs, Drugs, and Delinquency in a Survey of Urban Youth." *Criminology*, 31:565-589.

Esbensen, F.-A., D. Huizinga, and A.W. Weiher (1993). "Gang and Nongang Youth: Differences in Explanatory Factors." *Journal of Contemporary Criminal Justice*, 9:94-116.

Esbensen, F.-A., and D.P. Lynskey (2001). "Youth Gang Members in a School Survey." In M.W. Klein, H.-J. Kerner, C.L. Maxson, and E.G.M. Weitekamp (eds.), *The Eurogang Paradox: Street Gangs and Youth Groups in the U.S. and Europe*. Amsterdam: Kluwer.

Esbensen, F.-A., and L.T. Winfree, Jr. (1998). "Race and Gender Differences between Gang and Non-Gang Youth: Results from a Multi-Site Survey." *Justice Quarterly*, 15(4): 505-526.

Esbensen, F.-A., L.T. Winfree, Jr., N. He, and T.J. Taylor (2001). "Youth Gangs and Definitional Issues: When Is a Gang a Gang and Why Does It Matter?" *Crime & Delinquency*, 47:105-130.

Fagan, J. (1990). "Social Processes of Delinquency and Drug Use among Urban Gangs." In C.R. Huff (ed.), *Gangs in America*. Newbury Park, CA: Sage.

Fleisher, M. (1998). *Dead End Kids*. Madison, WI: University of Wisconsin Press.

Hagedorn, J.M. (1988). *People and Folks: Gangs, Crime, and the Underclass in a Rustbelt City*. Chicago: Lakeview Press.

Hagedorn, J.M. (1991). "Gangs, Neighborhoods, and Public Policy." *Social Problems*, 38:529-542.

Hawkins, J.D., T. Herrenkohl, D.P. Farrington, D. Brewer, R.F. Catalano, and T.W. Harachi (1998). "A Review of Predictors of Youth Violence." In R. Loeber and D.P. Farrington (eds.), *Serious and Violent Juvenile Offenders: Risk Factors and Successful Interventions*. Thousand Oaks, CA: Sage.

Hill, K.G., J.D. Howell, J.D. Hawkins, and S.R. Battin-Pearson (1999). "Childhood Risk Factors for Adolescent Gang Membership: Results from the Seattle Social Development Project." *Journal of Research in Crime and Delinquency*, 36:300-322.

Hindelang, M.J., T. Hirschi, and J.G. Weis (1981). *Measuring Delinquency*. Beverly Hills, CA: Sage.

Howell, J.C. (2003). *Preventing & Reducing Juvenile Delinquency: A Comprehensive Framework*. Thousand Oaks, CA: Sage.

Howell, J.C. (1999). "Youth Gang Homicides: A Literature Review." *Crime & Delinquency*, 45:208-241.

Huff, C.R. (2004). "Youth Violence: Prevention, Intervention, and Social Policy." In F.-A. Esbensen, S.G. Tibbetts, and L. Gaines (eds.), *American Youth Gangs at the Millennium*. Long Grove, IL: Waveland.

Huff, C.R. (1990). "Denial, Overreaction, and Misidentification: A Postscript on Public Policy. In C.R. Huff (ed.), *Gangs in America*. Newbury Park, CA: Sage.

Huizinga, D. (1997). "Gangs and the Volume of Crime." Paper presented at the annual meeting of the Western Society of Criminology, Honolulu, HI.

Huizinga, D., F.-A. Esbensen, and A.W. Weiher (1996). "The Impact of Arrest on Subsequent Delinquent Behavior." In R. Loeber, D. Huizinga, and T.P. Thornberry (eds.), *Program of Research on the Causes and Correlates of Delinquency: Annual Report 1995-1996*. Washington, DC: U.S. Department of Justice, Office of Juvenile Justice and Delinquency Prevention.

Huizinga, D., and K.F. Schumann (2001). "Gang Membership in Bremen and Denver: Comparative Longitudinal Data." In M.W. Klein, H.-J. Kerner, C.L. Maxson, and E.G.M. Weitekamp (eds.), *The Eurogang Paradox: Street Gangs and Youth Groups in the U.S. and Europe*. Amsterdam: Kluwer.

Klein, M.W. (1995). *The American Street Gang*. New York: Oxford University Press.

Klein, M.W., and L.Y. Crawford (1995). "Groups, Gangs, and Cohesiveness." In M.W. Klein, C.L. Maxson, and J. Miller (eds.), *The Modern Gang Reader*. Los Angeles: Roxbury.

Lipsey, M.W., and J.H. Derzon (1998). "Predictors of Violent or Serious Delinquency in Adolescence and Early Adulthood: A Synthesis of Longitudinal Research." In R. Loeber and D.P. Farrington (eds.), *Serious and Violent Juvenile Offenders: Risk Factors and Successful Interventions*. Thousand Oaks, CA: Sage.

Maxson, C.L., M.L. Whitlock, and M.W. Klein (1998). "Vulnerability to Street Gang Membership: Implications for Prevention." *Social Services Review*, 72:70-91.

Miller, J., and S.H. Decker (2001). "Young Women and Gang Violence: Gender, Street Offending, and Violent Victimization in Gangs." *Justice Quarterly*, 18:115-140.

Miller, W.B. (1958). "Lower Class Culture as a Generating Milieu of Gang Delinquency." *Journal of Social Issues*, 14:5-19.

Moore, J. (1991). *Going Down to the Barrio: Homeboys and Homegirls in Change*. Philadelphia: Temple University Press.

Mosher, C.J., T.D. Miethe, and D.M. Phillips (2002). *The Mismeasure of Crime*. Thousand Oaks, CA: Sage.

O'Brien, R.M. (1985). *Crime and Victimization Data*. Beverly Hills, CA: Sage.

Sampson, R.J., and J.H. Laub (1993). *Crime in the Making: Pathways and Turning Points Through Life*. Cambridge, MA: Harvard University Press.

Shaw, C.R., and H.D. McKay (1942). *Juvenile Delinquency and Urban Areas*. Chicago: University of Chicago Press.

Short, J.F., Jr. (1997). *Poverty, Ethnicity, and Violent Crime*. Boulder, CO: Westview Press.

Short, J.F., Jr., and F.L. Strodtbeck (1965). *Group Processes and Gang Delinquency*. Chicago: University of Chicago Press.

Snyder, H.N. (2003). *Juvenile Arrests 2001*. Washington, DC: U.S. Department of Justice, Office of Juvenile Justice and Delinquency Prevention.

Snyder, H.N., and M. Sickmund (1999). *Juvenile Offenders and Victims: 1999 National Report*. Washington, DC: U.S. Department of Justice, Office of Juvenile Justice and Delinquency Prevention.

Spergel, I.A. (1995). *The Youth Gang Problem*. New York: Oxford University Press.

Thornberry, T.P. (1998). "Membership in Youth Gangs and Involvement in Serious and Violent Offending." In R. Loeber and D.P. Farrington (eds.), *Serious and Violent Juvenile Offenders: Risk Factors and Successful Interventions*. Thousand Oaks, CA: Sage.

Thornberry, T.P. (1987). "Toward an Interactional Theory of Delinquency." *Criminology*, 25:863-891.

Thornberry, T.P., and J.H. Burch, II. (1997). *Gang Members and Delinquent Behavior. Juvenile Justice Bulletin*. Washington, DC: U.S. Department of Justice.

Thornberry, T.P., M.D. Krohn, A.J. Lizotte, and D. Chard-Wierschem (1993). "The Role of Juvenile Gangs in Facilitating Delinquent Behavior." *Journal of Research in Crime and Delinquency*, 30:5-87.

Thrasher, F.M. (1923/1967). *The Gang: A Study of One Thousand Three Hundred Thirteen Gangs in Chicago*. Chicago: University of Chicago Press.

Tolan, P.H., and D. Gorman-Smith (1998). "Development of Serious and Violent Offending Careers." In R. Loeber and D.P. Farrington (eds.), *Serious and Violent Juvenile Offenders: Risk Factors and Successful Interventions*. Thousand Oaks, CA: Sage.

U.S. Department of Health and Human Services (2001). *Youth Violence: A Report to the Surgeon General*. Rockville, MD: U.S. Department of Health and Human Services.

Vigil, J.D. (1988). *Barrio Gangs: Street Life and Identity in Southern California*. Austin: University of Texas Press.

Walker, S., C. Spohn, and M. DeLone (2000). *The Color of Justice: Race, Ethnicity, and Crime,* 2nd ed. New York: Wadsworth.

Warr, M. (2002). *Companions in Crime: The Social Aspects of Criminal Conduct.* New York: Cambridge University Press.

Warr, M., and M. Stafford (1991). "The Influence of Delinquent Peers: What They Think or What They Do?" *Criminology,* 29:851-865.

Wilbanks, W. (1987). *The Myth of a Racist Criminal Justice System.* Monterey, CA: Brooks/Cole.

Wilson, W.J. (1987). *The Truly Disadvantaged: The Inner City, the Underclass, and Public Policy.* Chicago: University of Chicago Press.

Winfree, L.T., Jr., F.-A. Esbensen, and D.W. Osgood (1996). "Evaluating a School-Based Gang Prevention Program: A Theoretical Perspective." *Evaluation Review,* 20:181-203.

Wolfgang, M.E., R.M. Figlio, and T. Sellin (1972). *Delinquency in a Birth Cohort.* Chicago: University of Chicago Press.

Zimring, F.E. (1998). *American Youth Violence.* New York: Oxford University Press.

CHAPTER 12

A Summary of Research on Drug-Related Violence

Helene Raskin White

There is clearly a statistical relationship between drug use and violence. Drug users are generally more violent than nonusers, and violent individuals are generally heavier drugs users than nonviolent individuals. However, correlation does not equal causation. Below I briefly review the empirical evidence for the drugs–violence association and alternative theoretical models to explain the connection. All the relevant literature cannot be covered in this short chapter, so the reader is referred to several excellent reviews for greater detail.[1]

Definitions of Drug-Related Violence

In trying to understand the nature of the drugs–violence connection, one has to keep in mind that this association varies across individuals, locations, historical periods, types of drugs and types of violent offenses. In fact, as Anthony and Forman (2002:42) note, there is no single drugs–crime relationship, but rather there are drugs–crime relationships, most of which are complex.

The term "drug-related violence" means different things in different studies. For example, drug-related homicide can include murders related to drug distribution, committed while using drugs, committed in the act of a crime

Portions of this paper were excerpted from White and Gorman, 2000. Preparation of this paper was supported, in part, by grants from the National Institute on Drug Abuse (DA/AA-03395 and DA 17552) and the Robert Wood Johnson Foundation (043747).

to get money for drugs, or that simply occur in high–drug use neighborhoods. In addition, in some official statistics and research reports, alcohol is included as a drug when estimating the level of drug-related crimes, whereas in others it is not. In addition, certain types of events, such as a man beating his wife for taking his drugs, may or may not be counted as drug-related violence (see Anthony & Forman, 2002; Miczek, DeBold, Haney, Tidey, Vivian & Weerts, 1994). Measurement of alcohol and other drug use varies greatly across studies; some studies measure acute use while others measure chronic use, and some measure drug-related problems while others measure dependence. Similarly, there is a lack of consistency of violence measures across studies, and few studies include measures of severity or degree of injury. See McBride and McCoy (1982) Roizen (1993), and White (1990) for additional issues in definitions and classification schema. Given this lack of agreement and consensus in definitions and measures, one must be cautious in making comparisons across studies and in evaluating the literature presented below.

For this chapter, I am defining drug-related violence as interpersonal violent behavior that occurs while an individual is using drugs, that is used to get drugs or money to buy drugs, or that is associated with drug distribution. Violence in this chapter focuses primarily on violent crimes (e.g., armed robbery, assault, homicide), although a brief discussion of domestic violence (child abuse and spouse abuse) is also included. In this chapter, I differentiate between alcohol use and illicit drug use and, where possible, I differentiate among illicit drugs (e.g., marijuana, cocaine, psychedelics, etc.).

State of the Knowledge about the Nature of the Association between Drugs and Crime

Alcohol-Related Violence

The empirical evidence supporting an association between alcohol use and violence is strong. While the rates of alcohol use by offenders at the time of an offense vary greatly across studies, in general they indicate that more than one-half of all homicides and assaults are committed when the offender, victim, or both have been drinking (see Collins & Messerschmidt, 1993; Roizen, 1993). In 1998, approximately 40 percent of offenders in jails and prisons reported that they had used alcohol prior to committing a violent offense (compared to about one-third for property crimes) (Greenfeld & Henneberg, 2001). More than 40 percent of prisoners used alcohol prior to committing murder and nearly one-half drank prior to committing an assault (Greenfeld & Henneberg, 2001). Recent survey data suggest that the role of alcohol in violent crime is decreasing, and this finding is consistent with decreases in U.S. per capita consumption and in alcohol-involved traffic fatalities (Greenfeld & Henneberg, 2001). Note, however, that reports of use at the time of offense commission may only indicate that offenders use alcohol often, rather than that their use causes them to commit the violent act. In fact, studies indicate that violent offenders have much higher rates of daily drinking, heavy drinking, and alcohol abuse than the general population (Greenfeld & Henneberg, 2001; White & Gorman, 2000). Note that such reports could be inflated to justify the violent behavior. In contrast, in one study, more than 50 percent of the adult assault offenders reported drinking at the time of their offense, but 59 percent of those drinking did not think that drinking was relevant to the commission of the crime (Collins & Messerschmidt, 1993).

Victimization studies also provide empirical support for the alcohol–violence relationship (Greenfeld & Henneberg, 2001; Pernanen, 1991). Although rates depend on victim perceptions, in 1998, 37 percent of all violent crime victims (who could make a judgment) reported that the offender had been drinking at the time of the offense. Rates were higher for intimates and family members than for acquaintances and strangers (Greenfeld & Henneberg, 2001). Note also that victims are often using alcohol or other drugs and actually may be the impetus for the violent encounter. In fact, it is difficult to separate the victim from the perpetrator in many instances (National Institute of Justice, 2002).

Alcohol plays an important role in domestic violence. According to the 1995 National Incident-Based Reporting System, one in four intimate assaults involved a perpetrator who had been drinking (Greenfeld, Rand, Craven, Perkins, Ringel, Warchol, Matson & Fox, 1998). In a 1992 national survey, 28 percent of men and 8 percent of women reported drinking at the time of a wife assault (Kantor & Asdigian, 1997). Leonard (2000) estimates that alcohol is involved in between 25 percent and 50 percent of all intimate partner violence (IPV) events. There is also an association between drinking patterns and IPV. Specifically, excessive drinkers and alcoholics are more likely to act violently toward their intimate partners (Leonard, 2000). Furthermore, a number of studies have found that heavy drinking predicts later domestic violence and that reductions in drinking among alcoholics are related to reductions in domestic violence (Leonard, 2000). The association between drinking behavior and IPV appears to hold for men and women even when common risk factors are controlled (Kantor & Straus, 1987; Leonard & Blane, 1992; Leonard & Senchak, 1996; White & Chen, 2002).

The evidence for a direct association between parental alcohol use and child abuse is mixed (Widom, 1993; Widom & Hiller-Sturmhöfel, 2001). However, there is some evidence that women who abuse alcohol compared to those who do not may be more likely to use harsh discipline on their children (Miller, Maguin & Downs, 1997). There is even stronger evidence of a link between parental alcoholism and sexual abuse of children; however, the perpetrator of the abuse is often another relative or stranger rather than the alcoholic parent. Therefore, parental alcohol abuse may leave children more vulnerable to abuse by others (Widom & Hiller-Sturmhöfel, 2001).

In a meta-analysis of studies examining all types of alcohol–violence relationships, Lipsey, Wilson, Cohen, and Derzon (1997) found significant, although very modest, effect sizes for both acute and chronic associations. They also found that the associations between alcohol and violent crime were weaker than those between alcohol and nonviolent crime. The relationships were stronger in criminal and psychiatric samples than in general population samples. Furthermore, when studies controlled for confounding variables, the alcohol–violence correlation was reduced substantially.

In addition to individual-level analyses, support for an alcohol–violence association comes from macro-level studies of the relationship between alcohol availability and rates of violence. Rates of homicide and other forms of violence have been related to alcohol availability and per capita consumption in international and U.S. state comparisons. However, the strength of the relationship is reduced when other variables, such as poverty, are controlled (Parker, 1993). Furthermore, efforts to reduce drinking (e.g., by increasing the tax on alcohol) have been shown to decrease violent crime (Cook & Moore, 1993). Several studies using city-level data have demonstrated an association between alcohol availability and various forms of violence even after controlling for confounding factors (Parker & Rebhun, 1995; Scribner, MacKinnon & Dwyer, 1995). However, Lipsey, Wilson, Cohen, and Derzon (1997) argue that the existing studies do not establish a causal relationship because the findings have been equivocal and the full range of possible confounding factors has not been examined. Furthermore, it may be the drinking context rather than the effects of alcohol on individuals that explains the association between alcohol availability and violence.

Drug-Related Violence

Data from the Arrestee Drug Abuse Monitoring Program (ADAM) in 1999 indicated that about two-thirds of adult and one-half of adolescent arrestees tested urine-positive for illegal drugs at the time of their arrest (Dorsey, Zawitz & Middleton, 2002). Marijuana was the drug most frequently detected for male adults and male and female juveniles, whereas cocaine was most frequently detected for female adults. However, data from adult arrestees and prisoners indicate a weaker association of drugs than alcohol to violence; alcohol use appears to be more strongly associated with violent crime, whereas drug use is more strongly associated with property crime (Harlow, 1998; Valdez, Yin & Kaplan, 1997). In 1997, about one third of state prisoners reported that they committed their crime under the influence of drugs; rates were higher for property than violent offenders (Dorsey, Zawitz & Middleton, 2002). Note that rates based on drug-testing results do not necessarily shed light on a causal relationship because such rates reflect drug use at the time of the arrest, not necessarily the offense. Thus, these data simply demonstrate that many criminal offenders are also drug users. In fact, criminal justice statistics indicate that offenders are heavier drug users than the rest of the population (Dorsey, Zawitz & Middleton, 2002; Kouri, Pope, Powell, Oliva & Campbell, 1997), and this finding holds for men and women (Graham & Wish, 1994) as well as for adolescents (Dembo, Williams, Wish, Berry, Getreu, Washburn & Schmeidler, 1990).

Adolescent arrestees' reports of crime commission under the influence are fairly equal for alcohol and drugs; approximately one-fourth reported committing property or violent crimes while under the influence of both alcohol and other drugs (Bureau of Justice Statistics, 1994). However, in a study of high-risk male adolescents, White, Tice, Loeber, and Stouthamer-Loeber (2002) found that aggressive acts were more often related to self-reported acute use of alcohol than to marijuana use (see also Huizinga, Menard & Elliott, 1989). After a review of the literature on alcohol, other drugs, and violence among youths, Osgood (1994:33) concluded that there was little evidence that substance use makes an independent contribution to adolescent violence (see also Carpenter, Glassner, Johnson & Loughlin, 1988; Elliott, Huizinga & Menard, 1989; White, 1997b). Derzon and Lipsey (1999) conducted a meta-analysis on marijuana use and delinquency and concluded that use of marijuana does not establish a developmental trajectory to aggressive behaviors (see also White, Loeber, Stouthamer-Loeber & Pandina, 2002).

The associations between different types of crime and different types of drug use do not support a unique effect of cocaine use on violence. In many ADAM sites, violent offenders were more likely to test positive for marijuana than cocaine, and property offenders were more likely to test positive for cocaine than marijuana (McBride, VanderWaal & Terry-McElrath, 2002:7). Nevertheless, cocaine is the drug most often related to homicide (Goldstein, Brownstein, Ryan & Bellucci, 1988; Lattimore, Trudeau, Riley, Lieter & Edwards, 1997). However, this association appears more likely due to drug-market violence rather than pharmacological effects of cocaine (MacCoun, Kilmer & Reuter, 2002; White & Gorman, 2000; see the section on "Systemic Violence" below).

White and Gorman (2000) examined trends in drug use in relation to trends in crime across 17 cities in the United States. They correlated ADAM data with data from the Uniform Crime Reports (UCR) on property and violent crime rates. Their findings indicated that there is no uniform association between any type of drug use and any type of crime. Research on the longitudinal associations between drug use and violence also presents mixed findings.[2] Note that gender, age, and race/ethnicity differences in the nature of the drugs–crime relationship have been observed (Collins & Messerschmidt, 1993; Nunes-Dinis & Weisner, 1997; Valdez, Yin & Kaplan, 1997; Wieczorek, Welte & Abel, 1990), but cannot be included in this review.

Theoretical Explanations for Drug-Related Violence

Although deviance theories, such as social learning theory and strain theory, have been applied to explain the etiology of substance use/abuse as well as violence, most of these theories have not been applied specifically to drug-related violence. One exception is routine activities theory. Proponents of the routine activities perspective argue that bars are crime "hot spots" because they bring together motivated offenders and suitable targets in the absence of effective guardianship (Roncek & Maier, 1991) .

The theoretical framework most often used for drug-related violence is the tripartite model (Goldstein, 1985). This model postulates that there are three ways in which drug use could cause violence: (1) through psychopharmacological effects of drugs on the individual, (2) by generating predatory crime to get money to pay for drugs, and (3) because of systemic violence involved in the illegal drug market. The tripartite model has been criticized, however, because it has not been tested often, is more applicable to homicide than to other types of violent crime, and is biased toward the systemic model (MacCoun, Kilmer & Reuter, 2002; Parker & Auerhahn, 1998).

The Psychopharmacological Model

The psychopharmacological model proposes that the effects of intoxication cause violent behavior (Collins, 1981; Fagan, 1990). In addition, chronic intoxication may also contribute to subsequent aggression due to factors such as withdrawal, sleep deprivation, nutritional deficits, impairment of neuropsychological functioning, or enhancement of psychopathologic personality disorders (Virkkunen & Linnoila, 1993). The psychopharmacological model has gained greater support in the alcohol literature than it has for other drugs. Controlled laboratory studies have consistently found that acute intoxication by alcohol (below sedating levels) is related to aggression when the subject is provoked (Bushman, 1997). However, it has also been demonstrated that the relationship between alcohol use and aggression is moderated by subject characteristics, experimental design conditions, and beverage characteristics (Chermack & Giancola, 1997; Gustafson, 1993; Ito, Miller & Pollock, 1996; Pihl, Peterson & Lau, 1993). Recent research suggests that increased aggression under conditions of alcohol intoxication in the laboratory cannot be explained by either physiological disinhibition of alcohol nor alcohol expectancies. Rather, alcohol increases aggression by causing changes within the person that increase the risk for aggression, such as reduced intellectual functioning, reduced self-awareness, reduced executive functioning, reduced self-attention, reduced attention to situational cues, and inaccurate assessment of risks (Bushman, 1997).[3]

The psychopharmacological explanation for the drugs–violence association has largely been refuted in the literature with regard to heroin and marijuana, but has received strong support for barbiturates and tranquilizers. (For an extensive review of specific drug effects on aggression in animals and humans, see Miczek, DeBold, Haney, Tidey, Vivian & Weerts, 1994; see also Parker & Auerhahn, 1998). Some studies have found that chronic use of marijuana, opiates, and amphetamines does increase the risk of violent behavior (Miczek, DeBold, Haney, Tidey, Vivian & Weerts, 1994). There is also some evidence that psychostimulant drugs (e.g., methamphetamine and cocaine) are associated with aggression at least in animals, although research findings are inconsistent (Anthony & Forman, 2002; Miczek, DeBold, Haney, Tidey, Vivian & Weerts, 1994). There is no conclusive evidence (except anecdotal and in small samples) that acute use of PCP (phencyclidine) and LSD (lysergic acid diethylamide) is associated with violent behavior, except when use enhances already existing psychopathology (Miczek, DeBold, Haney, Tidey, Vivian & Weerts, 1994; see also Fagan, 1990; Parker & Auerhahn, 1998). Goldstein (1998) has claimed that the intoxicating effects of all illicit drugs account for very little of drug-related violent crime, although few laboratory studies of drug effects on aggression have been conducted with the sophisticated controls that alcohol studies have included (MacCoun, Kilmer & Reuter, 2002). In sum, the psychopharmacological model appears relevant for explaining a potential causal relationship between alcohol and violence among adults, but little of the relationship between illicit drugs and violence. However, after a thorough review of the existing literature, Parker and Auerhahn (1998) concluded that the social environment is a more powerful contributor to violence than are the pharmacological effects of any drug, including alcohol.

The Economic Motivation Model

The economic motivation model assumes that drug users need to generate illicit income to support their drug habit. Thus, they engage in predatory crimes such as robbery and burglary to get drugs or the money to buy drugs. Support for the economic motivation model comes mostly from literature on heroin addicts that indicates that lowering the frequency of substance use among addicts lowers their frequency of crime, especially property crime (e.g., Anglin & Perrochet, 1998; Chaiken & Chaiken, 1990; Nurco, Shaffer, Ball & Kinlock, 1984). However, for the most part, reductions in criminality only occur for those individuals with previously low levels of criminal activity (Lipton & Johnson, 1998; Nurco, 1998). Furthermore, there appear to be ethnic/racial differences in the effects of treatment on crime reduction (Nurco, Hanlon, Kinlock & Duszynski, 1988).

Self-report data do not provide strong support that economic motivation accounts for much drug-related violence. In 1999, about 13 percent of jail inmates reported having committed a crime in order to get money for drugs, and more property than violent crimes were committed to get money for drugs (Dorsey, Zawitz & Middleton, 2002). Similarly, intensive drug users and highly delinquent youths do not report committing crimes to raise money for drugs (Altschuler & Brounstein, 1991; Carpenter, Glassner, Johnson & Loughlin, 1988; Johnson, Wish, Schmeidler & Huizinga, 1986). Across age groups, there appears to have been much less economically motivated predatory crime related to crack in the 1980s and 1990s than there was to heroin in the 1970s and 1980s. The reduction in property crime since the appearance of the crack epidemic supports this view. Drug dealing may have obviated the need to commit property crimes and income-generating violent crimes (Miczek, DeBold, Haney, Tidey, Vivian & Weerts, 1994), although this argument has been questioned (MacCoun, Kilmer & Reuter, 2002). In sum, much of the recent research dispels the assumption of economically motivated crime, once drug dealing is excluded (Harrison, 1992).

The Systemic Model

During the 1980s, attention began to focus on the systemic model (Goldstein, 1985), which posits that the system of drug distribution and use is inherently connected with violent crime. Systemic types of crimes surrounding drug distribution include fights over organizational and territorial issues, enforcement of rules, punishments of and efforts to protect buyers and sellers, and transaction-related crimes (Miczek, DeBold, Haney, Tidey, Vivian & Weerts, 1994). In addition, there is often third-party violence, such as bystander shootings or assaults on prostitutes who sell drugs.

The systemic model probably accounts for most of the recent violence related to illicit drug use, especially drug-related homicides, which increased significantly with the appearance of crack cocaine in 1985 (although they are currently declining) (Blumstein, 1995; Fagan & Chin, 1990; Goldstein, Brownstein, Ryan & Bellucci, 1989). However, MacCoun, Kilmer, and Reuter (2002) argue that at the low end of the market (in which selling is being done by users who are high on crack or cocaine), it might be difficult to distinguish systemic from pharmacological violence. MacCoun, Kilmer, and Reuter (2002) suggest that the crack market was particularly violent as compared to other drug markets because more youths participated in it, the drugs were very valuable and used frequently, and the intensity of enforcement raised the adverse consequences. Selective incarceration, the aging of participants, and deaths of the most violent individuals in conjunction with stabilization of the market may account for the recent decline in violence (Goldstein, 1998; MacCoun, Kilmer & Reuter, 2002).[4]

Nevertheless, the drug market may not be the cause of individuals becoming violent. Van Kammen and Loeber (1994) found that individuals drawn to dealing are already violent and delinquent, and once they are involved in drug use or dealing, their level of violent behavior (including weapons possession) increases (see also Fagan & Chin, 1990; Inciardi & Pottieger, 1991; Johnson, Natarajan, Dunlap & Elmoghazy, 1994). Johnson, Williams, Dei, and Sanabria (1990) argued that violence in the crack trade was a result of violent individuals selecting themselves or being recruited into this type of work. Overall, the literature suggests that violent individuals are attracted to drug selling rather than that drug selling causes individuals to become violent. Hence, these results support a common cause rather than a direct causal model (see below).

An Alternative Explanation for Drug-Related Violence

One alternative explanation for the association between drug use and violence is that violent behavior leads to drug use.[5] Another viable and well supported explanation is the common cause model, which postulates that substance use and violence do not have a direct causal link. Rather, they are related because they share common causes, such as hyperactivity, impulsivity, risk-taking, inability to delay gratification, abuse or rejection in family, lack of parental nurturance, early school failure, and peer rejection (Hawkins, Catalano & Miller, 1992; Reiss & Roth, 1993).[6] Given that these behaviors share several common causes, the same individuals would be expected to engage in both substance use and violence. Furthermore, the comorbidity between substance abuse, antisocial personality disorder, and other psychiatric disorders has been demonstrated in clinical and community samples (e.g., Collins, Schlenger & Jordan, 1988; Hesselbrock, Hesselbrock & Stabenau, 1985; Regier, Farmer, Rae, Locke, Keith, Judd & Goodwin, 1990). Therefore, it may be difficult to separate out the effects of drugs from the effects of psychological disorders on violence. In addition, subcultural norms may reinforce both violent behavior and substance use (Fagan, 1990).

Besides individual- and interpersonal-level influences, drug use and violence may share common environmental and situational causes. For example, rates of violent crime are high in neighborhoods that are poor, are densely populated, are racially segregated, and have a transient population (Bursik, 1988; Sampson, Raudenbush & Earls, 1997). Drug exposure opportunities and sustained use are also more common among residents of disadvantaged and disorganized neighborhoods, probably because the illicit drug market concentrates in such communities (Ensminger, Anthony & McCord, 1997). Certain types of places and situations also generate greater rates of both drug use and violence (Fagan, 1993). In sum, the connection between drug use and many violent crimes may not be causal.

Summary and Conclusions

It is obvious from the above review that one single model cannot account for the drugs–violence relationship among all people. Rather, there are some individuals for whom the acute, and possibly chronic, cognitive effects of some drugs, such as alcohol, increase the propensity toward violent behaviors. For others, aggressive behavior weakens bonds to conventional norms and increases involvement in deviant subcultures (including the illicit drug market) that provide opportunities and reinforcement for increased drug use. Finally, for others (probably a majority), biopsychological factors (e.g., temperament) and early parent–child interactions, in combination with socioenvironmental factors, increase the risk for involvement in all types of deviant behavior. As White and Gorman (2000) noted, the drug-using, crime-committing population is not homogeneous; rather, it is comprised of subgroups of individuals displaying different causal paths. Most drug users do not commit crimes, with the exception of obvious drug-related crimes (i.e., possession and dealing), and criminal offenders are heterogeneous in terms of their patterns of drug use. In addition, for most criminally involved drug users, drug use does not cause initial criminal involvement. Therefore, the task for future research is to understand why some drug users commit violent crimes and others do not and the conditions under which violence is more likely to ensue during episodes of drug use (Anthony & Forman, 2002; Brownstein & Crossland, 2002).[7]

Endnotes

[1]   Recommended reviews include: Chaiken and Chaiken, 1990; Chermack and Giancola, 1997; Fagan, 1990; Graham, Wells, and West, 1997; Harrison, 1992; MacCoun, Kilmer, and Reuter, 2002; McBride, VanderWaal, and Terry-McElrath, 2002; Miczek, DeBold, Haney, Tidey, Vivian, and Weerts, 1994; Osgood, 1994; Parker and Auerhahn, 1998; Watters, Reinarman, and Fagan, 1985; White, 1990, 1997a, 1997b; and White and Gorman, 2000.

[2]   The examination of temporal and developmental associations is beyond the scope of this paper. See Dembo, Williams, Getreu, Genung, Schmeidler, Berry, Wish, and La Voie, 1991; Farrington, 1995; Huang, White, Kosterman, Catalano, and Hawkins, 2001; Kaplan and Damphousse, 1995; White, Brick, and Hansell, 1993; White and Hansell, 1998; White, Loeber, Stouthamer-Loeber, and Farrington, 1999, for greater detail.

[3]   Numerous biological and neuropsychological mechanisms have been proffered to explain how alcohol use increases the risk of violence. For greater detail, see Fagan, 1990; Miczek, DeBold, Haney, Tidey, Vivian, and Weerts, 1994; Parker and Auerhahn, 1999; Pihl, Peterson, and Lau, 1993; and White, 1997a. For a review of laboratory studies and theoretical explanations for the association between alcohol and aggression, see Bushman, 1997; Chermack and Giancola, 1997; Ito, Miller, and Pollock, 1996; Lipsey, Wilson, Cohen, and Derzon, 1997; Parker and Rebhun, 1995; and Pihl and Peterson, 1995. For a review of the methodological issues in laboratory research, see White, 1997a.

[4]   See MacCoun, Kilmer, and Reuter, 2002, and McBride, VanderWaal, and Terry-McElrath, 2002, for greater detail on drug markets and their differential effects on violence.

[5]   Because this chapter focused on drug-related violence, I did not discuss the literature supporting the alternative causal model that violence leads to drug use (see Collins, 1993; Collins & Messerschmidt, 1993; Khantzian, 1985; White, 1990) or supporting reciprocal causation (see Collins, 1986; Fagan & Chin, 1990; White & Gorman, 2000; White, Loeber, Stouthamer-Loeber & Farrington, 1999).

[6]   The generality of deviance assumption has been questioned (see White & Labouvie, 1994), and several studies have found that there are different predictors of alcoholism, drug use, and violence (Brook, Whiteman & Cohen, 1995; McCord & Ensminger, 1997).

[7]   A complete list of recommendations for future research can be found in NIJ (2002) as well as individual papers by Anthony and Forman (2002); MacCoun, Kilmer, and Reuter (2002); and McBride, VanderWaal, and Terry-McElrath (2002).

Discussion Questions

1. What is meant by systemic violence? Provide three examples of systemic violence.

2. How would you apply routine activities theory to explain alcohol-related violence?

3. How would you distinguish the association between alcohol and violence from the association between illicit drugs and violence?

4. List five risk factors that predict violence and also predict drug use.

References

Altschuler, D.M., and P.J. Brounstein (1991). "Patterns of Drug Use, Drug Trafficking, and Other Delinquency Among Inner-city Adolescent Males in Washington, DC." *Criminology, 29* (November):589-622.

Anglin, M.D., and B. Perrochet (1998). "Drug Use and Crime: A Historical Review of Research Conducted By the UCLA Drug Abuse Research Center." *Substance Use and Misuse, 33* (July):1871-1914.

Anthony, J.C., and V. Forman (2002). "At the Intersection of Public Health and Criminal Justice Research on Drugs and Crime." In *Towards a Drug and Crime Research Agenda for the 21st Century,* National Institute of Justice [Online]: Available at: www.ojp.usdoj.gov/nij/drugscrime/194616.htm

Blumstein, A. (1995). "Youth Violence, Guns and the Illicit-drug Industry." In C. Block and R. Block (eds.), *Trends, Risks, and Interventions in Lethal Violence,* pp. 3-15. Washington, DC: National Institute of Justice.

Brook, J.S., M. Whiteman, and P. Cohen (1995). "Stage of Drug Use, Aggression, and Theft/Vandalism: Shared and Unshared Risks." In H.B. Kaplan (ed.), *Drugs, Crime, and Other Deviant Adaptations: Longitudinal Studies*, pp. 83-98. New York: Plenum.

Brownstein, H., and C. Crossland (2002). "Introduction." In *Towards a Drugs and Crime Research Agenda for the 21st Century*. National Institute of Justice [Online]: Available at: www.ojp.usdoj.gov/nij/drugscrime/194616.htm

Bureau of Justice Statistics (1994). *Fact Sheet: Drug Data Summary*. Washington, DC: U.S. Department of Justice.

Bursik, R.J., Jr. (1988). "Social Disorganization and Theories of Crime and Delinquency: Problems and Prospects." *Criminology*, 26 (November):519-551.

Bushman, B.J. (1997). "Effects of Alcohol on Human Aggression: Validity of Proposed Explanations." In M. Galanter (ed.), *Recent Developments in Alcoholism: Alcohol and Violence*, Volume 13, pp. 227-243. New York: Plenum.

Carpenter, C., B. Glassner, B.D. Johnson, and J. Loughlin (1988). *Kids, Drugs, and Crime*. Lexington, MA: Lexington Books.

Chaiken, J.M., and M.R. Chaiken (1990). "Drugs and Predatory Crime." In M. Tonry and J.Q. Wilson (eds.), *Drugs and Crime*, 13th ed., pp. 203-239. Chicago: University of Chicago Press.

Chermack, S.T., and P.R. Giancola (1997). "The Relation Between Alcohol and Aggression: An Integrated Biopsychosocial Conceptualization." *Clinical Psychology Review*, 17:621-649.

Collins, J.J. (1993). "Drinking and Violence: An Individual Offender Focus." In S.E. Martin (ed.), *Alcohol and Interpersonal Violence: Fostering Multidisciplinary Perspectives*, pp. 221-235. Rockville, MD: National Institute of Health.

Collins, J.J. (1986). "The Relationship of Problem Drinking to Individual Offending Sequences." In A. Blumstein, J. Cohen, J. Roth, and C.A. Visher (eds.), *Criminal Careers and "Career Criminals"*, pp. 89-120. Washington, DC: National Academy Press.

Collins, J.J. (ed.) (1981). *Drinking and Crime*. New York: Guilford.

Collins, J.J., and P.M. Messerschmidt (1993). "Epidemiology of Alcohol-Related Violence." *Alcohol Health and Research World*, 17:93-100.

Collins, J.J., W.E. Schlenger, and B.K. Jordan (1988). "Antisocial Personality and Substance Abuse Disorders." *Bulletin of the American Academy on Psychiatry Law*, 16:187-198.

Cook, P.J., and M.J. Moore (1993). "Economic Perspectives on Reducing Alcohol Related Violence." In S.E. Martin (ed.), *Alcohol and Interpersonal Violence: Fostering Multidisciplinary Perspectives*, pp. 193-212. Rockville, MD: National Institute of Health.

Dembo, R., L. Williams, A. Getreu, L. Genung, J. Schmeidler, E. Berry, E.D. Wish, and L. La Voie (1991). "A Longitudinal Study of the Relationships Among Marijuana/Hashish Use, Cocaine Use, and Delinquency in a Cohort of High Risk Youths." *Journal of Drug Issues*, 21:271-312.

Dembo, R., L. Williams, E.D. Wish, E. Berry, A. Getreu, M. Washburn, and J. Schmeidler (1990). "Examination of the Relationships Among Drug Use, Emotional/Psychological Problems, and Crime Among Youths Entering a Juvenile Detention Center." *International Journal of the Addictions*, 25:1301-1340.

Dorsey, T.L., M.W. Zawitz, and P. Middleton (2002). *Drugs and Crime Facts* (NCJ No. 165148). [Online]: Available at: www.ojp.usdoj.gov/bjs/pub/pdf/dcf.pdf

Derzon, J.H., and M.W. Lipsey (1999). "A Synthesis of the Relationship of Marijuana Use with Delinquent and Problem Behaviors." *School Psychology International,* 20:57-68.

Elliott, D.S., D. Huizinga, and S. Menard (1989). *Multiple Problem Youth: Delinquency, Substance Use, and Mental Health Problems.* New York: Springer-Verlag.

Ensminger, M.E., J.C. Anthony, and J. McCord (1997). "The Inner City and Drug Use: Initial Findings from an Epidemiological Study." *Drug and Alcohol Dependence,* 48 (December):175-184.

Fagan, J. (1993). "Set and Setting Revisited: Influence of Alcohol and Illicit Drugs on the Social Context of Violent Events." In S.E. Martin (ed.), *Alcohol and Interpersonal Violence: Fostering Multidisciplinary Perspectives*, pp. 161-191. Rockville, MD: National Institute of Health.

Fagan, J. (1990). "Intoxication and Aggression." In M. Tonry and J.Q. Wilson (eds.), *Drugs and Crime*, pp. 241- 320. Chicago: University of Chicago Press.

Fagan, J., and K. Chin (1990). "Violence as Regulation and Social Control in the Distribution of Crack." In M. De La Rosa, E.Y. Lambert, and B. Gropper (eds.), *Drugs and Violence: Causes, Correlates and Consequences*, pp. 8-43. Rockville, MD: National Institute on Drug Abuse.

Farrington, D.P. (1995). "The Development of Offending and Antisocial Behaviour from Childhood: Key Findings From the Cambridge Study in Delinquent Development." *Journal of Child Psychology and Psychiatry*, 36 (September):929-964.

Goldstein, P.J. (1998). "Drugs, Violence, and Federal Funding: A Research Odyssey." *Substance Use and Misuse*, 33 (July):1915-1936.

Goldstein, P.J. (1985). "The Drugs/Violence Nexus: A Tripartite Conceptual Framework." *Journal of Drug Issues*, 15 (Fall):493-506.

Goldstein, P.J., H.H. Brownstein, P.J. Ryan, and P.A. Bellucci (1989). "Crack and Homicide in New York City, 1988: A Conceptually Based Event Analysis." *Contemporary Drug Problems*, 16 (Winter):651-687.

Graham, K., S. Wells, and P. West (1997). "A Framework for Applying Explanations of Alcohol-Related Aggression to Naturally Occurring Aggressive Behavior." *Contemporary Drug Problems*, 24 (Winter):625-666.

Graham, N., and E.D. Wish (1994). "Drug Use Among Female Arrestees: Onset, Patterns, and Relationships to Prostitution." *The Journal of Drug Issues*, 24:315-329.

Greenfeld, L.A., and M.A. Henneberg (2001). "Victim and Offender Self-reports of Alcohol Involvement in Crime." *Alcohol Health and Research World*, 25(1):20-31.

Greenfeld, L.A., M.R. Rand, D. Craven, C.A. Perkins, C. Ringel, G. Warchol, C. Matson, and J.A. Fox (1998). "Violence by Intimates: Analysis of Data on Crimes by Current or Former Spouses, Boyfriends, and Girlfriends." Washington, DC: U.S. Department of Justice, Bureau of Justice Statistics.

Gustafson, R. (1993). "What Do Experimental Paradigms Tell Us about Alcohol-Related Aggressive Responding?" *Journal of Studies on Alcohol,* Supplement No. 11 (September):20-29.

Harlow, C.W. (1998). "Profile of Jail Inmates, 1996." Washington, DC: U.S. Department of Justice, Bureau of Justice Statistics.

Harrison, L.D. (1992). "The Drug-Crime Nexus in the USA." *Contemporary Drug Problems,* (Summer):203-245.

Hawkins, J.D., R.F. Catalano, and J.Y. Miller (1992). "Risk and Protective Factors for Alcohol and Other Drug Problems in Adolescence and Early Adulthood: Implications for Substance Abuse Prevention." *Psychological Bulletin,* 112:64-105.

Hesselbrock, V.M, M.N. Hesselbrock, and J.R. Stabenau (1985). "Alcoholism in Men Patients Subtyped by Family History and Antisocial Personality." *Journal of Studies on Alcohol,* 46 (January):59-64.

Huizinga, D.H., S. Menard, and D.S. Elliott (1989). "A Delinquency and Drug Use: Temporal and Developmental Patterns." *Justice Quarterly,* 6:419-455.

Huang, B., H.R. White, R. Kosterman, R.F. Catalano, and J.D. Hawkins (2001). "Developmental Associations Between Alcohol and Aggression During Adolescence." *Journal of Research in Crime and Delinquency,* 38:64-83.

Inciardi, J.A., and A.E. Pottieger (1991). "Kids, Crack, and Crime." *Journal of Drug Issues,* 21:257-270.

Ito, T.A., N. Miller, and V.E. Pollock (1996). "Alcohol and Aggression: A Meta-Analysis on the Moderating Effects of Inhibitory Cues, Triggering Events, and Self-Focused Attention." *Psychological Bulletin,* 120:60-82.

Johnson, B.D., M. Natarajan, E. Dunlap, and E. Elmoghazy (1994). "Crack Abusers and Non-crack Abusers: Profiles of Drug Use, Drug Sales and Nondrug Criminality." *Journal of Drug Issues,* 24:117-141.

Johnson, B.D., T. Williams, K.A. Dei, and H. Sanabria (1990). "Drug Abuse in the Inner City: Impact on Hard-Drug Users and the Community." In M. Tonry and J.Q. Wilson (eds.), *Drugs and Crime,* 13th ed., pp. 9-67. Chicago: University of Chicago Press.

Johnson, B.D., E. Wish, J. Schmeidler, and D.H. Huizinga (1986). "The Concentration of Delinquent Offending: Serious Drug Involvement and High Delinquency Rates." In B.D. Johnson and E. Wish (eds.), *Crime Rates Among Drug Abusing Offenders,* pp. 106-143. New York: Interdisciplinary Research Center, Narcotic and Drug Research.

Kantor, G.K., and N. Asdigian (1997). "When Women are Under the Influence: Does Drinking or Drug Use by Women Provoke Beatings by Men?" In M. Galanter (ed.), *Recent Developments in Alcoholism: Alcohol and Violence,* Volume 13, pp. 315-336. New York: Plenum.

Kantor, G.K., and M.A. Straus (1987). "The Drunken Bum Theory of Wife Beating." *Social Problems,* 34:213-230.

Kaplan, H.B., and K.R. Damphousse (1995). "Self-Attitudes and Antisocial Personality as Moderators of the Drug Use-Violence Relationship." In H.B. Kaplan (ed.), *Drugs, Crime, and Other Deviant Adaptations: Longitudinal Studies,* pp. 187-210. New York: Plenum.

Khantzian, E.J. (1985). "The Self-Medication Hypothesis of Addictive Disorders: Focus on Heroin and Cocaine Dependence." *American Journal of Psychiatry,* 142 (November):1259-1264.

Kouri, E.M., H.G. Pope, Jr., K.F. Powell, P.S. Oliva, and C. Campbell (1997). "Drug Use History and Criminal Behavior Among 133 Incarcerated Men." *American Journal of Drug and Alcohol Abuse,* 23:413-419.

Lattimore, P., J. Trudeau, K.J., Riley, J. Lieter, and S. Edwards (1997). *Homicide in Eight U.S. Cities: Trends, Context, and Policy Implications*. Washington, DC: National Institute of Justice.

Leonard, K. (2000). "Domestic Violence and Alcohol: What is Known and What Do We Need to Know to Encourage Environmental Interventions," Paper presented at the annual meeting of the National Crime Prevention Council, Alcohol and Crime: Research and Practice for Prevention, Washington, DC.

Leonard, K.E., and H.T. Blane (1992). "Alcohol and Marital Aggression in a National Sample of Young Men." *Journal of Interpersonal Violence*, 7:19-30.

Leonard, K.E., and M. Senchak (1996), "Prospective Prediction of Husband Marital Aggression within Newlywed Couples." *Journal of Abnormal Psychology*, 105:369-380.

Lipsey, M.W., D.B. Wilson, M.A. Cohen, and J.H. Derzon (1997). "Is There a Causal Relationship Between Alcohol Use and Violence? A Synthesis of Evidence." In M. Galanter (ed.), *Recent Developments in Alcoholism, Alcohol and Violence*, Volume 13, pp. 245-282. New York: Plenum.

Lipton, D.S., and B.D. Johnson (1998). "Smack, Crack, and Score: Two Decades of NIDA-Funded Drugs and Crime Research at NDRI 1974-1994." *Substance Use and Misuse*, 33 (July):1779-1815.

MacCoun, R., B. Kilmer, and P. Reuter (2002). "Research on Drugs-Crime Linkages: The Next Generation." In *Towards a Drugs and Crime Research Agenda for the 21st Century*, National Institute of Justice [Online]: Available at: www.ojp.usdoj.gov/nij/drugscrime/194616.htm

McBride, D.C., and C.B. McCoy (1982). "Crimes and Drugs: The Issues and Literature." *Journal of Drug Issues*, (Spring):137-151.

McBride, D.C., C.J. VanderWaal, and Y.M. Terry-McElrath (2002). "The Drugs-Crime Wars: Past, Present, and Future Directions in Theory, Policy, and Program Interventions." In *Towards a Drugs and Crime Research Agenda for the 21st Century*, National Institute of Justice [Online]: Available at: www.ojp.usdoj.gov/nij/drugscrime/194616.htm

McCord, J., and M.E. Ensminger (1997). "Multiple Risks and Comorbidity in an African-American Population." *Criminal Behaviour and Mental Health*, 7:339-352.

Miczek, K.A., J.F. DeBold, M. Haney, J. Tidey, J. Vivian, and E.M. Weerts (1994). "Alcohol, Drugs of Abuse, Aggression, and Violence," In A.J. Reiss and J.A. Roth (eds.), *Understanding and Preventing Violence*, 3rd ed., pp. 377-468. Washington, DC: National Academy Press.

Miller, B.A., E. Maguin, and W.R. Downs (1997). "Alcohol, Drugs, and Violence in Children's Lives," In M. Galanter (ed.), *Recent Developments in Alcoholism: Alcohol and Violence*, Volume 13, pp. 357-385. New York: Plenum.

National Institute of Justice (2002). *Towards a Drugs and Crime Research Agenda for the 21st Century*. National Institute of Justice: [Online]. Available at: www.ojp.usdoj.gov/nij/drugscrime/194616.htm

Nunes-Dinis, M.C., and C. Weisner (1997). "Gender Differences in the Relationship of Alcohol and Drug Use to Criminal Behavior in a Sample of Arrestees." *American Journal of Drug and Alcohol Abuse*, 23:129-141.

Nurco, D.N. (1998). "A Long-Term Program of Research on Drug Use and Crime." *Substance Use and Misuse*, 33 (July):1817-1837.

Nurco, D.N., T.E. Hanlon, T.W. Kinlock, and K.R. Duszynski (1988). "Differential Criminal Patterns of Narcotic Addicts over an Addiction Career." *Criminology,* 26 (August):407-423.

Nurco, D.N., J.C. Shaffer, J.C. Ball, and T.W. Kinlock (1984). "Trends in the Commission of Crime Among Narcotic Addicts Over Successive Periods of Addiction." *American Journal of Drug and Alcohol Abuse,* 10:481-489.

Osgood, D.W. (1994). "Drugs, Alcohol, and Adolescent Violence." Paper presented at the annual meeting of the American Society of Criminology, Miami, FL.

Parker, R.N. (1993). "The Effects of Context on Alcohol and Violence." *Alcohol Health and Research World,* 17:117-122.

Parker, R.N., and K. Auerhahn (1999). "Drugs, Alcohol, and Homicide: Issues in Theory and Research." In M.D. Smith and M.A. Zahn (eds.), *A Sourcebook of Social Research*, pp. 176-191. Beverly Hills, CA: Sage.

Parker, R.N., and K. Auerhahn (1998). "Alcohol, Drugs, and Violence." *Annual Review of Sociology,* 24:291-311.

Parker, R.N., and L. Rebhun (1995). *Alcohol and Homicide: A Deadly Combination of Two American Traditions.* Albany, NY: State University of New York Press.

Pernanen, K. (1991). *Alcohol in Human Violence.* New York: Guilford.

Pihl, R.O., and J. Peterson (1995). "Drugs and Aggression: Correlations, Crime and Human Manipulative Studies and Some Proposed Mechanisms." *Journal of Psychiatric Neuroscience,* 20:141-149.

Pihl, R.O., J.B. Peterson, and M.A. Lau (1993). "A Biosocial Model of the Alcohol-Aggression Relationship." *Journal of Studies on Alcohol,* Supplement No. 11:128-139.

Regier, D.A., M.E. Farmer, D.S. Rae, B.Z. Locke, S.J. Keith, L.L. Judd, and F.K. Goodwin (1990). "Comorbidity of Mental Disorders with Alcohol and Other Drug Abuse: Results from the Epidemiologic Catchment Area (ECA) Study." *Journal of the American Medical Association,* 264 (November):2511-2518.

Reiss, A.J., Jr., and J.A. Roth (1993), *Understanding and Preventing Violence.* Washington, DC: National Academy Press.

Roizen, J. (1993). "Issues in the Epidemiology of Alcohol and Violence." In S.E. Martin (ed.), *Alcohol and Interpersonal Violence: Fostering Multidisciplinary Perspectives*, pp. 3-36. Rockville, MD: National Institute of Health.

Roncek, D.W., and P.A. Maier (1991). "Bars, Blocks, and Crimes Revisited: Linking the Theory of Routine Activities to the Empiricism of 'Hot Spots'." *Criminology,* 29 (November):725-753.

Sampson, R.J., S.W. Raudenbush, and F. Earls (1997). "Neighborhoods and Violent Crime: A Multilevel Study of Collective Efficacy." *Science,* 277 (August):918-924.

Scribner, R.A., D.P. MacKinnon, and J.H. Dwyer (1995). "The Risk of Assaultive Violence and Alcohol Availability in Los Angeles County." *American Journal of Public Health,* 85 (March):335-340.

Valdez, A., Z. Yin, and C.D. Kaplan (1997). "A Comparison of Alcohol, Drugs, and Aggressive Crime Among Mexican-American, Black, and White Male Arrestees in Texas." *American Journal of Drug and Alcohol Abuse,* 23:249-265.

Van Kammen, W.B., and R. Loeber (1994). "Are Fluctuations in Delinquent Activities Related to the Onset and Offset in Juvenile Illegal Drug Use and Drug Dealing?" *The Journal of Drug Issues,* 24:9-24.

Virkkunen, M., and M. Linnoila (1993). "Brain Serotonin, Type II Alcoholism and Impulsive Violence." *Journal of Studies on Alcohol,* Supplement No. 11 (September):163-169.

Watters, J.K., C. Reinarman, and J. Fagan (1985). "Causality, Context, and Contingency Relationships Between Drug Abuse and Delinquency." *Contemporary Drug Problems,* 12:351-373.

White, H.R. (1997a). "Alcohol, Illicit Drugs, and Violence." In D.M. Stoff, J. Breiling, and J. D. Maser (eds.), *Handbook of Antisocial Behavior,* pp. 511-523. New York: John Wiley and Sons.

White, H.R. (1997b). "Longitudinal Perspective on Alcohol Use and Aggression during Adolescence." In M. Galanter (ed.), *Recent Developments in Alcoholism: Alcohol and Violence,* Volume 13, pp. 81-103. New York: Plenum.

White, H.R. (1990). "The Drug Use-Delinquency Connection in Adolescence." In R. Weisheit (ed.), *Drugs, Crime, and Criminal Justice,* pp. 215-256. Cincinnati: Anderson.

White, H.R., J. Brick, and S. Hansell (1993). "A Longitudinal Investigation of Alcohol Use and Aggression in Adolescence." *Journal of Studies on Alcohol,* Supplement No. 11 (September):62-77.

White, H.R., and P.H. Chen (2002). "Problem Drinking and Intimate Partner Violence." *Journal of Studies on Alcohol,* 63:205-214.

White, H.R., and D.M. Gorman (2000). "Dynamics of the Drug-Crime Relationship." In G. LaFree (ed.), *Criminal Justice 2000, Volume: The Nature of Crime: Continuity and Change,* pp. 151-218. Washington, DC: U.S. Department of Justice.

White, H.R., and S. Hansell (1998). "Acute and Long-term Effects of Drug Use on Aggression from Adolescence into Adulthood." *Journal of Drug Issues,* 28:837-858.

White, H.R., and E.W. Labouvie (1994). "Generality Versus Specificity of Problem Behavior: Psychological and Functional Differences." *The Journal of Drug Issues,* 24:55-74.

White, H.R., R. Loeber, M. Stouthamer-Loeber, and D.P. Farrington (1999). "Developmental Associations Between Substance Use and Violence." *Development and Psychopathology,* 11:785-803.

White, H.R., R. Loeber, M. Stouthamer-Loeber, and R.J. Pandina (2002). "Developmental Trajectories of Substance Use and Illegal Activity: Examining Dual Trajectory Models." Paper presented at the annual meeting of the American Society of Criminology, Chicago, IL.

White, H.R., P. Tice, R. Loeber, and M. Stouthamer-Loeber (2002). "Illegal Acts Committed by Adolescents Under the Influence of Alcohol and Drugs." *Journal of Research in Crime and Delinquency,* 39:131-152.

Widom, C.S. (1993). "Child Abuse and Alcohol Use and Abuse." In S.E. Martin (ed.), *Alcohol and Interpersonal Violence: Fostering Multidisciplinary Perspectives,* pp. 291-314. Rockville, MD: National Institute of Health.

Widom, C.S., and S. Hiller-Sturmhöfel (2001). "Alcohol Abuse as a Risk Factor for and Consequences of Child Abuse." *Alcohol Research and Health,* 25:52-57.

Wieczorek, W.F., J.W. Welte, and E.L. Abel (1990). "Alcohol, Drugs, and Murder: A Study of Convicted Homicide Offenders." *Journal of Criminal Justice,* 18:217-227.

CHAPTER 13

Modern Lynchings

Roberta Senechal de la Roche

Collective violence involving large crowds is comparatively rare in modern societies such as the United States. Small group violence, however, occurs with some frequency, including many so-called "hate crimes"— crimes said to be motivated by hatred of the victim's race, ethnicity, religion, or sexual orientation (see, e.g., Perry, 2001:7-11). In the early 1990s, for instance, more than two-thirds of hate crimes in the United States had two or more perpetrators (Levin & McDevitt, 1993:16).[1] Moreover, most who collectively threaten or commit violent hate crime are not members of formally organized "hate-groups" like the Ku Klux Klan, but instead are often related to the victims as fellow neighbors, prisoners, members of college fraternities, gang members, coworkers, or students (see, e.g., Levin & McDevitt, 1993; Perry, 2001).[2] Indeed, only about 10 to 15 percent of violent hate crimes in this period were committed by extremist groups (Levin & McDevitt, 1993; Perry, 2001:141-142).

In the popular conception of hate crime, bias and bigotry prompt attacks on others because of their membership in a different social category (Herek & Berrill, 1992:xiii; see also Berk, Boyd & Hamner, 1992:131; Levin & McDevitt, 1993:vii, ix-xi). It is sometimes said that anyone and everyone in certain social categories, such as African Americans or homosexuals, is equally vulnerable to attack. As one social scientist remarked, "The victims are interchangeable" (Perry, 2001:10). However, while it is true that some collective violence targets any and all members of a social category, much does not. For example, lynching and vigilantism usually target only specific

This paper was originally prepared for a Workshop on Theories of Violence, organized by Margaret A. Zahn and Anna Jordan, and sponsored by the National Institute of Justice, Violence and Victimization Division, Washington, DC, December 10-11, 2002. I thank Donald Black for comments on an earlier draft.

individuals whose conduct is defined as deviant. Moreover, strange as it may seem, a large amount of modern violence labeled as hate crime is actually a form of lynching—collective violence in which a group punishes an individual defined as deviant.[3] Modern lynchings differ greatly in one regard from the lynchings of earlier times: They are smaller. In this sense, they are *micro-lynchings*, yet they belong to the same sociological family as the more dramatic and familiar lynchings—usually of African Americans by whites—of a century ago in the American South (see, e.g., Brundage, 1993; Tolnay & Beck, 1995). The factors that produce large-scale lynchings and micro-lynchings are similar, but because some of those factors are present to a smaller degree in micro-lynchings, they produce smaller-scale and often less lethal violence. The phenomenon of micro-lynching is largely unrecognized among social scientists in the fields of collective violence and criminology, but it has occurred in diverse times and places, including many if not all modern societies such as the United States (see e.g., Berk, Boyd & Hamner, 1992:127; Senechal de la Roche, 2001; Shotland, 1976).

Definitions

Violence is threatened, attempted, or actual physical harm to a person or property. Some collective violence is predatory, such as when a group of robbers uses violence or the threat of violence to obtain money or goods, or when groups loot stores during a natural disaster. Some collective violence is recreational as well, such as when young people destroy property to celebrate a sports victory (Senechal de la Roche, 1997:66, note 7; see also Cooney & Phillips, 2002:75-108).[4] Most collective violence, however, is *social control*, a process that defines or responds to behavior as deviant (Black, 1976:2; 1983; 1984:1). Social control expresses a grievance, reacts to conduct deemed wrong or undesirable, and involves a pursuit of justice. It takes numerous forms. Someone with a grievance might, for example, engage in negotiation or seek out a third party (such as a legal official) to settle a dispute. Or someone might simply avoid the wrongdoer. But collective violence belongs to a form of social control known as self-help— the handling of a grievance with aggression (Black, 1990:44-49). Although collective self-help might entail physical injury to persons, it might also involve only lesser forms of aggression such as insults or vandalism, illustrated by a crowd booing an unpopular speaker or a referee at a sports event. Most violent self-help by groups is defined as crime in modern societies and is often deemed morally repugnant by observers. Even so, such aggression is itself moralistic, a case of social control against one or more deviants (see Black, 1983).

Collective violence differs along two dimensions: its *degree of organization* and its *breadth of liability*. Collective violence may be highly organized, such as that of street gangs or terrorist organizations, or the amount of organization may be relatively low, illustrated by spontaneous crowds that gather briefly to lynch or riot, then disperse. Liability is accountability for a deviant act, such as the vulnerability of a burglar to punishment for his crime or a motorist to the payment of damages for an accident. It may be individual (when only a single person is accountable for his or her conduct) or collective (when members of a social category or group are accountable for the conduct of a fellow member) (see, e.g., Koch, 1984; Moore, 1972). Variation along both dimensions—the degree of organization and breadth of liability—distinguishes at least four forms of violent self-help by groups: lynching, rioting, vigilantism, and terrorism. Lynching and rioting have a low degree of organization, but lynching entails individual liability (punishing a particular offender) whereas rioting entails collective liability (attacking any and all members of a social category). Vigilantism and terrorism have a high degree of organization, but vigilantism entails individual liability while terrorism entails collective liability (see Figure 13.1).[5]

Figure 13.1
Four Forms of Collective Violence*

		Liability	
		individual	collective
Organization	low	lynching	rioting
	high	vigilantism	terrorism

From Senechal de la Roche (1996). "Collective Violence as Social Control." *Sociological Forum*, 11:105. Reprinted with permission.

In sum, whether large or small, *lynching is a form of collective violence characterized by informal organization and a logic of individual liability*. Although a lynching might involve some planning or organization, it is typically spontaneous and temporary, sometimes lasting only a few minutes. Lynchers punish only an alleged wrongdoer (or perhaps several wrongdoers at once) and disregard uninvolved people associated with the offender (Senechal de la Roche, 1996; 1997:50-51). Thus, lynching is not peculiarly American or Southern, nor is it a relic of the past. It has appeared across the world—in countless tribal and earlier societies (for references, see Senechal de la Roche, 1997:51-52; 2001). And both large and small lynchings still occur in rural areas, suburbs, and cities in Latin America, Australia, Europe, the United States, and elsewhere (see, e.g., Benevides & Ferreira, 1991; Human Rights and Equal Opportunity Commission, 1991; Martins, 1991; Senechal de la Roche, 1997:70, note 7; 2001:139-140).

The Geometry of Lynching

Central questions for any theory of violence include: From one conflict to the next, when is violence likely to occur? Why is the severity of violence greater in one case than another? Even killings vary in severity from a quick dispatch to prolonged and painful torture. Finally, why in particular does violence take the form of a lynching rather than, for example, a homicide involving only the killer and the target? Donald Black's "pure sociology" of conflict and violence (see, e.g., 1998; Chapter 9, this volume) provides a new and useful theoretical approach applicable to these questions. Black suggests that every form of social control has its own distinctive multidimensional social geometry. That geometry includes the social characteristics of all the parties in a case of conflict: offenders, complainants, and third parties with knowledge of the conflict.[6] What, then, is the social geometry that explains lynching? First consider the general theory of lynching—a theory that I later apply to micro-lynchings in modern America.

Three major elements of the social geometry of a conflict increase the likelihood and severity of lynchings: *social polarization*, *strong and unequal partisanship*, and *third-party solidarity* (Senechal de la Roche, 2001). To elaborate:

1. ***Social polarization of the adversaries***. A lynching is more likely when the alleged offender and aggrieved party are separated by considerable social distance along at least some of the following social dimensions:

   —*Relational distance* is "the degree to which [people] participate in one another's lives" (Black, 1976:40-48), measured by such factors as the nature and number of ties between people, the frequency and scope of contact between them, and the age of their relationship. All else constant, including the nature of the offense and other relevant variables, a lynching is more likely and more likely to be severe when the principal parties are relationally distant from one another. Hence, conflict between strangers is more conducive to lynching than is conflict between relatives, friends, or acquaintances.

   —*Cultural distance* refers to differences in the symbolic aspect of social life, such as differences in language, religion, and dress. The greater these differences, the greater is the likelihood and severity of a lynching.

   —*Functional interdependence* is the degree to which people cooperate and depend upon one another for their survival or well-being. The more interdependent the principal parties to a conflict, the less likely is a lynching between them.

—*Inequality of status* refers to differences in wealth or any other form of social status, such as respectability, conventionality, or integration. For example, someone who has a criminal record or who has been shunned by others is less respectable than someone who has not faced such actions. In addition, those who are conventional have more social status than those who are unconventional, and those who are integrated and close to the center of social life have more social status than marginal people with few if any links to others. The greater the inequality of social status of any kind between the parties in a conflict, the greater the likelihood and severity of a lynching. Moreover, when an offense is upward—committed by a social inferior against a social superior—it is more likely to attract a lynching than if the offender's social status is higher than the aggrieved party's (Senechal de la Roche, 1997:56-58; for a detailed discussion of all the above variables, see Black, 1976: Chapters 2-6).

Conflicts that are highly polarized—with the parties separated by a great deal of relational and cultural distance, independence, and inequality—are most conducive to lynchings of great severity. Such was the social geometry of most late nineteenth- and early twentieth-century lynchings of African Americans by whites in the South. As the social polarization of conflict lessens, however, so do the likelihood and severity of lynchings. Thus, a lynching of any kind is highly unlikely where the principal parties are intimate, culturally similar, equal, and interdependent (see, e.g., Senechal de la Roche, 1997). And if one does occur between such close parties, it is less likely to be lethal.

2. ***Strong and unequal partisanship.*** Violence becomes collective only when third parties decisively take sides and provide strong support for one adversary against another. If third parties fail to rally to either side, the aggrieved party is left to handle the conflict alone. Whether third parties remain neutral and possibly serve as mediators or peacemakers, or quickly and forcefully take the side of one of the adversaries, depends on their own location in the social geometry of a conflict (Black, 1998:125-143).

   Lynchings arise only when third parties provide strong partisanship to one side. This happens when third parties are socially close (intimate, culturally similar, interdependent) to the aggrieved party but are socially distant from the alleged wrongdoer. For example, if a member of an intimate circle of culturally similar friends is victimized by a culturally distant stranger, the friends are likely to support their aggrieved associate (Black, 1998:125-143). If they do so violently, their support becomes a lynching. Second, *lynchings arise only where partisanship is unequal.* Here the individual accused of misconduct has few or no supporters—perhaps because he or she is a stranger or culturally alien—while the offended party enjoys strong support from his or her socially close partisans (Senechal de la Roche, 2001). If the culturally and relationally distant offender lacks anyone socially close enough to take his or her side in the conflict, he or she must face the group of avenging friends alone. Such is the plight of anyone who is lynched.

3. ***Third-party solidarity***. Lynchers must be highly solidary among themselves—relationally and culturally close and functionally interdependent. If they are not solidary—if, say, they are relationally and culturally distant from one another—concerted action is unlikely to occur. Members of a street gang, for instance, are typically relationally close to one another, culturally homogeneous, and have cooperative ties to one another. Because their solidarity is so high, their capacity for collective social control, including group violence is high as well. In contrast, if the associates of, say, a middle-aged resident of modern suburbia are culturally diverse, scattered, and not interdependent with one another, their solidarity is much lower, and for them to help this resident by participating in a lynching is almost impossible to imagine. Without tightly knit partisans, then, lynchings do not occur (Senechal de la Roche, 2001).

Micro-Lynchings

Although micro-lynchings are frequent in modern America, most have a low degree of severity. Typically they involve only a threat of violence or an attack involving only pushing and shoving, a few punches or kicks, and the like. In American high schools and colleges, for example, students have often inflicted micro-lynchings on other students, especially those who were visibly homosexual or members of minorities (see, e.g., Berrill, 1992:32-34; Human Rights Watch, 2001; Hunter 1992:76-79; Levin & McDevitt, 1993:126-127). In these cases, the degree of social polarization between an alleged wrongdoer who is a homosexual or a minority group member and those of the group who mete out punishment is moderate: The adversaries are likely to be culturally distant (in the case of a minority group member) and functionally independent, but some relational closeness may be present as well. High school and college micro-lynchers and those they attack sometimes even have regular contact—in hallways, classes, dining halls, or dormitories. However brief and superficial, such regularized contact increases intimacy and thereby reduces the severity of any collective violence that might occur (e.g., Black, 1990:43-47; Senechal de la Roche, 1990:143-147; 1996:106-111; 1997:52-55). Accordingly, in high schools and colleges, homosexuals have more often faced insults and threats than beatings, and have been more likely to be spat upon or otherwise mildly harassed than attacked and wounded with a weapon (e.g., Berrill, 1992:32-33).[7] They have rarely if ever been killed.

Other elements of the geometry of a lynching were present as well. Those with grievances had strong support from solidary third parties, while the individual they deemed deviant had few or no partisans who openly took his or her side. Micro-lynchers are usually solidary groups of young men, such as members of close-knit friendship groups who share the same neighborhood or, in colleges, members of the same athletic team or fraternity. Indeed, fraternities are among the only settings on modern college campuses where solidarity is so high. Each fraternity resembles a clan in a larger tribe: Members are relationally close (commonly living and eating together), culturally similar (very homogeneous), and interdependent (with a high degree of cooperation among the "brothers"). Their social exclusiveness and relative lack of ties with others outside their group also distances them from the larger student population. Any member of a fraternity offended by a socially distant outsider, then, is likely to attract quick and strong collective support. This high level of solidarity and partisanship helps explain why fraternities have earned notoriety for varied acts of collective violence on campuses, including many micro-lynchings (Levin & McDevitt, 1993:128-130; Southern Poverty Law Center, 2000; Wiener, 1989). As one specialist in hate crime notes, "There is a consensus by many law enforcement agencies that these crimes are proportionate to the percentage of fraternity members on campus . . . the higher the percentage of fraternity membership, the greater potential for hate crimes" (Winbush, 1999).

As mentioned earlier, lynching arises where partisanship is unequal, particularly where those deemed wrongdoers have no support at all. Thus, we find that those subject to modern micro-lynchings are generally socially isolated at the time they are attacked. For instance, in one case an African-American woman at Brown University was kicked and hit in the face by "three drunken white males" who became angry because she refused to open a locked dormitory door for them (Southern Poverty Law Center, 2000).[8] Had the distribution of supporters in this case been more equal, something other than a micro-lynching would probably have occurred. If African-American friends of the young woman had been present to take her side, for example, an exchange of insults or threats or even brawling between the two sides might have taken place—or possibly nothing at all would have happened. Particularly isolated and vulnerable have been visibly homosexual students with a style of life both culturally and morally distant from most others, such as fellow students, faculty, school officials, police, and possibly family members (Human Rights Watch, 2001:4-5, 20-21). As one study of aggression toward homosexuals in high schools concluded, "The most common response to harassment . . . is no response" (p. 80). Making public one's deviant sexual orientation, or exhibiting patterns of dress, speech, or comportment that communicate such an orientation may have also attracted multiple verbal or physical attacks from varied groups of students against the same individuals.

Many micro-lynchings in public places have involved violence against deviant individuals who were maximally relationally distant—complete strangers—and possibly culturally distant and socially inferior as well. These polarized cases generate comparatively more severe violence. For example, micro-lynchings by solidary groups of youths against homosexuals who are strangers have more often been lethal (see, e.g., Comstock, 1991:26, 46-47, 57-62). Severely beating a female homosexual because she rebuffs a sexual advance by a male, or beating a male homosexual to death, however, has rarely occurred among fellow students, coworkers, or others more closely connected to the deviant individual (Comstock, 1991:13, 69-70).

Micro-lynchings in modern America have also been relatively numerous in ethnic enclaves of the working class and poor. In particular, many have been inflicted by members of street gangs and other youth groups who share both ethnicity and neighborhood and who have high levels of solidarity and strong supporters close at hand. In one New York City neighborhood in the 1970s (and probably later as well), for instance, some Italian-American youths served as "a proxy police force" that occasionally harassed and beat African-American strangers accused of wrongdoing (Rieder, 1985:178-179; see also Levin & McDevitt, 1993:79-83).[9] Likewise, in one highly publicized incident in Howard Beach, New York, in 1986, a small group of white friends attacked three African-American men who had allegedly insulted one of them, resulting in the death of one and serious injuries to another (Levin & McDevitt, 1993:5-7). Because the three black men were culturally distant, independent, and strangers to the young white man they had offended, the conflict was highly polarized and the severity of the lynching was greater. African-American street gangs (both inside and outside of prisons) respond with similar severity to socially distant and socially isolated individuals they regard as deviant—sometimes including lone whites or Asian Americans (Anderson, 1990:39, 174-175; Jankowski, 1991:184-186; Useem & Kimball, 1989:60-63, 95, 105-107, 192-193). Those who lack close ties to peers, however, typically do not commit micro-lynchings, regardless of their social distance from anyone who might offend them (Senechal de la Roche, 2001:139-140; see also Maxson, 1999:239-240, 248-249).

Residents of solidary ethnic enclaves have also occasionally inflicted micro-lynchings on minority families who moved into their neighborhoods. These conflicts have had a social geometry conducive to lynching as well: a high degree of social polarization between the parties (newcomers versus long-term residents), strong support for the aggrieved side, and numerous third parties (neighbors and friends) whose social closeness and solidarity leads them to act collectively against a deviant who has few or no allies. Small groups of residents have thus sometimes engaged in threats, vandalism, firebombing, and physical assaults against isolated families regarded as "invaders" (see e.g., Levin & McDevitt, 1993:76-87; Rieder, 1985:200-202).

Minority families who settle in such neighborhoods with little trouble from the established residents still, at least over the short term, remained socially distant and isolated. For this reason, even seemingly trivial offenses— barking dogs, trash thrown over a fence, or an exchange of angry words— might trigger a micro-lynching against them (see, e.g., Human Rights and Equal Opportunity Commission, 1991:76-77, 162-163, 215-216). In contrast, the residents in socially atomized settings such as middle-class American suburbs largely lack solidarity and therefore virtually never come together to inflict micro-lynchings upon minority newcomers or others deemed undesirable. Suburbanites tend to stay aloof from others' conflicts and "mind their own business" (Baumgartner, 1988).

Conclusion

Micro-lynching is a small version of a more dramatic form of social control that once occurred in the American South and other settings in various societies. It also occurs under similar conditions in modern America—where the adversaries are socially distant and where the aggrieved parties attract strong partisanship from solidary supporters against socially isolated wrongdoers. Although the empirical literature on so-called "hate crime" provides many examples of micro-lynchings, it also includes diverse forms of predatory and recreational violence—and individual violence as well as collective violence. As one writer notes, "very different kinds of events" are "commonly aggregated under a particularly alarming title" (Berrill, 1992:138-139). Hate crime is thus not a unitary phenomenon that can always be explained with the theory of lynching outlined above. Some require a theory of predatory violence, for instance, and some a theory of moralistic but individualized violence. Each form of collective violence—whether lynching, gang war, brawling, or terrorism— requires its own theory as well (see Senechal de la Roche, 2001). We have only just begun to determine the frequency and distribution of the various forms of collective violence across different social settings, and to uncover the social geometry of each.

Endnotes

[1]   Various studies have found that between 57 and 88 percent of violent attacks on homosexuals were committed by two or more persons (Berrill, 1992:29-30).

[2]   Collective violence in the United Kingdom and Australia manifests a similar diversity of participants (see, e.g., Human Rights and Equal Opportunity Commission, 1991).

[3]   Bilateral violence—such as brawling or gang warfare—arises under different conditions from those conducive to a unilateral form such as lynching. For example, bilateral violence occurs between adversaries who are equal in status (Black, 1990: 44-49; 1995:855, note 130; Senechal de la Roche, 1996:13, 112-113).

[4]   For discussion of contemporary recreational violence, see, for example, Levin & McDevitt, 1993: Chapter 5; Perry, 2001:99-102.

[5]   Consider several scenarios in which the various forms of collective violence might appear in microscopic versions. If an African-American high school student insults or strikes a white student, and the latter's friends find and beat the offender, that reaction would be a *micro-lynching*—the focus of the present chapter. If the avenging white students instead beat uninvolved African Americans in response to the offense (a collective liability scenario) and then dispersed for good, that would be a *micro-riot*. If, for example, in the face of a series of interracial conflicts, white students formed an organization to punish a series of alleged African-American offenders over time, that would qualify as *micro-vigilantism*. And if white students formed an organization to respond to a chronic act of deviance (such as the integration of blacks into their school), and repeatedly used violence against uninvolved African Americans (a collective liability scenario), that would qualify as *micro-terrorism*.

[6]   For descriptions of Black's strategy of pure sociology and its more general application to a theory of social control, see Black, 1976; 1990; 1995; 1998. Conflict here refers to clashes over right and wrong rather than to clashes of interest arising from competition for scarce resources (see Black, 1998:xiii-xxi).

[7]   Ridicule and threats by a group—micro-lynching with a low degree of severity—sometimes resemble the collective shaming rituals known as charivaris in many places in Europe until the nineteenth century (see, e.g., Bohstedt, 1983:8-9; Ingram, 1984). Charivaris often entailed groups making noise and singing rowdy songs outside offenders' homes, or groups symbolically desecrating their houses to publicize the inmates' wrongdoing. Some modern acts of group ridicule have been similarly designed to publicly humiliate deviants and draw attention to their wrongdoing. One hate crime study reports, for example, that gay and lesbian high school students sometimes have had their families' houses, trees, and automobiles wrapped with toilet paper and festooned with trash and shaving cream (Human Rights Watch, 2001:47).

Discussion Questions

1. What is one major difference between lynching and rioting?

2. What is social control?

3. Give an example of a case of conflict where the principal parties are socially polarized.

4. What specific elements of solidarity are present among members of a sports team or fraternity?

5. Why is group violence against homosexuals and minorities in high schools and colleges relatively less severe than that seen outside of these social settings?

References

Anderson, E. (1990). *Streetwise: Race, Class, and Change in an Urban Community*. Chicago: University of Chicago Press.

Baumgartner, M.P. (1988). *The Moral Order of a Suburb*. New York: Oxford University Press.

Benevides, M., and R.F. Ferreira (1991). "Popular Responses and Urban Violence: Lynching in Brazil." In M.K. Huggins (ed.), *Vigilantism and the State in Modern Latin America: Essays on Extralegal Violence*, pp. 33-45. Westport, CT: Praeger.

Berk, R.A., E.A. Boyd, and K.M. Hamner (1992). "Thinking More Clearly about Hate-Motivated Crimes." In G.M. Herek and K.T. Berrill (eds.), *Hate Crimes: Confronting Violence against Lesbians and Gay Men*, pp. 123-143. Newbury Park, CA: Sage.

Berrill, K.T. (1992). "Anti-Gay Violence and Victimization in the United States: An Overview." In G.M. Herek and K.T. Berrill (eds.), *Hate Crimes: Confronting Violence Against Lesbians and Gay Men*, pp. 19-45. Newbury Park, CA: Sage.

Black, D. (1998). *The Social Structure of Right and Wrong*, rev. ed. San Diego: Academic Press.

Black, D. (1995). "The Epistemology of Pure Sociology." *Law and Social Inquiry*, 20:829-870.

Black, D. (1990). "The Elementary Forms of Conflict Management." In *New Directions in the Study of Justice, Law, and Social Control*, pp. 43-69. Prepared by the School of Justice Studies, Arizona State University. New York: Plenum.

Black, D. (1984). "Social Control as a Dependent Variable." In D. Black (ed.), *Toward a General Theory of Social Control*, Volume 1, *Fundamentals*, pp. 1-36. Orlando, FL: Academic Press.

Black, D. (1983). "Crime as Social Control." *American Sociological Review*, 48:34-45.

Black, D. (1976). *The Behavior of Law*. New York: Academic Press.

Bohstedt, J. (1983). *Riots and Community Politics in England and Wales, 1790-1810*. Cambridge, MA: Harvard University Press.

Brundage, W.F. (1993). *Lynching in the New South: Georgia and Virginia, 1880-1930*. Urbana, IL: University of Illinois Press.

Comstock, G.D. (1991). *Violence Against Lesbians and Gay Men*. New York: Columbia University Press.

Cooney, M., and S. Phillips (2002). "Typologizing Violence: A Blackian Perspective." *International Journal of Sociology and Social Policy*, 22:75-108.

Herek, G.M., and K.T. Berrill (eds.) (1992). *Hate Crimes: Confronting Violence Against Lesbians and Gay Men*. Newbury Park, CA: Sage.

Human Rights and Equal Opportunity Commission (1991). *Racist Violence: Report of the National Inquiry into Racist Violence in Australia*. Canberra: Australian Government Publishing Service.

Human Rights Watch (2001). *Hatred in the Hallways: Violence and Discrimination Against Lesbian, Gay, Bisexual, and Transgender Students in U.S. Schools*. New York: Human Rights Watch.

Hunter, J. (1992). "Violence Against Lesbian and Gay Male Youths." In G.M. Herek and K.T. Berrill (eds.), *Hate Crimes: Confronting Violence Against Lesbians and Gay Men*, pp. 76-82. Newbury Park, CA: Sage.

Ingram, M. (1984). "Ridings, Rough Music and the 'Reform of Popular Culture.'" *Past and Present*, 105:79-113.

Jankowski, M.S. (1991). *Islands in the Street: Gangs and American Urban Society*. Berkeley, CA: University of California Press.

Koch, K. (1984). "Liability and Social Structure." In D. Black (ed.), *Toward a General Theory of Social Control*, Volume 1, *Fundamentals*, pp. 95-129. Orlando, FL: Academic Press.

Levin, J., and J. McDevitt (1993). *Hate Crimes: The Rising Tide of Bigotry and Bloodshed*. New York: Plenum.

Martins, J. (1991). "Lynchings—Life by a Thread: Street Justice in Brazil, 1979-1988." In M.K. Huggins (ed.), *Vigilantism and the State in Modern Latin America: Essays on Extralegal Violence*, pp. 21-32. Westport, CT: Praeger.

Maxson, C.L. (1999). "Gang Homicide: A Review and Extension of the Literature." In M.D. Smith and M.A. Zahn (eds.), *Homicide: A Sourcebook of Social Research*, pp. 239-254. Thousand Oaks, CA: Sage.

Moore, S.F. (1972). "Legal Liability and Evolutionary Interpretation: Some Aspects of Strict Liability." In M. Gluckman (ed.), *The Allocation of Responsibility*, pp. 51-107. Manchester, UK: Manchester University Press.

Perry, B. (2001). *In the Name of Hate: Understanding Hate Crimes*. New York: Routledge.

Rieder, J. (1985). *Carnarsie: The Jews and Italians of Brooklyn Against Liberalism*. Cambridge, MA: Harvard University Press.

Senechal de la Roche, R. (2001). "Why Is Collective Violence Collective?" *Sociological Theory*, 19:126-144.

Senechal de la Roche, R. (1997). "The Sociogenesis of Lynching." In W.F. Brundage (ed.), *Under Sentence of Death: Lynching in the South*, pp. 48-76. Chapel Hill, NC: University of North Carolina Press.

Senechal de la Roche, R. (1996). "Collective Violence as Social Control." *Sociological Forum*, 11:97-128.

Senechal de la Roche, R. (1990). *The Sociogenesis of a Race Riot: Springfield, Illinois, in 1908*. Urbana, IL: University of Illinois Press.

Shotland, R.L. (1976). "Spontaneous Vigilantes." *Society,* 13:30-32.

Southern Poverty Law Center. "Hate Goes to School." Available at: www.splcenter.org/intelligenceproject/ip-arch.html, November 28, 2002.

Tolnay, S., and E.M. Beck (1995). *A Festival of Violence: An Analysis of the Lynching of Blacks in the American South, 1882-1930*. Urbana, IL: University of Illinois Press.

Useem, B., and P. Kimball (1989). *States of Siege: U.S. Prison Riots, 1971-1986*. New York: Oxford University Press.

Wiener, J. (1989). "Reagan's Children: Racial Hatred on Campus." *The Nation*, 248: 260-264.

Winbush, R.A. (1999). "Campus Hate Crimes: Fruit on the American Tree of Violence." *The Black Collegian* Online. Available at: www.black.collegian.com/news/special-reports/hatecrimes1999.1st.shtml, December 1, 2002.

CHAPTER 14

Hate Violence

Mark S. Hamm

Definition of Hate Violence

"Hate violence" is a form of hate crime, which is a crime motivated by prejudice based on the *symbolic status* of a victim. Violence is perpetrated against a victim because of what that person represents. These symbolic statuses can include race, religion, ethnicity, nationality, sexual orientation, disability, or political organization. The burning of a synagogue in Tunisia is one example. Gay bashing in America is another example. Religious riots in Iraq is still another. Hate violence is, therefore, an extremely heterogeneous phenomenon that occurs in nearly all human communities.

The motives behind this violence are not unique to hate crime perpetrators. To be sure, the symbolic status of victims is often the motivation for terrorism as well. (Accordingly, there is considerable overlap in criminological studies of hate crime and terrorism.) In the United States, terrorism is defined by the federal government as "a violent act or an act dangerous to human life in violation of the criminal laws, to intimidate or coerce a government, the *civilian population*, or any segment thereof, in the furtherance of political or social objectives" (U.S. Department of Justice, 1993:25, emphasis added). Even though the motivations may be similar, hate violence and terrorism are not the same thing.

For example, the 1995 Oklahoma City bombing was clearly an act of terrorism. It was "a violent act" intended to "intimidate or coerce" the U.S. government in the furtherance of a political objective. In this crime, Timothy McVeigh targeted the victims of the Murrah Federal Building because of their symbolic status as federal employees (Hamm, 1997). Like hate crime perpetrators, McVeigh selected his victims because of what they represented. In contrast, when Aaron McKinney kidnapped and pistol-whipped gay

University of Wyoming student Matthew Shepard, leaving him to die on a fence post near Laramie in 1998, he did not commit terrorism because the homicide had no larger objective. Therefore, not all acts of terrorism are considered hate violence, and hate violence is not necessarily terrorism unless it has a political or social foundation.

In summary, people routinely make invidious distinctions between groups based on individual and social characteristics. As Richard Berk (1994:v) points out, "the need to distinguish between 'us' versus 'them' is standard equipment for the human psyche." Yet relatively few individuals are equipped with the psyche to raise human distinctions to the level of bitter and concentrated hatred necessary for violence against symbolic targets. Where, then, does such righteous hatred come from and why does it take such a deadly form? That is the central question of this chapter.

Description of the State of Knowledge

Studies of hate violence suffer from a lack of social scientific consensus on the meaning of hate crime. This lack of consensus stems from the fact that definitions of a hate crime are primarily a function of local norms and politics. In today's Germany, for example, most hate violence is alternatively defined by scholars and policymakers as *right-wing violence* or *xenophobic violence*. In Belgium, the Netherlands, Norway, and Sweden it is referred to as *racist violence*. In Britain and France, it is called *racial violence*. In Ireland, it is called *political violence*. In Israel, the preferred term is *terrorism*. Still other countries, such as Italy and Russia, do not consider the symbolic status of victims or the motivation of perpetrators and simply treat the problem with existing criminal statutes (Hamm, 1998).

In the United States, hate crimes are defined by the FBI as "crimes that manifest evidence of prejudice based on race, religion, sexual orientation, or ethnicity." Violent categories include murder, non-negligent manslaughter, forcible rape, aggravated assault, and arson. However, because participation in the FBI's annual Hate Crime Statistics report is voluntary, only 23 states fully comply with this definition. Some states refuse to include sexual orientation as a victim category, other states add victim categories (e.g., color and ancestry, labor union membership) and offenses (e.g., cross-burning), and still other states do not report hate crimes at all. It is possible, then, for the states to accept in full the FBI's definition of hate crime, to add victim classifications, to delete those parts of the definition they deem inconsistent with local traditions, or to ignore the definition altogether.

All of this becomes important when we try to interpret official statistics on hate violence. For instance, each year human rights organizations document hundreds of violent hate crimes against gays and lesbians in states that do not include sexual orientation in their hate crime laws. As a result, these acts of anti-gay violence do not appear in the Uniform Crime Reports covering hate crime.

With these sorts of caveats in mind, some empirical patterns *do* emerge from official reports.

1. In Western Europe, the most frequent victims of "hate crimes" are Eastern European, Asian, Pakistani, and third-world immigrants.

2. Groups of young white males are most often the aggressors; and

3. Among these aggressors, neo-Nazi skinheads are responsible for the most serious acts of violence (see Hamm, 1994).

4. In the United States, hate crimes motivated by a victim's race are the most frequent (62% of total incidents), and the target is most often a black person.

5. Crimes motivated by a victim's religion are the second most frequent (17% of total), and the target is most often a Jew.

6. Sexual orientation is the third most frequently reported (11%), and most of these crimes are committed against homosexuals.

7. Ethnicity is the least frequently reported characteristic (10%), and the most likely victim is a Hispanic.

8. A relatively small percentage of hate crimes are violent (about 18%), and

9. Incidents of violent hate crimes often produce multiple offenses, involving multiple victims and multiple offenders—the vast majority of whom are white males. In 1998, for example, there were 11 hate-motivated murders involving 22 offenders; 13 hate-motivated rapes involving 17 offenders; and 1,044 cases of hate-motivated aggravated assault involving 2,395 offenders. In other words, violent hate crimes are typically group projects perpetrated by white males, suggesting that they share a conspiratorial motive for their violence.

The Neo-Nazi Skinheads: A Case Study of Hate Violence

The patterns presented above are consistent with criminological research on hate violence (see Aronowitz, 1994; Fangen, 1998; Kuhnel, 1998). My own study of American neo-Nazi skinheads shows that violence is widespread within this subculture. More than one-half of the skinheads in the study (52%) had been involved in at least three self-reported fights in the previous two-year period. In total, these youths committed roughly 120 acts of violence during the period, and more than one-half were directed against persons of another race (Hamm, 1993). These acts of hate violence were all undertaken as group projects, and they included two homicides, two attempted homicides, and more than 50 assaults.

Although organized white supremacy groups may account for only a fraction of all hate crimes (see Levin & McDevitt, 1993), understanding the organizational dynamics behind this violence may provide a theoretical framework for comprehending other cases in which white males perpetrate crimes against others because of their symbolic status. First, I offer a few words on skinheads.

The subculture of hate violence. The skinheads constitute a unique criminal subculture for three reasons. First, while scholars have found that gangs are a largely immigrant, adolescent, underclass phenomenon, they have not found racism to be an organizing principle for gang membership. Skinhead membership is an explicit function of racism. Like the Ku Klux Klan, the whole point of being a skinhead is to maintain not only white power but white male power.

Second, scholars point out that violence, like racism, plays a minor role in gang behavior patterns; where it does exist, violence is related to turf wars, socioeconomic disadvantage, social disorganization, or drugs. For skinheads, violence is often their trademark, and they use it for the explicit purpose of instilling fear in enemies or in innocent people.

Finally, violent gangs are conceived as natural, lower-class interstitial institutions, resulting mainly from the weakness of secondary institutions (schools, communities, etc.). Skinheads have emerged under various social conditions. They do not share a common street corner or neighborhood culture. Rather, skinheads are a homologous international youth subculture with a common *ideology* (neo-Nazism), supported and sustained by a specific paramilitary *style* (shaved or closely cropped hair, "white-power" regalia, combat boots, and flight jackets), and *musical expression* of ideology and style. For these reasons, the skinheads constitute what can best be described as a terrorist youth subculture.

My theory begins with a postulate from functionalist sociology: Terrorist youth subcultures are the product of working-class families. These families assume the existence of a dominant ideology that stresses the achievement of economic goals. Children who grow up in these families conform to this ideology and, as they mature, they set realistic goals that are well within their reach. Typically, these youths are successful high school students; because of their working-class heritage, however, they are committed to blue-collar employment. They become common laborers or artists. They are not frustrated by this; hence, they are not upwardly mobile in the traditional sense. They lay claim to a working-class consciousness because it is a natural reaction to their upbringing.

At this point, these young people are no different than millions of working-class youths throughout the world. Some have engaged in delinquency, but most have not. Their path to extremism begins to take shape when they are introduced to white-power rock music.

White-power rock exposes youths to the raw and vitriolic language of racial and ethnic hatred. It does so by presenting an elaborate fantasy wherein minorities and Jews are portrayed as agents in a conspiracy to threaten the well-being of the average blue-collar worker. It does so with such powerful emotion that youths begin to link musical messages to their focal concerns about employment. Through daily exposure to songs such as "Hail, the New Dawn" and "Die! Liberal Scum," these youths are transformed into adherents of a modern form of Nazism.

This transformation process occurs at a metaphysical level through a sort of seat-of-the-pants shamanism. That is, players in white-power bands transform themselves from ordinary musicians to extraordinary ones through the expression of highly forbidden messages and symbols that are part of a larger and widely known consciousness. Consumers of this music, in turn, seek to transform themselves from their ordinary realities to something wider, something that enlarges them as people. They become skinheads.

Neo-Nazism is the ideology of the international skinhead subculture. At the basis of this ideology operates a well-developed paranoia that working-class whites will have their self-respect, power, and economic well-being usurped by racial and ethnic minorities. This paranoia not only has a well-developed musical expression but also a vibrant underground press. Exposure to this literature further serves to entrench neo-Nazi ideology in the minds of youths. This is often accomplished through extravagant cartoons depicting grotesque images of young black males, Jews, and homosexuals. Publishers of this underground press have capitalized on advances in technology, and now there are roughly 500 Internet web sites promoting racial hatred.

Drawing from these abstractions created by others (often adult bigots), youths then carve out a social world of their own that is a literal and imaginative representation of white supremacy. With other "true believers" they form strong family-type bonds. They are not besieged by anomia. In fact, at this point they are synanomic—youths are hyperactively bonded to the dominant social order (especially to images of nationalism and militarism) and to one another.

During this period of development, skinheads become fascinated with firearms and paramilitary training. Riding the powerful waves of ideology, style, music, guns, and male bonding, skinheads then mix in the most potent elixir contained within this theory: beer. (Each case of hate violence in my study was perpetrated by two or more skinheads and in each case perpetrators reported that they had been drinking beer prior to the attack.) All of this comes together to trigger the vitality, the emotions, and the excitement necessary for skinheads to "go beserk" on their perceived enemies. These acts of hate violence, then, reflect the moral transcendence recognized by Jack Katz in his acclaimed book, *Seductions of Crime.* "For skinheads," writes Katz (1988:128), "violence is essential so that membership may have a seductively glorious significance . . . Being in this world of experience is not simply a matter of detailing posture and using violence to raise the specter of terror. It is also a contingent sensual involvement."

Which Theories Are Used Most Often to Explain Hate Violence?

Theories represent generalizations about a specific phenomenon. Hate violence, like terrorism, is a unique area of criminological inquiry because little primary research exists on individuals and groups responsible for committing this sort of criminality. Walter Laqueur argues that the major question associated with theories of political violence "is not whether great caution should prevail with regard to generalizations; the real issue is to what extent generalizations are at all possible. We shall know the answer once there are more systematic studies of *specific terrorist groups*, which . . . are virtually nonexistent" (1987:162, emphasis added). What follows is a brief review of my research on one specific group, and the theoretical perspectives that can help us understand its criminality.

This study focuses on the intersection of the skinhead and militia movements, and the contemporary trend toward apocalyptic violence. Drawing on trial transcripts, court records, original interviews, a secret diary, journalistic accounts, and my own ethnography, the research examines a white supremacist gang called the Aryan Republican Army (ARA) and its connection to Timothy McVeigh and the Oklahoma City bombing (Hamm, 2002). The ARA's story centers around a string of professionally executed bank robberies, the purpose of which was to support a series of anti-government attacks including armored truck heists, sabotaging pubic utilities, derailing trains, assassinations, and bombings.

Several conclusions from this study confirm the theory on skinheads discussed earlier. Other conclusions point to the efficacy of more traditional criminological theories.

Containment Theory

Containment theory focuses on the ability of individuals to resist crime by maintaining a positive self-image in the face of environmental pressures toward crime (Reckless, 1940). The men of the ARA failed to do this. Why? To begin with, their violence was rooted in a complex mix of social pressures (including childhood trauma, alcohol and other drug abuse, economic insecurity, family dysfunction, and perceived social inequity), social pulls (criminal subcultures and propaganda), and psychological pushes (shame, humiliation, and rage). For the ARA, hate violence was largely an outward expression of inner turmoil. However, this varied a great deal. Some ARA members experienced profound humiliation and rage (resulting from childhood abandonment, prison rape, and failures in the military), but several members avoided these experiences. Nevertheless, they continued to engage in hate violence.

Therefore, the most important task may not be explaining the obvious bigots—those who commit hate violence as part of an ongoing criminal career—but explaining how normal people suddenly became perpetrators of hate violence. Several ARA members had never committed a crime in their lives, then one day they began robbing banks with assault weapons and pipe bombs—all in an effort to support the violent overthrow of the government.

Recent events suggest that these types of offenders may pose the greatest danger to society today. Four of the seven ARA members had no criminal background. The same can be said of Timothy McVeigh and Terry Nichols, a co-conspirator in the Oklahoma City bombing. The same applies to such violent ideologues as Chevie Kehoe (who was tied to more acts of terrorism than any other right-wing extremist of the 1990s) and Eric Rudolph (suspected of the 1996 Centennial Olympic Park bombing). The same applies to the serial and mass murderers Benjamin Smith (a neo-Nazi skinhead whose Midwestern killing spree left six minorities dead), Eric Harris and Dylan Klebold (the Columbine killers), and the Washington, DC–area sniper John Lee Malvo. Still the same can be said of the 9/11 hijackers. None of these individuals had prior criminal histories of any significance, yet they killed thousands of innocents, terrifying an entire nation.

The task for theoretical criminology, then, is to explain how it is that seemingly normal, decent people become involved in social movements that seek to annihilate civilizations. We must explain how the Timothy McVeighs of this world fall victim to the inevitable pull of human shallowness. How their decency becomes co-opted, dulling their sense of right and wrong. Two leading theories can offer important insights here.

Social Learning Theory and Techniques of Neutralization

By extending Ronald Akers's theory of social learning (see Chapter 1 of this volume) to hate violence, we can begin to study the ways in which the cultures of racism in society teach the skills, the ideology, and the dedication to a cause necessary for such behavior to occur. Further studies are needed on how pro-terrorism messages are transmitted through interpersonal contact, and through racist music, books, and newsletters, as is an understanding of virtual means of communication (the Internet) by extremist groups.

Identifying these connections is useful only if it tells us something about the extent to which a person engages in denial while telling himself or herself that he or she is doing something to advance a noble cause. Terrorists and hate crime perpetrators often believe themselves to be innocent of wrongdoing, even if their acts result in the murder of millions (Laqueur, 2001; Lifton, 1999). James Aho (1994) has written insightfully about paramilitary survivalists of the Aryan Nations who discuss bomb-building techniques at potluck dinners. I once saw a group of skinhead women decorating a birthday cake with a swastika, as their children played innocently in the foreground. Such moral indifference is the meaning of Hannah Arendt's concept of the *banality of evil*. Arendt warned that evil can result from a constellation of ordinary human qualities. These include not fully realizing the immorality of your actions; being as normal as your peers doing the same thing; having motives that are dull, unimaginative, and commonplace; and retaining long afterwards the facade of pseudo-stupidity about your actions (see Cohen, 2001).

We can begin to unpack this quandary by applying Gresham Sykes and David Matza's (1964) well-known "techniques of neutralization." By interviewing imprisoned terrorists and perpetrators of hate violence, researchers can work "backward" to understand the rationalizations that were seen as valid by the person at the time of their violence, rationalizations that made it possible to protect the offender from the restraining voice of conscience.

Hamm's Explanation of Hate Violence

I believe that there is much to learn about terrorism and hate violence from containment theory, social learning theory, techniques of neutralization, as well as Katz's theory of moral transcendence. As useful as they are, however, I also believe that these theories overlook an important point. Namely, they fail to take into account the importance of subculture. Criminologists have long acknowledged that actions labeled criminal are typically generated within the boundaries of deviant subcultures (Cloward & Ohlin, 1960; Cohen, 1955; Sutherland & Cressey, 1978). Hate violence is no different (and neither is terrorism). We do not study these criminals for who they are, but for what they do. Ideologically motivated violence is, more often than not, subcultural behavior. Aryan Republican Army, al Qaeda, and Ku Klux Klan—all name subcultural networks as much as individual identities.

As such, future studies must move beyond existing theoretical orientations to provide an analytical framework for understanding the relative importance of subcultural by-products—music, literature, symbolism, and style—among people who become active in hate movements. To do so is to delineate the confluences of cultural and criminal dynamics that cause hate violence—or, more precisely, to articulate a cultural criminology.

Discussion Questions

1. What are the differences between skinheads and street gangs?

2. How does the banality of evil concept help us understand hate violence?

3. Some argue that criminologists should not even study "evil" because it is a religious term, not a sociological one. What do you think?

4. There are important differences between hate violence and other forms of interpersonal violence. What are they?

5. What role does subculture play in hate violence and terrorism?

References

Aho, J.A. (1994). *This Thing of Darkness: A Sociology of the Enemy.* Seattle: University of Washington Press.

Aronowitz, A.A. (1994). "Germany's Xenophobic Violence: Criminal Justice and Social Responses." In M. Hamm (ed.), *Hate Crime: International Perspectives on Causes and Control*, pp. 37-70. Cincinnati: Anderson.

Berk, R. (1994). "Foreword." In M. Hamm (ed.), *Hate Crime: International Perspectives on Causes and Control*, pp. v-x. Cincinnati: Anderson.

Cloward, R., and L. Ohlin (1960). *Delinquency and Opportunity: A Theory of Delinquent Gangs.* New York: Free Press.

Cohen, A. (1955). *Delinquent Boys: The Culture of the Gang.* New York: Free Press.

Cohen, S. (2001). *States of Denial: Knowing About Atrocities and Suffering.* Cambridge, UK: Polity.

Fangen, K. (1998). "Living Out Our Ethnic Instincts: Ideological Beliefs Among Right-Wing Activists in Norway." In J. Kaplan and T. Bjorgo (eds.), *Nation and Race: The Developing Euro-American Racist Subculture*, pp. 202-230. Boston: Northeastern University Press.

Hamm, M.S. (2002). *In Bad Company: America's Terrorist Underground.* Boston: Northeastern University Press.

Hamm, M.S. (1998). "Terrorism, Hate Crime, and Anti-Government Violence: A Review of the Research." In H. Kushner (ed.), *The Future of Terrorism: Violence in the New Millennium*, pp. 59-96. Thousand Oaks, CA: Sage.

Hamm, M.S. (1997). *Apocalypse in Oklahoma: Waco and Ruby Ridge Revenged.* Boston: Northeastern University Press.

Hamm, M.S. (ed.) (1994). *Hate Crime: International Perspectives on Causes and Control.* Cincinnati: Anderson.

Hamm, M.S. (1993). *American Skinheads: The Criminology and Control of Hate Crime.* Westport, CT: Praeger.

Katz, J. (1988). *Seductions of Crime.* New York: Basic Books.

Kuhnel, W. (1998). "Hitler's Grandchildren? The Reemergence of a Right-Wing Social Movement in Germany." In J. Kaplan and T. Bjorgo (eds.), *Nation and Race: The Developing Euro-American Racist Subculture*, pp. 148-174. Boston: Northeastern University Press.

Laqueur, W. (2001). "Left, Right, and Beyond: The Changing Face of Terror." In G. Rose and J. Hoge (eds.), *How Did This Happen? Terrorism and the New War*, pp. 71-82. New York: Public Affairs.

Laqueur, W. (1987). *The Age of Terrorism.* Boston: Little, Brown.

Levin, J., and J. McDevitt (1993). *Hate Crimes: The Rising Tide of Bigotry and Bloodshed.* New York: Plenum.

Lifton, R.J. (1999). *Destroying the World To Save It: Aum Shinrikyo, Apocalyptic Violence, and the New Global Terrorism.* New York: Metropolitan.

Reckless, W. (1940). *Criminal Behavior.* New York: McGraw-Hill.

Sutherland, E., and D. Cressey (1978). *Criminology,* 10th ed. Philadelphia: Lippincott.

Sykes, G.M., and D. Matza (1964). "Techniques of Neutralization: A Theory of Delinquency." *American Sociological Review*, 22(6):664-70.

U.S. Department of Justice (1993). *Terrorism in the United States.* Washington, DC: Federal Bureau of Investigation.

CHAPTER 15

Terrorist Violence

Christopher Hewitt

Definition of Terrorist Violence

Terrorism can be distinguished from the other types of violence examined in this book in terms of the motivations of the terrorists. Terrorist violence is violence for a social/collective purpose rather than a personal/individual purpose. As Richard Williams, a member of the United Freedom Front, argued during his trial "What differentiates us from criminals—what makes us political prisoners—is that criminal action is done for some type of personal gain" (George & Wilcox, 1996:160). The United Freedom Front robbed banks, but used the money to fund its bombing campaign against government and corporate targets. An ordinary criminal robs banks and uses the money for personal gain.

A narrower definition of terrorism restricts the term to attacks against civilian targets, so that an IRA sniper who shoots a British soldier would be an urban guerrilla and not a terrorist. (Presumably the members of the Black Liberation Army, who gunned down police officers in cities throughout the United States also regarded themselves as urban guerrillas rather than terrorists). However, most of the official definitions of terrorism used by United States government agencies emphasize the social motivations of those involved and implicitly include attacks on noncivilian targets. The Federal Bureau of Investigation (FBI) defines terrorism as "the unlawful use, or threatened use of violence against persons or property to intimidate or coerce a government, the civilian population, or any segment thereof, in furtherance of political or social objectives," while the State Department considers terrorism to be "premeditated, politically motivated violence by subnational groups or clandestine agents, usually intended to influence an audience." The usage in this paper is compatible with both definitions; terrorism is organized violence by substate actors in pursuit of political or social goals. Violence by individuals is considered terrorism if it is premeditated and if there is evidence that it was motivated primarily by political or social goals.

Because terrorism is socially motivated violence, most typologies classify terrorists according to their political and social goals. A useful breakdown should distinguish between three broad categories: (1) nationalist-separatist groups, (2) revolutionary-leftist groups, and (3) reactionary-rightist groups. These categories are typically distinctive in terms of the social characteristics of the terrorists, their campaigns, and their targets. Terrorist victims are primarily selected for ideological reasons, and unlike other forms of violence, terrorist campaigns (as opposed to isolated acts of terrorism) require a significant degree of social support.

In this chapter two types of terrorism will be examined and compared, national-separatist and revolutionary-leftist. National-separatists seek territorial changes, involving new political identities for particular regions, while revolutionary-leftists seek a revolutionary transformation of the *status quo* within the boundaries of an existing state. Five major foreign cases will be examined. The examples of national-separatist terrorism are EOKA in Cyprus (1955-1959), the IRA in Northern Ireland (1970-1998), and ETA in the Basque provinces of Spain (1975-present).[1] The revolutionary-leftist cases include the Tupamaros of Uruguay (1963-1972) and the Red Brigades in Italy (1975-1982). The third type of terrorism, which can be labeled as rightist or reactionary terrorism, will not be considered in this paper.[2] This is terrorism in defense of the *status quo*, or which seeks to return to a previous *status quo*. Under this heading I would include the Ku Klux Klan in its various incarnations, Loyalist groups in Northern Ireland, and neo-Fascist and neo-Nazi groups in Italy, Germany, and Spain.

Description of the State of Knowledge

In describing what is known about terrorism, the material will be grouped under three headings: the social characteristics of foreign terrorists, the campaigns and victims of foreign terrorism, and the parallels between foreign terrorism and terrorism within the United States.

Social Characteristics of the Terrorists

There is an obvious similarity in the class background of revolutionary-leftist terrorists. They are disproportionately drawn from the ranks of the educated middle class. As regards the Tupamaros of Uruguay, Porzecanski (1973), D'Oliveira (1973), and a 1972 report published by the Ministry of the Interior (Uruguay Ministerio del Interior, 1972) agree that about one-third were students and one-third were professionals. Given that the Tupa-maros were an avowedly Marxist group, the small number of genuine "pro-letarians" is striking. In D'Oliveira's sample, only 5 percent were blue-collar and in the Ministry report the figure was 12 percent. Porzecanski classifies 32 percent as "workers," but most of these held white-collar jobs as civil servants or bank clerks.

The Italian Red Brigades had a similar occupational profile. Of 37 left-ist terrorists listed by Galleni (1981) as killed in action, 11 were students, seven were factory workers, six were unemployed, and the remainder had jobs such as teacher or clerk. According to della Porta, who has gathered the most comprehensive occupational data, of 1,362 leftists arrested for ter-rorist offenses, about one-fourth (25.8%) were students, another one-fourth (26.1%) were "proletarians," while most of the remainder held professional or other white-collar jobs (36.4%).[3]

Nationalist terrorists are very different from revolutionary terrorists in terms of their occupational profile, and at first glance differ from one another. In Cyprus, the EOKA leaders were from comfortable middle-class backgrounds, but the rank-and-file guerrillas were peasants or of the work-ing class. Markides (1977:18) describes them as having jobs as "carpenters, mechanics or electricians" and an elementary education. Loizos (1978:317-318) found that of 68 EOKA members killed in action, only two were uni-versity graduates, and only 24 had a secondary education. The most common occupations were peasants (13), craftsmen (12), clerks (7), and laborers (4).

The socioeconomic background of the IRA killed in action is lower work-ing-class, with the most commonly listed job being unskilled laborer. Eighty-nine percent of the IRA men killed in Belfast came from those wards defined as "areas of special need." According to an analysis of those arrested for terrorist offenses, the occupational distribution is similar to that of the general Catholic population, although professionals are underrepresented.[4]

Clark (1984:143-147) examined the social class of a sample of ETA members, and found that about one-third came from a working-class back-ground and another one-third from a lower middle-class background. He con-cludes that the class composition of ETA reflects that of the Basque region, except that the working class is "slightly under-represented" while there are relatively few from upper-class occupations. Given that the working class in the Basque region contains a large number of immigrants from other parts of Spain, this suggests that the ETA members are essentially a cross-section of the ethnic Basques, as the IRA are of Northern Irish Catholics. The nationalist terrorist profile reflects that of the ethnic community from which they are drawn.[5] The occupational class of nationalist terrorists compared to the general population is addressed in Table 15.1.

Table 15.1
Occupational Class of Nationalist Terrorists Compared to General Population (%)

	Professionals	Clerical	Skilled	Semi-skilled	Unskilled
IRA	3	9	22	19	33
N.I. Catholics	9	12	23	25	32

	Upper Class	Middle Class	Lower Middle	Working Class
ETA	2.5	12.3	29.6	30.9
Basque provinces	6.0	12.4	23.6	47.2

As regards age and sex, terrorists are generally young and predominantly male. The median ages in years for the different groups is as follows: IRA killed in action (20), EOKA arrested for terrorist offenses (21), ETA members (24), Red Brigades captured or killed (27), and Tupamaros captured or killed (27). The proportion of males in each group was reported as: EOKA (100%), IRA (99%), Red Brigades (95%), ETA (93%), and Tupamaros (75%). These statistics are similar to those found for other crimes of violence. The differences between the cases in the proportion of women result from both the ideology of the groups and the culture of the societies where the violence occurred. Revolutionary-leftist groups are predictably more progressive on feminist issues and therefore not only allowed women to join but also had women in leadership roles. For example, the original leaders of the Red Brigades were Renato Curcio and his wife Margherita Cagol.[6] On the other hand, the virtual absence of women in EOKA, the IRA, and ETA reflects the traditional nature of the Greek Cypriot, Irish Catholic, and Basque communities. Grivas, the leader of EOKA, remarks in his autobiography that "some girls asked me for permission to form a guerrilla group but this I did not allow" (Grivas, 1965:15). Clark (1984:144) describes ETA's pronounced antipathy to women in the organization. As one etarra (supporter of ETA) put it, ". . . ETA opposed women in the organization because their place was in the home and they talked too much."

Campaigns and Victims

Nationalist terrorists see their land as being occupied by foreigners and seek to drive them out by raising the costs of the occupation. One obvious way of doing this is to kill the soldiers, police, and officials who symbolize this domination. In all three cases, a majority of those killed by the terrorists were in this category. Both the IRA and ETA also bombed civilian targets outside the contested region itself. The IRA set off bombs in England, and ETA set off bombs in Madrid. Other ways of raising the costs include bombing businesses or tourist areas in an attempt to hurt the economy.[7]

Although most bombings were not intended to produce civilian casualties, large numbers of civilians died because inadequate warnings were given. Table 15.2. shows the victims of the three nationalist terrorist groups classified by status/reason for attack.

Table 15.2
Victims of Nationalist Terrorism Classified by Type (%)

	EOKA (1955-1959)	ETA (1968-1980)	IRA (1969-1993)
Military and Police	39.6	68.0	55.7
Former members of	—	—	5.5
Civilians working for	—	—	1.9
Informers	36.0	5.6	3.6
Elite individuals*	7.9	8.0	1.9
Factional	—	—	2.5
Other selected civilians	3.0	4.2	1.0
Ethnic/sectarian	4.3	—	8.5
During robberies	—	—	—
0.2			
Unintended victims**	9.2	10.5	19.2
[Total deaths]	[394]	[287]	[1795]

*Politicians, government officials, judges, business
**Mainly bombing victims, but includes other accidental deaths due to crossfire, etc.

Sources: Clark (1984); Crawshaw (1978); Sutton (1994).

The strategy of revolutionary terrorists is very different. They seek to create a revolutionary situation by acts of "armed propaganda" aimed at inspiring the oppressed masses, or by the so-called "provocation-repression" strategy in which the state is provoked into overreacting against the general public.[8] It is hoped that this will lead the masses to realize that the government is the enemy, and thus increase support for revolution. Tactically this requires the terrorists to strike at targets selected for their symbolic value. The Tupamaros kidnapped British and American diplomats and created a Robin Hood image of themselves by distributing the proceeds of their "expropriations" (i.e., robberies) in slum neighborhoods. The Red Brigades killed or wounded corporate officials, judges, and politicians. In their most famous action they kidnapped and tried Aldo Moro as an enemy of the people, and then "executed" him. Consequently, the terrorism of the Tupamaros and the Red Brigades was highly selective and far less deadly than the terrorism of the nationalist groups. Table 15.3. shows the victims of the two leftist terrorist groups classified by status/reason for attack. Because the number of those killed is relatively small compared to those killed by nationalist terrorists (26 by the Tupamaros, 84 by Italian leftists), the totals include those kidnapped and wounded as well as killed.

Table 15.3
Victims of Leftist Terrorism Classified by Type (%)

	Tupamaros (1963-1972)	Red Brigades (1975-1982)
Military/Police	50.7	30.9
Informers	—	0.3
Business	18.7	31.3
Politicians	4.0	14.7
Journalists/academics	5.3	6.1
Judges/ lawyers	1.3	6.4
Diplomats	5.3	0.3
During robberies	4.0	—
Accidental/crossfire etc	4.0	—
Other/unknown	6.7	9.9
[Total victims]	[75]	[265]

Sources: Calculated by author from Galleni (1981) and Mayans (1971).

The American Experience With Terrorism

There are obvious similarities between foreign leftist and nationalist terrorists and comparable groups within the United States, regarding both their social characteristics and their campaigns. Members of the Weathermen and other revolutionary groups that sought to overthrow the status quo were generally from socially privileged backgrounds. They were the sons and daughters of corporate executives, lawyers, and other professionals, who had gone to prestigious elite schools. For example, the three Weathermen who perished in a March 1970 explosion that destroyed a Greenwich Village town house were graduates of Bryn Mawr College, Columbia University, and Kenyon College, while the two survivors were graduates of Swarthmore College and Bryn Mawr College. Only a minority came from blue-collar or lower white-collar backgrounds. As with foreign leftist groups, women played a significant role in both the Symbionese Liberation Army and the Weathermen. In addition, like the Tupamaros and the Red Brigades, terrorism by American revolutionary-leftists involved selective attacks on symbolic targets, and consequently claimed few victims.

The examples of nationalist/separatist terrorism fall into two clusters: the Puerto Rican *independistas,* and black groups such as the Nation of

Islam, Black Panthers, Republic of New Afrika (RNA), Black Liberation Army (BLA), and so on. The black militants were drawn primarily from lower working-class backgrounds, while some could even be described as underclass, having been career criminals and/or drug addicts before joining the Black Panthers or the Nation of Islam. This is not surprising because both organizations deliberately recruited on the streets and in the prisons. However, the Panthers and other left-wing nationalists differed from the black Muslims in their ability to attract a minority of college-educated middle-class individuals. The New Afrikan Freedom Fighters arrested in October 1984 were led by a *cum laude* graduate of Harvard University, and the eight defendants and their spouses held a total of 10 college degrees and six postgraduate degrees, including three in law, two in education, and one in medicine. Except for the leader of the group, who was working toward his doctorate, all were employed. One woman held a clerical job, the others were professionals or civil servants (Larsen, 1985). Overall, like other nationalist-separatist groups, black militants were (in class terms) a cross-section of the black community.

The victims of nationalist/separatist terrorism in America are also similar to the victims of other nationalist campaigns. The Puerto Rican nationalists killed American soldiers in Puerto Rico, and bombed civilian targets in U.S. cities. The BLA and the Panthers targeted the police, who they saw as an occupation force in the ghettos, while Black Muslim splinter groups (the Death Angels in San Francisco and the Yahweh cult in Miami) murdered randomly selected whites.

Explaining Terrorism

Early attempts at explaining terrorism focused on psychological factors, seeking to discover a "terrorist personality," while contemporary media accounts often imply that terrorists are psychologically disturbed losers. In fact most terrorists appear quite normal. Because terrorism is motivated by sociopolitical goals, this suggests that the best predictor of terrorism is the sociopolitical context, particularly public support for the terrorists and their goals. This again differentiates terrorism from other forms of crime, in which there is rarely a direct link between public attitudes and criminal activity.

Terrorism and public opinion are linked in two important ways. First, terrorists aim to change public opinion by their actions. Revolutionary terrorists hope to create a revolutionary consciousness in the masses, while nationalist terrorists seek to destroy the morale of their foreign enemies. Second, in order to sustain their campaigns, terrorists require a nontrivial degree of popular support. Terrorists are most effective when they can rely on the members of the general public to shelter them or at least to turn a blind eye to their activities. Two measures of public support for terrorism are available: favorable perceptions of the terrorists and voting for political parties linked to the terrorists. Both measures are likely to change in response to the overall political situation, to what the terrorists do, and to the counter-terrorism policies adopted by the state.[9]

In Uruguay, surveys asked whether the Tupamaros were well-intentioned revolutionaries or common delinquents. In Italy, respondents were asked which phrase best applied to the Red Brigade. Three phrases were negative (instruments controlled from on high, dangerous assassins, crazy), one was ambivalent (pursuing a just end with the wrong means), and one was positive (fighting for a better society). In the Basque provinces, surveys asked whether ETA members were patriots, idealists, madmen, criminals, or individuals manipulated by outside forces. In Northern Ireland, the question was whether or not IRA members were basically patriots and idealists. In each country, a significant minority had a favorable view of the terrorists, with the proportion ranging from 47 percent in the Basque Provinces, to 39 percent in both Northern Ireland and Uruguay, while even in Italy the figure was 28 percent. Their fellow ethnics are likely to view nationalist terrorists particularly favorably, with almost one-half (48%) of Northern Irish Catholics holding a positive image of the IRA and a majority of ethnic Basques (66%) having a a positive image of ETA.

Voting provides another measure of support for the terrorists in the Basque Provinces and Northern Ireland. In the Basque regional parliament, Herri Batasuna, regarded as the political wing of ETA, won about 15 percent of the vote throughout the 1980s and 1990s, and its successor, Euskal Heritarrok, won 18 percent in the 1998 elections. Sinn Fein, the political wing of the IRA, first contested elections in 1982, when it won 10 percent of the Northern Irish Assembly vote. Since then it has steadily increased its share of the vote, winning 16 percent of the vote in 1997 and overtaking the moderate Irish nationalist party (the Social Democratic and Labour Party) in 2003.

But why do people support terrorism? A popular explanation sees such support as a response to various grievances. "We are the answer to an unjust system," declared the Tupamaro manifesto, while the Catholic minority supposedly supports the IRA because of Protestant discrimination. The problem with this interpretation is that the countries that have experienced the most significant revolutionary terrorism are on the whole relatively prosperous, democratic, and egalitarian. In Latin America, the countries that suffered the most from revolutionary terrorism were Uruguay, Argentina, and Venezuela—not Bolivia or Paraguay. In addition, the terrorists were drawn not from the poor but from the educated middle class. Halperin (1976) has suggested a more cynical but plausible theory for Latin American terrorism. He argues that it is the oversupply of liberal arts and social science university graduates that creates support for revolutionary groups. "These movements express the despair of young members of the administrative class radicalized and alienated from society by the deterioration of their career prospects in countries with stagnant economies. If successful, the movements offer political power and a new role for the administrative class" (p. 52).

Similarly, the most serious cases of nationalist terrorism are not found where ethnic minorities are especially oppressed in either a political or economic sense. There are several cases of ethnic minorities whose position was very similar to that of Northern Irish Catholics, but whose communities had negligible or nonexistent ethnic violence. French-speakers in Quebec and in New Brunswick, or the South Tyrolese in Italy could (and did) make equally valid claims of discrimination.[10] Indeed, because both Irish nationalists and Quebec separatists compared themselves to black Americans, it raises the question of why the level of black nationalist violence in the United States has been so low.[11] Table 15.4 ranks seven multi-ethnic societies in terms of the relative income of the nationalist ethnic group compared to the rest of the population. It is striking that—contrary to the grievance hypothesis—it is the relatively *advantaged* ethnic groups that are the most violent.

Table 15.4
Relative Income by Ethnicity (%)

Greek Cypriots/Turkish Cypriots	125
Basques/Spaniards	110
NI Catholics/Protestants	85
Tyrolese/Italians	79
New Brunswick French/English	70
Quebec French/English	64
U.S. Blacks/Whites	59

Note: First named group's per capita income divided by that of second group. (Roche & Barton, 1991:31).

The root cause of terrorism seems to lie in the political culture and the manner in which revolutionary-leftist and militant nationalist ideologies are transmitted from generation to generation. As one Irish nationalist describes it, "We came very early to our politics. One learned quite literally at one's mother's knee that Christ died for the human race and Patrick Pearse for the Irish section of it" (McCann, 1974:4). Political socialization in the school seems to be a common factor in both Northern Ireland and Cyprus. Bernadette Devlin (1969:62) says that her "militantly republican school . . . turned me into a convinced republican," while Grivas, the EOKA leader, describes how in his village school "the glories of Greek history always took first place" and notes that his secondary school "like all the others in Cyprus was staffed with teachers from Greece who brought fresh fervor to our nationalism" (1965:3).

Personal Reflections: The Threat of Terrorism in America

Karl Popper (2002) argued that the best theories are those which make "risky predictions," and predictions about the terrorist threat to the United States are intrinsically risky. In order to assess the likelihood of a major attack by Islamic terrorists *within* America, I would argue that because terrorism is a political phenomenon, any theory must focus on such political and social factors as the goals of the terrorists, the degree of popular support they have, and the counter-terrorist policies of the government.

Many see Islamic terrorism as a new kind of terrorism, and classify groups such as al Qaeda as "fundamentalist." Supposedly, fundamentalists are hostile to, and threatened by modernization, and the United States is hated because it symbolizes the essential characteristics of modern society—freedom, pluralism, and secularism.[12] It is claimed that religiously motivated terrorists are more willing than secular terrorists to carry out mass attacks against civilian targets, because the victims are unbelievers and infidels (Stern, 2001).

However, an alternative interpretation of the motivations and strategy of Islamic terrorists can be found by paying attention to Osama bin Laden's communications. Terrorism is violence with a message, and the message of Islamic terrorists is very clear. Bin Laden articulated his grievances against America in a *fatwa* issued in February 1998. The United States was occupying Saudi Arabia and its holy places (Mecca and Medina), blockading Iraq, and supporting Israel in its oppression of the Palestinian people. Osama bin Laden went on to declare that "to kill Americans and their allies—civilians and—is an individual duty for every Muslim" (Lewis, 1998), and his followers have attacked both military and civilian targets. Attacks on military targets include the 1993 ambush of marines in Somalia; the 1996 bombing of a United States military complex in Dhahran, Saudi Arabia; the 1998 bombing of United States embassies in Kenya and Tanzania; and the bombing of the U.S.S. Cole in Aden in 2000.

They have also shown no qualms about attacking civilian targets in the United States. This was clear even before the September 11, 2001, attack. The 1993 bombing of the World Trade Center was intended to kill thousands of ordinary Americans.[13] The old saying that "terrorists don't want lots of people dead, they want a lot of people watching" does not hold for groups that want to maximize the suffering of their enemy. The reason why it is the duty of every Muslim to kill American soldiers and civilians is explained by Osama bin Laden, later in the declaration. Americans are to be killed "until the Aqsa Mosque [in Jerusalem] and the Haram Mosque [in Mecca] are freed from their grip and their armies, shattered and broken-winged, depart from all the lands of Islam." Couched in religious language, this is a classic nationalist manifesto, and the action that it calls for is clearly a standard nationalist terrorist strategy: hurt your enemy until he stops occupying your land.

It is significant that we have not had any Islamic terrorist attacks in the United States since September 11, 2001, and several reasons for this can be suggested. First, the invasion of Afghanistan and consequent disruption of the al Qaeda network must have reduced their capabilities. Second, increased security within the United States and along the border has made it harder for terrorists to carry out attacks within America. For example, in December 1999, an Algerian was arrested with explosive materials in his car when he tried to cross the border from Canada. He told police that he planned to bomb Los Angeles International Airport. The recent Code Orange alert may have foiled an attempt to skyjack foreign airplanes in a variant of the 9/11 attack.

However, it is hard to believe that al Qaeda does not have some remaining sleeper cells in place or that al Qaeda operatives could not slip into the country, with whatever devices and material they require to carry out some type of terrorist attack. After all, the United States is a country with an estimated eight to 14 million illegal immigrants, and into which several tons of illegal drugs are smuggled each year. Surely if the goal is to spread terror among ordinary Americans, or to hurt the economy, al Qaeda could bomb shopping malls, tunnels and bridges, or amusement parks. Instead, it appears that al Qaeda is not trying very hard to carry out such attacks.

Let me suggest two reasons why attacks within the United States may not be strategically desirable for Islamic extremist groups in the immediate future. The 9/11 attack was spectacularly successful in terms of its impact on the Middle East and the Muslim world. The targets were chosen for their symbolic significance to bin Laden's constituency, and the attacks were intended to inspire and radicalize them. The terrorists struck at America's financial center and at the Pentagon. Presumably the target of the third plane was some equally significant symbol of American power such as the Capitol or the White House. The number of such symbolic targets is very limited and they are now well-guarded. Not only does al Qaeda probably lack sufficient resources for another such attack, but the law of diminishing returns would come into effect. The propaganda value of an attack on the Golden Gate Bridge or Disney World would be far less, and such attacks would probably stiffen American resolve. Moreover, the 9/11 attack provoked the United States into an invasion of the Arab heartland. Not only has this increased anti-American sentiments within the region, but American soldiers are now involved in a guerrilla insurgency. From Osama bin Laden's point of view, this may have been one of the purposes of the original 9/11 attack—to provoke the United States into a costly involvement under unfavorable conditions.

Endnotes

1   The acronyms stand for Ethnike Organosis Kyprion Agoniston (National Organization of Cypriot Fighters), Irish Republican Army, and Euzkadi ta Askatasuna (Homeland and Freedom).

2   Mark Hamm's chapter on hate crimes is to a large extent focused on rightist terrorism.

3   Information supplied privately to author by Donatella della Porta.

4   As reported in the Belfast news-magazine *Fortnight,* May 7, 1976.

5   All EOKA members were Greek, and I have never seen any reliable evidence that there are any Provisional members of the IRA, although the Official IRA did have at least one Protestant member. However, Clark (1984:147) found that a large proportion (38%) of ETA members are of mixed Spanish and Basque descent.

6   Margherita was no figurehead, and when her husband was captured she led a successful attack on the prison where he was held, and freed him.

7   In Northern Ireland, the United Kingdom government pays compensation for property damage so the IRA bombing of factories and other businesses raised the costs to Britain in a very direct way, with payments totaling $750 million for the 1969-1987 period alone. In 1979 and again in 2001, ETA waged a "vacation war" setting off bombs in Spanish coastal resorts.

8   This provocation/repression strategy was also adopted by ETA (Clark, 1984:123). Insofar as police and soldiers are of a different ethnicity from the terrorists and their supporters, it is very likely that counter-terrorist policies will lead to ethnic polarization and thus generate more support for the terrorists.

9   For sources and more detail, see Hewitt (1990). There were no contemporary polls on Greek-Cypriot attitudes toward EOKA, but most writers acknowledge that it had widespread support.

10   See Aunger (1981) for a comparison of New Brunswick and Northern Ireland. Czikann-Zichy (1978) gives a description of the situation in the South Tyrol.

11   Liam de Paor (1970:5) described Northern Catholics as "blacks who happen to have a white skin." Pierre Vallieres, the intellectual voice of the Front de Liberation du Quebec, described French-Canadians as "Negres blancs d'Amerique" (1971).

12   For examples of such media interpretations of the September 11th attacks by both liberals and conservatives, see Hewitt (2003:7-9).

13   The 1993 bombing of the World Trade Center was intended to topple the towers when full of people, and in the same year the FBI arrested a group planning to blow up other New York buildings and set off bombs in the Lincoln and Holland tunnels.

Discussion Questions

1. After September 11, 2001, many people feared that other terrorist attacks would follow. Do you think that there will be more terrorist attacks within the United States? If so, what kinds of attacks do you anticipate, and from what kinds of groups?

2. Compare and contrast any two domestic terrorist groups.

3. In 2001, Washington, DC, was "terrorized" by two snipers who killed. Would the FBI consider this a terrorist incident? Should the definition of terrorism be extended to include such incidents?

4. Who were the victims of the anthrax letters sent a few days after September 11, 2001, and what does this suggest about the group or individual responsible?

References

Aunger, E. (1981). *In Search of Political Stability*. Toronto: McGill.

Clark, R. (1984). *The Basque Insurgents: ETA 1952-80*. Madison: University of Wisconsin Press.

Crawshaw, N. (1978). *The Cyprus Revolt*. London: Allen and Unwin.

Czikann-Zichy, M. (1978). *Turmoil in the South Tyrol*. New York: Macmillan.

de Paor, L. (1970). *Divided Ulster*. Harmondsworth: Penguin.

Devlin, B. (1969). *The Price of my Soul*. London: Pan.

D'Oliveira, S. (1973). "Uruguay and the Tupamaro Myth." *Military Review*, 53:25-36.

Galleni, M. (1981). *Rapporto sul Terrorismo*. Milano: Rizzoli.

George, J., and L. Wilcox (1996). *American Extremists: Militias, Supremacists, Klansmen and Others*. Amherst, NY: Prometheus Books.

Grivas, G. (1965). *Memoirs*. New York: Praeger.

Halperin, E. (1976). *Terrorism in Latin America*. Beverly Hills, CA: Sage.

Hewitt, C. (2003). *Understanding Terrorism in America; From the Klan to al Qaeda*. New York: Routledge.

Hewitt, C. (1990). "Terrorism and Public Opinion: A Five Country Comparison." *Terrorism and Political Violence*, 2:145-170.

Larsen, J. (1985). "Son of Brinks." *New York*, May 6.

Lewis, B. (1998). "License to Kill: Osama bin Ladin's Declaration of Jihad." *Foreign Affairs*, November/December.

Loizos, P. (1975). *The Greek Gift*. New York: St Martins Press.

Markides, K. (1977). *The Rise and Fall of the Cyprus Republic*. New Haven, CT: Yale University Press.

Mayans, E. (1971). *Tupamaros*. Cuernavaca, Mexico: Cuernavaca Centro Intercultural de Documentation.

McCann, E. (1974). *War and an Irish Town* Harmondsworth, UK: Penguin.

Popper, K.R. (2002). *Conjectures and Refutations: The Growth of Scientific Knowledge*. London: Routledge.

Porzecanski, A. (1973). *Uruguay's Tupamaros*. New York: Praeger.

Roche, P., and B. Barton (1991). *The Northern Ireland Question Myth and Reality*. Brookfield, VT: Avebury.

Stern, J. (2001). *The Ultimate Terrorists*. Cambridge, MA: Harvard University Press.

Sutton, M. (1994). *Index of Deaths 1969-1993*. Belfast: Beyond the Pale.

Uruguay Ministerio del Interior (1972). *7 Meses de Lunch Antisubversion*. Montevideo: Uruguay Ministerio del Interior.

Vallieres, P. (1971). *White Niggers of America*. New York: Monthly Press.

PART IV

The Need for a Theory of Violence

Shelly L. Jackson
Margaret A. Zahn
Henry H. Brownstein

Theories and Violence Research: An Evaluation and Agenda for the Future

The original goal of this book was to bring together some of the best current social explanations for violence and to assess current evidence regarding these explanations for specific forms of violent behavior. This coming together, we hoped, would allow a fruitful integration of points of view, thus garnering a comprehensive theory of violence and a clear picture of next steps in the empirical testing of ideas related to the causes of violence. The picture that emerges, however, is far muddier than that and suggests that a comprehensive evidence-based theory of violence faces significant challenges at this time.

It is important to reiterate here that theory has several important functions. One of these functions is to suggest propositions about relationships among social variables that can be tested through the research process (Chafetz, 1978:92). Theory is critically important as it forms the foundation for research. Theories assist in developing hypotheses to be tested (and, consequently, in conceptualizing the ideas, limiting the scope of research, and making predictions) and in assisting in the interpretation of the findings.

This book has presented theories that explain violence. The question we now ask is: Can we develop one integrated theory that can explain all violence? Every decade or two this question is raised, and an attempt is made to integrate theories of violence. In this chapter, we address (1) an evaluation of the theories, (2) challenges to the integration of existing prominent theories, and (3) future directions for the study of violence.

Evaluation of Existing Theories

We thought it would be important to apply scientifically agreed-upon criteria to the theories presented in this book. In this section, we examine the five criteria of a good theory: parsimony, originality, generalizability, testability (i.e., the level of empirical support for the theories), and validity (in the context of the utilization of the theories by violence researchers).

Five Criteria of a Good Theory

Parsimony. Parsimony is met when simple statements offer the greatest explanatory power. If a theory is to explain a phenomenon, it must be stated in a way that adds clarity rather than confusion. Some theories use few explanatory variables to explain a tremendous amount of information and thus are said to be parsimonious. For example, see Akers and Silverman on learning theory or Black on the social geometry of violence. Other theories are considerably more complex; see Tittle on control balance theory or Marcus Felson on routine activities theory. If two theories are equal in all other ways, the most parsimonious theory is preferred. It can be said with confidence that the chapters varied tremendously in terms of parsimony.

Originality. A theory of violence that has originality offers ideas that provide an explanation of violent activity or behavior that advances previous theories. New is not necessarily better, but a good theory of violence needs to advance our understanding of violence. Original theories advance our understanding of violence by making us consider new variables that were not considered in previous theories. For example, feminist theory raises issues of patriarchy and hierarchy that otherwise might not be considered. Similarly, Lynch's radical criminology theory includes biological and chemical variables that social scientists typically do not include in their theories.

Testability. A theory must be testable if it is to be useful. Thus, we often look to empirical support to determine a theory's usefulness. Few of the theories in this book have substantial empirical support. Two exceptions are Akers and Silverman's social learning theory and Bursik's social disorganization theory. These theories each have extensive empirical support. Agnew's strain theory, on the other hand, has a moderate amount of empirical support.

The remaining theories, however, have much less empirical support. We learned that Tittle's theory was introduced in 1995, and little research has been done since that time. He informs us that the theory is complex and nonlinear, making empirical testing challenging. However, in 2004, he redesigned the theory and expects testing to begin shortly.

Richard Felson has little direct empirical support for his theory. Instead, he relied on refuting existing frustration-aggression research, positing that there are alternative explanations for the findings that fit his theory. Similarly, Lynch reviewed the literature from divergent fields (not all having to do with violence) and makes logical connections among them to explain violence. Black relied primarily on logic and borrowed from anthropological work to support his theory. And finally, Renzetti confessed that feminist theory has not been well tested.

Because Marcus Felson's work is more of an approach than a theory, it is difficult to ascertain whether it has empirical support. Practical applications of this approach or perspective have been used extensively with great success by law enforcement and others concerned with public safety. However, the theory itself has not been subjected to systematic empirical research.

Generalizability. As noted by others, collective violence theory has lagged far behind psychological, interpersonal, and even structural theories of violence. Therefore, each theorist was asked to discuss whether his or her theory was applicable to collective violence. With varying degrees of success, most theories were able to incorporate the phenomenon of collective violence (although most have not directly tested this relevance). Richard Felson strongly asserts that collective violence is no different than individual violence: Both involve a grievance, except that group processes play a role in collective violence. Akers and Silverman also cogently argue that their theory is applicable to collective violence (e.g., terrorism). Tittle incorporates collective violence directly into his theory. Black's theory explains all forms of moralistic violence, including collective violence, because it relies on violent structures rather than individuals. Bursik's social disorganization theory deals extensively with groups and thus may be readily applicable to collective violence. Finally, Agnew argues that strain theory may be useful in explaining collective violence, but such application has not yet been thoroughly developed.

Renzetti notes that feminist theorists have not applied their theory to the study of terrorist violence, although feminist theory might be useful in explaining women's lack of involvement in terrorist organizations. Although Lynch and Marcus Felson did not directly address this issue, their theories may be readily applicable to collective violence. Lynch's focus on class, race, and economic deprivation as explanations for violence clearly applies to collective violence. Finally, because Marcus Felson's routine activities approach concentrates on the event rather than the individual, it would also aptly apply to collective violence.

Validity. There are a variety of types of validity, but the most basic form is face validity. Does a theory seem reasonable on its face? The use of theories in violence research would be one possible test of validity.

In examining which theories are used by violence researchers, we found that only two of the researchers used theories in this book. Dutton's review of violence against women relies predominantly on ecological theory, though also on feminist theory as written by Renzetti, and Senechal de la Roche uses Black's violent structures theory to explain modern lynching. The remaining research chapters, however, used a variety of other theories to explain the phenomena they addressed.

Specifically, Hamm, Esbensen, and White used varying theories to explain specific types of violence. Hamm is developing his own theory of hate violence that incorporates the concept of subcultures with more traditional criminological theories (e.g., containment theory, Akers's social learning theory, techniques of neutralization, and moral transcendence). Esbensen notes that the study of youth violence includes extensive research on risk and protective factors, but at present there are no causal linkages in the form of a coherent theory of youth violence. He asserts that integrated theoretical models hold the most promise for explaining youth evidence. Finally, White outlines five theoretical models that have been used to explain drug-related violence. They are the psychopharmacological model, the economic compulsive model, the systemic model, the possibility that violent behavior leads to drug use, and the possibility that violence and drug use are related because they share common causes (individual, interpersonal, environmental, and situational factors) rather than being causally related.

Thus, it appears that violence researchers are not using many of the theories in this book. This book did not include every theory or every topic of research, but it is interesting that of the forms of violence reviewed in this book, only two explicitly used established theories. There seems to be a disconnect between the violence research and the violence theory—possibly because the theories were originally theories of crime rather than violence.

It is further clear from this analysis that violence researchers are still struggling with how to explain their particular types of violence. General theories may be helpful in starting to think about a social problem, but as more facts become known, these general theories may not sufficiently take into account phenomena associated with a specific social problem. A new or integrated theory may be needed to account for all the known facts of a social problem such as violence.

The Need for Theories of Violence

There is a strong disconnect between the existing theories and the empirical studies of types of violence. With the exception of studies of intimate partner violence, which is strongly linked to feminist theory, many empirical studies of violence—for example, violence in the drug trade, violent hate crime—are not linked to the theoretical presentations currently popular in criminology.

For the most part (Donald Black's theory is the notable exception), these existing theories treat violence as a variation of crime or deviance rather than as a subject to be addressed on its own merits. Learning theory, strain theory, and control balance theory all treat violence as a variation of illegal or non-normative behavior. This approach has proven to be problematic. By focusing on behavior as criminal or deviant, theorists assume that the behavior in question (violent behavior) is not normative. However, some forms of violence are normative according to time or place. For example, spanking children, now viewed by some as "violence," has often been pre-scribed socialization treatment for raising children. In addition, throughout much of the world, hitting women is a normative means of control used by male partners and is not against the law. Thus, theories that treat violence as a subset of crime or deviance often miss the mark because of faulty assumptions. Furthermore, crime and deviance as the object of investiga-tion, rather than violence *per se*, has made it difficult to deal with inter-personal as well as collective forms of violence in the same theory. Again, Black's theory and some variants of radical theory overcome this problem by taking violence, rather than crime or deviance, as the object of study.

Violence, even though some forms of it may be criminal, is behavior deserving of attention, in and of itself, rather than as a subtype of criminal or deviant behavior. If it is a genre of behavior apart from aggression, there must be some consensus regarding the nature of the genre. Here too, theorists and researchers differ on what constitutes violence.

Definitions of Violence

Defining violence is a critical first step in developing an effective the-ory. How theorists define violence directly impacts what concepts are included in the theory.

Typically, we think of violence as physical force used against another and resulting in harm. Yet, as you may have deduced from reading these chap-ters, there is no concept of violence upon which all agree.

Definitions of violence vary along a number of dimensions. What sep-arates definitions of violence is: (1) the level of the action or behavior—indi-vidual, interpersonal, or collective; (2) the nature and degree of force—whether it is physical or not, such as threats, attempts, verbal assault, invasion, insult, intimidation, pressure; (3) the outcome of the force—whether it results in injury or not; (4) the injury might be of one type or degree—such as physical, hurting, degrading, depriving one's control over contact with others; (5) the targets—recipients of force might be intended or incidental or may be persons or property such as individual(s), places, property with strong symbolic significance (such as a place of worship), liv-ing creatures, civilian targets, certain hated groups, dating partners; and (6) intentionality—whether harm or injury is intended or not.

Below we look specifically at the definitions of violence posited by the authors of the chapters in this book. Because all of these definitions include the core elements of violence as a form of forceful activity or behavior for the purpose of domination or control, we focus on differences and show how the definitions together cover a broad range of social activity that we know as violence. For example, some definitions refer to the aggressive behavior of perpetrators of violence in general, others to examples of illicit or illegal behavior specifically in the form of violent crime. Some definitions focus on individual forms of violence, others on collective violence. Some definitions emphasize the act, others the outcome.

As mentioned, definitions of violence vary in terms of how they view the nature and degree of force. For Akers and Silverman, violence can range from suicidal to interpersonal to the collective, but they specifically refer to physical threat and harm against persons and places. For Agnew, violent acts are usually intentional, or at least the result of negligence or recklessness. Black views violence as the use of physical force against people and property, most often as moralistic in that it is a form of social control, but he recognizes that the force might also be used for predatory, recreational, or even ritualistic purposes. Bursik defines violence in legalistic terms, such as "crimes against persons," which might include illegal activities that result in or have the potential to result in the victim's physical injury or even loss of life. Richard Felson suggests that violence is different from aggression. Aggression is a social psychological phenomenon referring to the intentional harm of people by others, and it becomes violence when it involves the use of or threat to use physical force.

While most definitions of violence emphasize force that is physical, some do not. Describing the contribution of feminist theory to our understanding of violence, Renzetti suggests that violence need not be physical. Feminist research has identified violence that is sexual, psychological, and economic. Similarly, Senechal de la Roche suggests that in addition to physical force, violence may include lesser forms of aggression, such as insults or vandalism.

In addition to differing in their view of the nature and degree of force, definitions of violence vary by the level of the action or behavior to which they refer. For example, violence may occur on an interpersonal or a collective level. While most theories of violence emphasize the interpersonal dimension, some deliberately pay attention to collective violence. Writing about the relationship between drugs and violence, White refers specifically to interpersonal violence. Hewitt writes about terrorism as violence and argues that its intent is collective harm for social or political purposes rather than personal harm for individual purposes. Senechal de la Roche distinguishes collective violence as having a greater degree of organization and breadth of liability as compared with interpersonal violence. Renzetti distinguishes interpersonal violence not from collective violence, but from structural violence, which she says is perpetrated by social institutions rather than by persons.

Whether violence is interpersonal or collective, it may also be the product of legal or illegal activity or behavior. Most theorists emphasize the criminal forms of violence. Akers and Silverman acknowledge that the principles of their theory may apply to both conforming and deviant behavior, but in their explanation, they emphasize behavior that is illegitimate. Agnew suggests that as an example of violence, his general strain theory emphasizes criminal violence. Similarly, Bursik's theory focuses heavily on illegal activities or behavior.

Theories of violence are also distinguished by the way they look at the outcome of the force or its recipient. The force used in violent action or behavior may or may not result in injury. If there is injury, it may be more or less serious, even fatal in some cases. The recipient of the force may be intended or incidental to the activity or behavior. Agnew points out that for the recipients of violence, the harm is usually unwanted. Yet, as Tittle suggests, the perpetrator intends for violence to result in physical pain or damage, and a question for students of violence is why some people or groups engage in violence and others do not. Hewitt says that in the case of terrorist violence, the victims are often civilian or noncombatant targets, though not everyone agrees. For Hamm, the victims are selected for their symbolic value, as a target of hate.

Renzetti suggests that feminist theorists have brought attention to the perception and experience of victims of violence—and especially to their psychological harm. Dutton also points out that sexual violence can have a psychological impact on the victim.

At the heart of each of these definitions is one or more actors using force (threat or actual) of some sort against one or more targets resulting in some harm. However, it is clear from this analysis that theorists and researchers have defined violence differently in important ways. These differential definitions challenge our ability to integrate the theories and the research findings.

Focus of Theories of Violence

In the chapters of this book, the authors suggest ways to define and explain violence. Theories vary from the structural to the interpersonal to the psychological. Some theories are built around a belief in the free will of human beings, others around a belief that external forces determine human behavior. Some focus on social variables, such as gender or class, others on psychological variables, such as intention and motivation. Still others emphasize ecological variables, such as time of day or setting.

Most explanations of violence focus on perpetrators of the violence, although some give more attention to the recipient or victim. Others may emphasize the characteristics or circumstances of the violent event itself, the social and ecological time and space in which the perpetrator and victim find themselves together. Others focus directly on the social structure and its relation to violence.

Theories that are generally perpetrator-centered include control balance, strain, social learning, and radical ecology theory. For example, social learning theory is most concerned with how an individual learns to be violent. Violence is the product of social exchange in which the words, responses, presence, and behavior of others directly reinforce how an individual will behave.

Victim-centered theories of violence include some critical theories, such as radical and, notably, realist theories. Perhaps, however, feminist theory gives the greatest attention to victims in understanding and explaining violence. Feminist theories have explicitly expanded the definition of violence to emphasize the perceptions and experiences of violence. By drawing attention away from physical violence and legal codes, they have shown the importance of recognizing the impact of the behavior on its recipient or victim in order to understand violence. In addition, feminist theories emphasize the conditions under which victims use violence against perpetrators as a way of preventing future victimization.

There are also theories that are event-focused, most of which are included in the category of routine activities theory. In terms of these theories, the propensities of individuals to violence are peripheral to the characteristics and circumstances of an event. These theories focus on violence prevention in the context of environmental design.

Finally, there are theories that emphasize social structure and its relationship to violence. The emphasis of these theories is on social conflict and the social geometry of this conflict. The social geometry attracts different kinds of social life to a situation and thus defines the location and direction of the conflict. Social geometry determines when a situation generates a violent response. One example of how social geometry explains violence is classic blood feuds or, in more contemporary terms, gang violence. Likewise, Bursik's theory posits that the structural variation in three types of networks within neighborhoods (private, parochial, and public) has an effect on crime.

Clearly, then, we are faced with the challenge of integrating theories with divergent perspectives. Given the differences among these theories, the task of integration becomes more daunting.

Analysis of Explanatory Variables

Finally, we look at the explanatory variables that each theory uses. Examination of the theories in this book reveals some stark similarities and contrasts. If we examine the structural and event-focused theories, we find that Bursik's social disorganization theory, Black's pure sociological theory, Marcus Felson's routine activities approach, and Lynch's radical theory all contend that factors other than individuals contribute to violence. While these theories rely on social structures of one sort or another to explain violence, each uses a different set of variables to explain violence. Bursik explains crime by examining neighborhood-level variables such as interactional networks (private, parochial, and public) as sources of social control.

Black uses variables such as relational and cultural distance, social elevation, and organizational dimensions. Felson, however, uses the concept of routine activities to analyze violence. Lynch, as mentioned above, uses class, race, and economic position to explain violence.

The remaining theories explain the use of violence used by individuals or groups of individuals (i.e., collectives). A desire for change is at the root of each of these theories. That is, violence is used as the means to get someone or something to change. Agnew, Tittle, Richard Felson, and Hewitt each posit theories in which someone perceives that they are being treated negatively, and violence is the response they use to bring about some change. Again, however, the explanatory variables used to explain this phenomenon vary tremendously.

In Agnew's theory, when a person is treated badly, it results in negative emotions, and corrective action—in the form of violence—is taken to reduce the negative feelings. In Tittle's control balance theory, individuals who perceive control balance deficits (e.g., from debasement or humiliation) may use violence to achieve a better control ratio. (Interestingly, the theory posits that everyone is born with a latent desire to overcome control deficits, often with violence). Richard Felson says that in dispute-related violence, anger resulting from mistreatment or humiliation overrides inhibitions leading to the use of violence (he asserts, however, that a specific biological urge is not needed to explain the use of violence). He contends that aversive stimuli in the form of personal attacks and offensive behavior lead to aggression (he is careful to use the word aggression, i.e., intentional harm, rather than violence, i.e., the use of force). Finally, Hewitt's terrorist theory also seeks to effect change on a collective scale. In each of these cases, some form of grievance is the perceived cause.

In contrast to the theories above, feminist theory asserts that violence (most often directed against women) has less to do with grievance *per se* and more to do with power and control. This theory's explanatory variables include gender, sexism, and patriarchy. That is, violence is used against women because our society permits the use of violence against women. Thus, for Renzetti, gender is the central organizing component of social life and is the primary explanatory variable. Nonetheless, some feminist theorists conceive of violence by victims toward perpetrators in terms similar to those used by Agnew, Tittle, or Felson, that is, as a means of stopping unwanted treatment. Conversely, Richard Felson was the only theorist to assert explicitly that gender does not matter in any way in theorizing about violence.

In sum, we do not have a way to unify these theories because of significant differences in their definitions of violence, variables, underlying assumptions, and evidentiary bases. In addition, bodies of research on violent behaviors, such as hate violence and drug violence, do not share sufficient commonality to facilitate a general understanding of violence. Therefore, substantial work remains before we can reach an understanding of violence that fully encompasses the many lines of theoretical work.

Future Directions

In the field of violence studies, then, there are multiple theories. These theories are difficult to integrate into a parsimonious explanation because they define the phenomenon differently; use multiple levels of analysis and multiple variables that frequently do not cross over from one theory to another; the underlying assumptions differ; and evidentiary bases exist in various bodies of literature that are not easily linked to each other or to existing theories. These difficulties are compounded by many theorists' attempts to deal only with violence that is defined as criminal or deviant, rather than focusing on the harm itself, independent of its legal status. (For additional review of this difficulty, see Jackman, 2002).

What, then, will help us come to an evidence-based, parsimonious theory of violence?

First, we should focus on theories intended to explain violence as such rather than as a manifestation of crime and deviance.

Second, theories that deal with individual dispositions to violence—for example, learning theory, strain, control balance—might be profitably integrated into one social explanation for individual propensities for violent behavior. The works of Elliott, Ageton, and Canter (2003) and Tittle (1985) represent an attempt in this direction (see also Braithwaite, 1989; Colvin, Cullen & Vanderven, 2002; Tittle, 2004, for arguments concerning theoretical integration).

Third, violence theories should focus on relationships, not on individual dispositions. Violence always involves a relationship between a person, group, or nation that is physically harmed at the hands of another person, group, or nation. Specifying relational types and collecting data on these types would seem most productive. In the field of homicide studies, for example, causal understanding moved forward most when the field began differentiating one type of homicide from another, often based on degree of intimacy of the participants (e.g., family versus stranger). Causes for these relationally different types may be distinct from each other.

Similarly, it would be helpful to identify types of violence. Black, for example, has offered to distinguish moralistic violence from predatory violence. For instance, moralistic violence may exist between two individuals (a husband asserting dominance over a wife because of belief in patriarchy), between groups (terrorist groups who believe in the superiority of one religion), or between nations (communism versus free-enterprise states). Additional types of violence may include recreational and incidental categories.

The typology to be used would certainly be in question. Many have been suggested—by Black, Durkheim (1951, see his discussion of egoistic, altruistic, and anomic suicide), and others. Focusing on differing types of violence and the distinct causes for each, however, may prove to be the most parsimonious way to eventually reduce violence-related harm to individuals, groups, and whole societies. In a society now at war against terror, where homicide rates are far higher than in other developed nations, and where violence against women remains a pressing problem, the need to advance violence theory with a coherent foundation of evidence could not be greater.

References

Braithwaite, J. (1989). *Crime, Shame, and Reintegration*. New York: Cambridge University Press.

Chafetz, J.S. (1978). *A Primer on the Construction and Testing of Theories of Sociology*. Itaska, IL: F.E. Peacock.

Colvin, M., F.T. Cullen, and T. Vanderven (2002). "Coercion, Social Support, and Crime: An Emerging Consensus." *Criminology*, 40:19-42.

Durkheim, E. (1951). *Suicide: A Study in Sociology*. Tr. by J.A. Spaulding and G. Simpson. Edited with Introduction by George Simpson. New York: Free Press. (Originally published in Paris by F. Alcan, 1897.)

Elliott, D.S., S.S. Ageton, and R.J. Canter (2003). "An Integrated Theoretical Perspective on Delinquent Behavior." In F.T. Cullen and R. Agnew (eds.), *Criminological Theory: Past and Present*, pp. 489-502. Los Angeles: Roxbury.

Jackman, M.R. (2002). Violence in Social Life. *Annual Review of Sociology*, 28:387-415.

Tittle, C.R. (forthcoming). "Refining Control Balance Theory." *Theoretical Criminology*.

Tittle, C.R. (1985). "The Assumption That General Theories Are Not Possible." In R.F. Meier (ed.), *Theoretical Methods in Criminology*, pp. 93-121. Beverly Hills, CA: Sage.

Editors' Biographical Information

Margaret A. Zahn is a Professor of Sociology at the North Carolina State University and Director of the Crime, Justice Policy and Behavior Program at RTI International. She previously served as Dean of Humanities and Social Sciences at North Carolina State and was Director of the Violence and Victimization Division at the National Institute of Justice, where the idea for this book was originally conceived. She has studied violence, especially homicide, during much of her career and has co-edited a number of books on that topic, including *Homicide: A Sourcebook of Social Research*, co-edited with M. Dwayne Smith. She is past president of the American Society of Criminology and is also an elected Fellow of that society.

Henry H. Brownstein is the Director of the Center on Crime, Drugs, and Justice at Abt Associates, Inc., a government and business research and consulting firm. Prior to joining Abt Associates, he was the Director of the Drugs and Crime and International Research Division at the National Institute of Justice, the research, development, and evaluation agency of the U.S. Department of Justice. He has also been a Professor of Criminology, Criminal Justice, and Social Policy, and Director of the Graduate Program in Criminal Justice at the University of Baltimore, and Chief of Statistical Services for the New York State Division of Criminal Justice Services. His research has mostly been in the areas of drugs and violence, homicide, and the relationship between research and public policy. He has published numerous articles and book chapters on various subjects, including drug-related violence, homicide by women, and the social construction of public policy and social problems. His most recent books are *The Problems of Living in Society* (2003) and *The Social Reality of Violence and Violent Crime* (2000). He earned his Ph.D. in sociology in 1977 from Temple University.

Shelly L. Jackson is an Assistant Professor of Research Psychiatry at the Institute of Law, Psychiatry and Public Policy, University of Virginia, and Lecturer in the Psychology Department, University of Virginia. For the past 10 years, she has been involved in family violence research, with a particular interest in child maltreatment, both within the federal government and in academia. Jackson, along with her colleagues, is beginning a three-year study on prison rape sponsored by the National Institute of Justice.

Contributors' Biographical Information

Robert Agnew is Professor of Sociology and Violence Studies at Emory University in Atlanta, Georgia. His research focuses on the causes of crime and delinquency, especially his general strain theory of crime and delinquency. He has just published two books: *Why Do Criminals Offend? A General Theory of Crime and Delinquency* (2005) and *Juvenile Delinquency: Causes and Control* (2nd ed., 2005).

Ronald L. Akers is Professor of Criminology and Sociology and Associate Dean of Faculty Affairs in the College of Liberal Arts and Sciences at the University of Florida. CLAS. He is author of several books including *Criminological Theories* (4th ed., 2004, with Christine Sellers), *Deviant Behavior: A Social Learning Approach* (3rd ed., 1985), and *Social Learning and Social Structure: A General Theory of Crime and Deviance* (1998), and co-editor with Gary Jensen of *Social Learning Theory and the Explanation of Crime* (2003). He is also author of more than 80 chapters and articles in major criminology and sociology journals. His major research and scholarly work has been on developing and testing his social learning theory of crime and deviance as well as other theories and on many substantive, empirical, and policy issues in crime, deviance, law, and justice.

Donald Black is the University Professor of the Social Sciences at the University of Virginia. A theoretical sociologist, he previously held appointments at Harvard University and Yale University. His books include *The Behavior of Law* (1976), *The Manners and Customs of the Police* (1980), *Toward a General Theory of Social Control* (1984, two volumes), *Sociological Justice* (1989), and *The Social Structure of Right and Wrong* (1993; revised edition, 1998).

Robert J. Bursik, Jr is a Curator's Professor of Criminology and Criminal Justice at the University of Missouri-St. Louis. He is a Fellow of the American Society of Criminology and a former editor of *Criminology*. Although he has published papers in a variety of substantive areas, most of his research has focused on the relationship between neighborhood dynamics and crime rates. He currently is involved in a project on immigration and crime, and soon will be exploring the rural poverty/crime association in Appalachia.

Mary Ann Dutton, Ph.D., is a clinical psychologist who has specialized in the area of intimate partner violence and other forms of interpersonal violence over the past 24 years. She is a professor in the Department of Psychiatry, Georgetown University, where she is currently involved in research focusing on interpersonal trauma and low-income and minority women's health and mental health issues. Dutton is Principal Investigator on several federally funded studies that focus on coping, health outcomes, revictimization, and coercive control among women who have been in recent violent and abusive relationships. She is currently developing community-based, low-cost, accessible, and culturally competent interventions for partner violence victimization. Dutton has trained audiences of lawyers, judges, advocates, and health professionals concerning physical violence and sexual assault, both nationally and internationally. Her workshops and lectures have focused on understanding the dynamics, traumatic impact, and interventions. She has published numerous articles, book chapters, and books on these topics.

Finn-Aage Esbensen is the E. Desmond Lee Professor of Youth Crime and Violence in the Department of Criminology and Criminal Justice at the University of Missouri-St. Louis. He is past Editor of *Justice Quarterly* and he has served as Principal Investigator of two multi-year quasi-experimental evaluations of school-based violence and gang prevention programs. His publications include a textbook, *Criminology: Explaining Crime and Its Context*, (5th ed., 2004, with Stephen E. Brown and Gilbert Geis), a gang reader, *American Youth Gangs at the Millennium* (2004, with Stephen G. Tibbetts and Larry Gaines), and numerous book chapters and journal articles.

Marcus Felson is Professor at the School of Criminal Justice, Rutgers University. He has also served as a professor at the University of Southern California and the University of Illinois at Urbana-Champaign. He is very interested in how everyday life produces crime opportunities. His practical concern is how to use situational prevention measures to reduce crime opportunities and thus lower crime rates. He is author of *Crime and Everyday Life* (3rd ed., 2002).

Richard B. Felson is Professor of Crime, Law, and Justice and Sociology at The Pennsylvania State University. He is the author of *Violence and Gender Reexamined* (2002), *Violence, Aggression & Coercive Actions* (1994, with J. Tedeschi), and two co-edited books, all published by the American Psychological Association. His articles have appeared in a variety of journals, including *Criminology*, *Journal of Personality and Social Psychology*, *Social Forces*, and *Social Psychology Quarterly*. He research is concerned with a variety of topics including situational factors in homicide and assault, motives for rape and domestic violence, and reporting assaults to the police.

Mark S. Hamm is a criminology professor at Indiana State University. He has published widely on terrorism and hate violence. Hamm is the author, most recently, of *In Bad Company: America's Terrorist Underground* (2001). He is currently exploring transnational crimes committed by such terrorist groups as al Qaeda.

Christopher Hewitt is a Professor of Sociology at the University of Maryland Baltimore County. He has written extensively on terrorism and political violence. His publications include *The Effectiveness of Anti-Terrorist Policies* (1984), *Consequences of Political Violence* (1993), *Encyclopedia of Modern Separatist Movements* (2000), and *Understanding Terrorism in America: From the Klan to al Qaeda* (2003). His current research is on how those carrying out terrorist attacks within the United States were identified and captured, based on an examination of more than one thousand cases.

Michael J. Lynch is a Professor in the Department of Criminology at the University of South Florida. His areas of interest include: environmental crime and justice, corporate crime and regulation, radical theories of crime, and racial bias in the criminal justice system. His recent publications have appeared in a variety of journals including: *The Archives of Pediatric and Adolescent Medicine, Sociological Quarterly, The British Journal of Criminology, Mankind Quarterly, Social Science Quarterly, The Social Science Journal, Criminal Justice Review, Critical Criminology, The Journal of Black Studies,* and *Crime, Law and Social Change.* His most recent book is *Environmental Crime: A Sourcebook* (2004, with Ronald G. Burns).

Helene Raskin White is a Professor of Sociology with a joint appointment at the Center of Alcohol Studies and Sociology Department at Rutgers, the State University of NJ. Her longitudinal research focuses on the comorbidity of drug use, delinquency, violence, and mental health problems over the life course in normal and high-risk samples. She has co-edited two books and published more than 100 articles and book chapters. White serves on several advisory and editorial boards and as a grant reviewer for NIH. Currently, she is implementing and evaluating substance abuse prevention programs for college students.

Claire M. Renzetti is Professor of Sociology at St. Joseph's University in Philadelphia. She is editor of the international, interdisciplinary journal *Violence Against Women,* co-editor of the *Violence Against Women* book series (Sage Publications), and editor of the *Gender, Crime and Law* book series (Northeastern University Press). She has authored or edited 13 books as well as numerous book chapters and articles in professional journals. Her current research focuses on the violent victimization experiences of women public housing residents. Renzetti has held elected and appointed positions on the governing bodies of several national professional organizations, including the Society for the Study of Social Problems, the American Society of Criminology, and the Eastern Sociological Society.

Roberta Senechal de la Roche is Associate Professor of History at Washington and Lee University. Her writings include *The Sociogenesis of a Race Riot: Springfield, Illinois, in 1908* (1990); "Collective Violence as Social Control," *Sociological Forum* (1996); "The Sociogenesis of Lynching," in W. Fitzhugh Brundage, ed., *Under Sentence of Death: Lynching in the South* (1997); and "Why Is Collective Violence Collective?," *Sociological Theory* (2001). She also recently edited the symposium, *Theories of Terrorism for Sociological Theory* (2004).

Adam L. Silverman received his Ph.D. in Political Science/Criminology, from the University of Florida where is he is currently Breier Post-Doctoral Fellow. He specializes in research on terrorism, counter-terrorism, security administration and policy, religion and political violence/politics, violence, and deviance. He is the author of several articles, chapters, and conference papers on the social behavioral dynamics and the social structural factors in terrorism.

Charles Tittle is a Professor in the Department of Sociology and Anthropology at North Carolina State University. In 2000, he was appointed the Goodnight/Glaxo-Wellcome Endowed Chair of Social Science there. His first appointment was at Indiana University, Bloomington. Subsequently he served on faculties at Florida Atlantic University, Boca Raton, and Washington State University in Pullman. Tittle's research interests include the sociology of crime and deviance, sociological theory, and urban sociology.

Name Index

Subject Index